DATE DUE

Separation of Powers
and Good Government

The Ashbrook Series on Constitutional Politics

Sponsored by the John M. Ashbrook Center for Public Affairs at Ashland University

General Editors: Peter W. Schramm and Bradford P. Wilson

American Political Parties and Constitutional Politics

Separation of Powers and Good Government

The American Judiciary and Constitutional Politics

Separation of Powers and Good Government

Edited by

Bradford P. Wilson
and Peter W. Schramm

ROWMAN & LITTLEFIELD PUBLISHERS, INC.

AVI 0996-0/2

ROWMAN & LITTLEFIELD PUBLISHERS, INC.

Published in the United States of America
by Rowman & Littlefield Publishers, Inc.
4720 Boston Way, Lanham, Maryland 20706

3 Henrietta Street, London WC2E 8LU, England

British Cataloging in Publication Information Available

Library of Congress Cataloging-in-Publication Data

Separation of powers and good government / edited by Bradford P.
Wilson and Peter W. Schramm.
p. cm. — (The Ashbrook series on constitutional politics)
"This volume grew out of a conference on separation of powers and
good government held at Ashland University in November 1991 and
sponsored by the John M. Ashbrook Center for Public Affairs"—Pref.
Includes bibliographical references and index.
1. Separation of powers—United States. 2. United States—Politics
and government. I. Wilson, Bradford P. II. Schramm, Peter W.
III. Series.
JK305.S467 1994 320.473—dc20 94–7185 CIP

ISBN 0–8476–7899–7 (cloth : alk. paper)
ISBN 0–8476–7900–4 (pbk. : alk. paper)

RECEIVED

JUL 1 3 1995

Printed in the United States of America

™ The paper used in this publication meets the minimum requirements of
American National Standard for Information Sciences—Permanence of
Paper for Printed Library Materials, ANSI Z39.48–1984.

CONTENTS

PREFACE

OUR AGE IS ONE in which constitutional democracy is gaining ground. Many peoples recently liberated or now struggling for civil and political freedom are facing the daunting task of framing constitutional arrangements that will be both free and competent, both moderate and democratic. Serious attention is being paid to the institutional arrangements of political orders in which self-government has been established or re-established.

In addition to being the world's oldest constitutional democracy, the United States is widely regarded as the most successful one. The sources of that success are many, but the design of the American Constitution has a strong claim to preeminence. This book is offered as an aid to understanding and evaluating that design.

James Madison wrote in *The Federalist* that "no political truth is certainly of greater intrinsic value, or is stamped with the authority of more enlightened patrons of liberty" than the "maxim that the legislative, executive, and judiciary departments ought to be separate and distinct." In what manner separate and in what manner distinct were meant to be answered by the Constitution but have been a matter of considerable debate ever since.

Not until the second century of the Constitution's existence did the critics of the Framers' design begin to call into question the principle of separation itself. Beginning with Woodrow Wilson's critique of the separation of powers, the dominant perspective in American political science has been that the separation of powers is an obstacle to government's "getting things done," i.e., to progress.

This book takes a fresh look at this agitated issue. It attempts a review and analysis of the theory and practice of the American separation of powers from the Founding to the present time. It represents no school of thought, no consensus of opinion. As there are different authors, so there are different views and scholarly interests represented. We do think it fair to say, however, that all the authors in this book approach their subject with a common assumption: the Framers' argument that the separation of powers is an essential ingredient of good government deserves to be taken seriously, more so than has generally been the case in this century's scholarship.

This volume grew out of a conference on Separation of Powers and Good Government held at Ashland University in November 1991 and sponsored by the John M. Ashbrook Center for Public Affairs. All of the authors in this book participated in that conference. We are grateful to the Lynde and Harry Bradley Foundation for its support of the conference, and to the late Marjorie Clark Ingmand for her support of this publication. We are also grateful to The Johns Hopkins University Press for permission to republish Harvey C. Mansfield's essay from his book *America's Constitutional Soul*. Finally, thanks are due to Gregory Dunn for his editorial assistance along the way.

Bradford P. Wilson
Peter W. Schramm

PART I

On the Founding

Separation of Powers in the American Constitution

Harvey C. Mansfield

SEPARATION OF POWERS is the chief of the "auxiliary precautions" necessary against oppression by government, according to James Madison in *Federalist* 51. It is especially a precaution against government, but also, as will be seen, a necessary means to effective government. As a precaution, it is auxiliary to "dependence on the people" or to representation, the primary precaution. In *The Federalist,* in which separation of powers is best expounded, the American Constitution is shown to be republican government that is wholly popular, because all parts of it are derived from the people, and yet wholly representative, because in no part do the people govern directly. Separation of powers is the form or structure of republican government in which the people are revealed as not governing directly. While Madison in *Federalist* 10 refers to representation and extensive size as a republican remedy for republican diseases, separation of powers might best be described as a non-republican auxiliary to republicanism, its "interior structure," as Madison says in *Federalist* 51.

Separation of powers, according to Alexander Hamilton in *Federalist* 9, is a modern invention, indeed an invention of modern political science. Although as a doctrine separation of powers is indebted to the medieval parliaments and modern, limited monarchies whose practices give substance to abstract categories, it did not emerge as it were naturally from the conflict of social groups for political power. In this regard and as a whole, separation of powers must be distinguished from the mixed regime dear to ancient political philosophers such as Plato, Aristotle, Polybius, and Cicero. Set forth as a guide to statesmen, the mixed regime results from an assessment of the rival claims to rule of social groups or classes in which each claim is found to be partial, hence in need,

3

and yet worthy of being mixed with its rivals to achieve a better or truer whole. This assessment presupposes both an existing whole and the existing political parties that claim to rule it. But the doctrine (for such it is) of the separation of powers begins with a theoretical analysis dividing political power into categories not found in uninstructed political practice. For it was clear from the first that legislative, executive, and judicial powers do not correspond exactly, and often not even roughly, to the actual powers of parliaments, kings, and judges. This analysis, then, is critical in its initial stance and not merely after consideration. *The Federalist* presents its version of the separation of powers not as emerging from the practice of republics, let alone of the English monarchy, but as one cure for the weakness and disorders of previous republics, including the American states which had been independent since 1776 and above all the federal government under the Articles of Confederation. Although it borrows from practice, separation of powers was originally, and remains essentially, a theory—but not, as we shall see, a utopian theory.

The most famous theorists of the separation of powers, besides the authors of *The Federalist*, are Locke and Montesquieu. But the theory had its origin in certain writers who published before Locke during the English Civil War, and, surprisingly, its essential precondition in the political science of Thomas Hobbes. Hobbes was the furthest of any political thinker from believing that power ought to be separated, but he prepared the theory of separation of powers by arguing that power pure and simple, without reference to the ends for which it will be used, is and should be the central concern of politics. Hobbes's political science reduces the social claims to rule heard in politics, which are the basis of a mixed regime, to individual desires for power. Reasoning from these desires, men create a sovereign or government that is wholly artificial and wholly representative, presupposing no prior society or social group. This sovereign is defined by his power to make laws for his subjects unlimited by any claims of their subjects to rule.

As Hobbes was writing during the English Civil War, and to some extent with a view to his absolutist solution, the separation of powers first appeared in the 1640s as a distinction between legislative and executive powers in writings by Philip Hunton, John Sadler, John Milton, and (later: 1656) Marchamont Nedham on the parliamentary side. Thus, the original and perhaps essential separation of powers was twofold, between legislative and executive, not threefold as we know it today. It was made for a double purpose: to separate the executive power (which was usually held to include the judiciary) from the legislative and, not incidentally, to subordinate the executive to the legislative. In both respects the end was to maintain the rule of law, so that the one or those who made the law could not apply it, and the one or those who applied it could not change it to suit themselves. But since the executive in Britain was the king (and would be likely anywhere to be one or few), and since "executive" means carrying out the will of someone else, the king was by implication reduced to a subordinate, and the doctrine of separation of powers, despite the seeming impartiality of its end, had from its origin a republican bias. More radical writers, such as the Levelers Isaac Penington and Sir Henry Vane, used it to criticize the invasions of a republican executive (Cromwell) or republican legislature (the Long Parliament), but this usage hardly made it less a republican doctrine. Moderate royalists at this time, such as Charles Dallison and George Lawson, also used it in defense of the king, but to do so they had to combine it with some version of the mixed regime in order to elevate the king from the rank of mere executive.

The problem of the separation of powers in its original statements was its republican animus against the executive: this animus made it subversive in a monarchy and, as Americans were to discover from bitter experience with weak executives in the federal government and in the states from 1776 to 1787, useless and dangerous in a republic. The doctrine itself was self-defeating, for how could the executive power be kept separate from the legislative if the legislative was encroaching and the executive was subordinate? To turn to a "mixed monarchy" or a "balanced constitution" was an inconsistent, makeshift arrangement because it admits the claims to rule of several parties and thus is forced to mix powers to satisfy the parties as well as separate powers to promote the rule of law. Harmony gets in the way of security, and it is not clear which comes first.

Locke and Montesquieu, the two greatest promoters of separation of powers (Madison called Montesquieu the oracle on the subject), saw this problem clearly and attempted solutions. They were obliged to add a third power, to compromise the purity of the separated powers, and to "fortify" the executive (Madison's expression) well beyond the literal meaning of the word. But when they complicated the original twofold distinction, they did it for the sake of that distinction, and while complicating it, they clarified its end.

Locke achieved a synthesis of Hobbes's political science and the constitutionalist opinion of the 1640s and 1650s. In his *Two Treatises of Government* Locke makes the same beginning as Hobbes from a prepolitical state of nature, and thus, like Hobbes, obviates all claims to rule that might proceed from existing groups and that might justify a mixed regime. But in contrast to Hobbes, Locke believed that men could be governed by "declared Laws," hence that they need not be required to consent to government regardless of its lawlessness. The reasonable desire of each to know what is his, and to keep it secure, can and should be satisfied with such laws. Locke thought it safe to define the legislative power as sovereign rather than insist, as Hobbes did, that every act of the sovereign be considered a law. Rule of law in Locke's understanding is the rule of the lawmaking power, governed only by the natural law that society must be preserved and not by any higher law containing specific commands or prohibitions. When formulated in this way, as rule by legislation, rule of law calls for a separation between legislative power and executive power to ensure that the legislature is not exempt from the laws it will often be making.

Yet, mindful of the weakness of a subordinated executive, Locke added a third power, the federative, dealing with foreign affairs, which he called the natural power because it corresponds to the power every man had in the state of nature. This power was conceptually distinct from the executive, yet since it required the whole force of society for its exercise, as did the executive, the two powers were placed in the same hands. They are distinct, Locke says, because laws can direct the exercise of the executive, whereas the federative must be left in great part to prudence. As Locke discerns a practical alliance between two powers against a "sovereign" third, he justifies a prudence that can support the rule of law but cannot be directed by law. This appreciation of discretion, as distinct from law, culminates in *prerogative*, which is acting for the public good without direction from a law or even against the law. Prerogative applies to domestic as well as foreign affairs; so the need for discretion, which supports executive power, becomes an equal, countervailing, and complementary consideration to the rule of law, which demands the sovereignty of the legislative.

We see that Locke's seemingly abstract constitutional doctrine makes a very practical appeal to the two sides of the Civil War—legislative supremacy for the Whigs and prerogative for the Tories. But although each side can recognize its slogan in Locke's argument, it will not find that Locke endorses either claim to rule. Neither the law-abidingness of Parliament nor the virtue of the king is presupposed. Instead, Locke traces the three separate powers to be found in civil society to one general power, called "political power," which in turn he derives from the power that each man has in the state of nature to execute the law of nature, his natural right and duty conjoined. Underneath the supremacy of legislative power in civil society is the fundamental executive power in the state of nature.

This fundamental power, which reminds us of Hobbes, becomes divided in civil society between lawful power and discretionary power (these are not Locke's terms) in a balance that reminds us of the constitutionalist writers. But Locke, while avoiding the extremism and absolutism of Hobbes, clarifies the inconsistency of the constitutionalist inventors of separation of powers. With the notion of the state of nature, borrowed from Hobbes, he provides a ground for the separated powers exercised by government in civil society, and thus also a limitation on government through its wholly representative character. And since government has no right or power of its own, his political science can apportion its powers more from an analysis of the nature of political power than from a need to satisfy the demands of existing powers. Locke shows that separation of powers and representation are necessary to each other, and that both are necessary for limited government.

The influence of Locke can be seen in a small group of early eighteenth-century radicals, including John Trenchard, Anthony Hammond, John Toland, Walter Moyle, and William Hay, called "Commonwealthmen." They opposed corruption of the House of Commons by the king's ministers through "placemen," members of Parliament given offices and pensions to influence their votes and to secure their loyalty to the ministers. The arguments against such corruption (and also against standing armies that might overawe Parliament) were made on behalf of the independence of the legislative power, but not so as to subordinate the executive. Indeed a Tory, Henry St. John, Viscount Bolingbroke, could use the same arguments to promote the policy of a "Patriot King" who would govern independently of Parliament without resort to "corruption" and without regard to parties.

These writers have mechanized Locke's more subtle and complicated ordering in a government in which legislative and executive powers are balanced so as to be kept independent of each other. Speaking generally, one might say that the seventeenth-century clash of monarchical and republican regimes, moderated by appeals to a mixed regime, had become a dispute between powers of government to be resolved by finding a balance. The older claims to rule were now advanced, as they are today, in terms of Lockean political science, and parties, rather than claiming to rule the whole regime, formed around the two visible powers within a limited government in order to redress its balance—as Montesquieu remarked.

Montesquieu's contribution to the theory of separation of powers was above all in his formulation of the invisible, or less visible, power, the judicial. In reaction to Hobbes and Machiavelli, and in some degree to Locke, Montesquieu denied that fear could have a prominent and positive role in free government. He accepted the Lockean understanding of the rule of law as requiring government limited to the securing of rights, and he insisted more than Locke on the mildness and moderation of such a government. "A constitution," he said in the *Spirit of the Laws* (1748), "can be such that no one will be constrained to do things the law does not oblige him to do, and not to do things the law permits him" (11.4). Its end should be political liberty, defined as "that tranquility of spirit that comes from the opinion each has of his safety" (11.6). The government must be such that one citizen will not fear another citizen. To achieve this, the separation of the "three sorts of powers" is necessary, and particularly the independence of the "power of judging." The latter punishes crimes or judges differences among individuals, and it must be separated from the other two powers so that the judge neither legislates nor has the force of an oppressor.

Montesquieu makes it clear that the power of judging had its origin in the executive power (they were together in Locke), and thereby draws our attention especially to that separation. He remarks that European governments are moderate because the prince, who has the first two powers, leaves to his subjects the exercise of the third. When subjects themselves exercise the power of judging—in juries—that power, "so terrible among men . . . becomes so to speak invisible and null." Citizens fear the magistracy, but not the magistrates: in accordance with political liberty, they do not fear other citizens. At the same time, since punishment has been subtracted from the executive power, that power no longer appears to have the "force of an oppressor."

Montesquieu transfers the terrifying aspect of government from the executive to judging, and from judges to juries, so that it nearly disappears from view. This is perhaps why he speaks of the *power of judging*, not the *judicial power* as did Lawson and Bolingbroke, who anticipated him in describing the three powers as we do today. The third power is different in nature from the other two; lacking a will of its own, it is the power that hides power. In this respect it seems to epitomize the mildness of free government, and Montesquieu seems to suggest that the separation of the third power from the other two, and particularly from the executive, is the essential separation.

Yet Montesquieu cannot leave the power of judging without political strength against the other two powers and against the people. So he allows the hereditary nobility (in the House of Lords) to stand up for it, defending itself while defending the power of judging. It is to have a negative "faculty of preventing," as opposed to a "faculty of enacting," at least in taxation. For the sake of securing the independence of judging, Montesquieu compromises its separation from the legislature and also admits, contrary to the principle of wholly representative government, a distinct hereditary interest in government—though not because "nobles" are noble. Such compromising moderation was not inconsistency, but it was not agreeable to Americans, who borrowed much else from Montesquieu. Separation of powers was originally a republican doctrine that Locke and Montesquieu rationalized, neutralized, and cleansed of its partisan animus. But to do so they reinterpreted the English Constitution rather than abstracted from it, and in their political science they left items of unreason, unacceptable to rational republicans, such as prerogative and the House of Lords. Certain improvements remained for grateful Americans to effect so that the separation of powers could be adapted, not to the peculiar circumstances of America but to the universal requirements of an experiment "on the capacity of mankind for self-government" (*Federalist* 39).

At the time of the Revolution, Americans were agreed on the necessity of separation of powers, but unclear as to what separation meant. Their colonial inheritance was a hostility to executive power in the royal governors which they often expressed in the language of the radical Commonwealthmen, using *separation of powers* to demand the end of executive corruption in the appointment of "placemen" from the assemblies to serve on governor's councils. Then, in the Articles of Confederation and in their state constitutions made immediately after the Revolution began, Americans reverted to the weak executive of seventeenth-century republicanism. After sad experience during the war with domineering or hesitant legislatures (felt and denounced by Thomas Jefferson among others), they were ready to be instructed in a design that for the first time would justify a strong executive to a republican people. But those favoring a strong executive could not make it seem fully republican, for example, Theophilus Parsons in the "Essex Result" (1778), who advocated representation for property as well as men, and also John Adams in his *A Defence of the Constitutions of Government of the United States of America* (1787), who combined separation of powers with balance of the natural orders of society—one, few, and many. Yet the Antifederalists, who recognized the difficulty and were more dedicated republicans, could find no convincing republican justification for a strong executive and a complex structure of offices (for example, *The Federal Farmer*, Letter 14).

Through common deliberation the Framers of the Constitution came to a better solution and a clearer understanding. Comparing the government they had made with Britain's mixed government, James Wilson said that in principle the new government was "purely democratical. But that principle is applied in different forms; in order to obtain the advantages, they exclude the inconveniences, of the simple modes of government." Madison argued in *Federalist* 10 and 51 that a certain material basis of diverse sects and interests was required for a successful republic. But this material basis is called forth and kept in being by the "different forms" of the Constitution, so that the Constitution does not depend on a certain prior social order. Its material basis is diversity rather than hereditary conventions. Nonetheless, as was said above, part of its formal structure—the separation of powers—is not distinctively republican.

Two arguments for separation of powers appear in *The Federalist*, but one of them, which is closer to republican distrust of outstanding men, is much more obvious. This argument is that separation of powers is needed as a precaution against the ambition of those holding power. It refers to the "encroaching" (a word used frequently) nature of power as such, and does not examine sorts of powers. It is satisfied when power is checked by power, and its concern is negative, the prevention of tyranny. In Madison's famous statement (*Federalist* 47): "The accumulation of all powers legislative, executive, and judiciary in the same hands, whether of one, few, or many, and whether hereditary, self-appointed, or elective, may justly be pronounced the very definition of tyranny." He assumes (with Montesquieu), not that all men are hungry for absolute power (as Hobbes), but that absolute power actually held will be abused. In this matter he departs from the classical tradition that holds open the possibility of a wise man who would not abuse absolute power.

The other argument for separation of powers, less obvious in *The Federalist* but implied by Hamilton's mention of the "regular" distribution of power (*Federalist* 48), is that separation makes the powers work better. In this mode power is not generalized but kept distinct in sorts or classes and understood as power to perform some definite function (well). Montesquieu is the source of the first argument, Aristotle (in his discussion of the parts of a constitution at the end of *Politics*, book 4) the source of the second. While maintaining both, and without departing from republicanism, *The Federalist* gradually shifts its main reliance from the first to the second.

In *Federalist* 47 and 48 Madison refutes the simplistic republican doctrine of separating powers that says that each power should be located in its own branch and kept in isolation from the other powers in their branches. Such a doctrine overlooks precisely the encroaching nature of power that republicans ought to fear. Because power encroaches, and powers do not merely work at their own functions in isolation, the three branches must be given means of self-defense to ward off encroachment. Such means necessarily involve the branches with one another, but only for the sake of the independence of each. Independence is secured not by innocent reliance on "parchment barriers," but only by mutual checks, such as the president's veto and the Senate's consent to executive appointments and treaties, requiring legitimate contact in order to prevent illegitimate collusion. The simplistic doctrine in fact leaves the legislature dominant and unchecked, "drawing all power into its impetuous vortex." Thus, the simplistic doctrine is the one confused.

If power encroaches, Madison's argument continues, it must be because men love it, or have ambition. But the spirit needed for defense is the same as the motive behind encroachment. Separation of powers by the self-defense of each, then, makes use of the ambitious in order to watch over the ambitious. The principle is "Ambition must be made to counteract ambition" (*Federalist* 51). Although republicans distrust ambition, Madison has brought them, by means of their distrust, to see that ambition is useful, perhaps indispensable, to republics at least by counteracting itself. One might also reflect that ambition is in a sense republican, being hostile to fixed, hereditary interests in the community. Although ambitious individuals constitute a class, as a class they help maintain diversity. Ambitious persons distinguish themselves by leading groups of men to do new and different things. Again, we see that the forms of separated powers create their own social support.

The negative argument in *Federalist* 47–51 shows the advantage that separation of powers presents to the people: a precaution against oppression by their rulers. It speaks to their distrust by setting forth a "policy of supplying by opposite and rival interests, the defect of better motives." But this statement, as it were to the people, already suggests opportunities for the ambitious. Ambition counteracting ambition means ambition *vying* with ambition, not thwarting it. Unlike simplistic republicans and the Antifederalists, Madison does not frown upon ambition. The argument in *Federalist* 51, as David Epstein has pointed out, "cannot be considered a summary of the whole book" (*The Political Theory of "The Federalist,"* 1984, p. 146). The rest of *The Federalist,* describing the three branches of government and the different qualities required for success in each, speaks to the ambitious as well as to the common people, and not merely to their ambition. In its positive argument for separation of powers, *The Federalist* evokes "better motives" than ambition by dwelling on the qualifications required to succeed in each constitutional situation. This is neither empty exhortation to virtue nor rash reliance on virtue: as the negative argument connects private interest to defense of one's constitutional place, the positive one connects private interest to virtue in carrying out one's constitutional duty.

The Federalist does not make a theme of its discrimination of the separate powers. To do so might seem to endorse the claims to rule of those who claim virtue in those powers, in the manner of the Aristotelian mixed regime. Instead, *The Federalist* presents those virtues through an analysis of the two modes of power, energy and stability. The forms of power—legislative, executive, and judicial—must be constructed with these two modes and with an eye to their difference and their balance. Energy and stability are categories of political science (indeed of natural science), not political opinion. In directing the virtues of politicians through scientific categories *The Federalist* makes them means to a republican and constitutional end; virtue is encouraged but subordinated to liberty. Liberty is understood as the end of a distribution of power in the Constitution which gives not only security from fear of other citizens but also, through elections, a share in rule for all and an opportunity for ambition in some. Although scientific, the system is not mechanical, and does not merely connect selfish interests seeking calculated utility on the model of a free market.

Thus, the "fit characters" Madison mentioned in *Federalist* 10 as likely to emerge in greater number from a large republic are called to the tasks of the three branches, not so much for what they are as for what they will do. The merits required in each branch are, in turn, described as the expected consequences of merely formal characteristics: the relatively lengthy term and small size of the House of Representatives (relative, that is, to republican tradition and Antifederalist objections); the number and term of senators and of the executive; and the lifetime tenure of judges. As with all constitutions, the ordering of quantities produces probable qualities (Aristotle, *Politics,* book 4, chs. 11–13), but *The Federalist* is careful not to identify the result in terms of a regime. Its argument moves from what is republican to what is good for republican government, leaving it to be inferred that "the more permanent branches"—the Senate, the executive, and the judiciary (*Federalist* 52)—are not the ones republicans would claim as their own even though they enable republics to be more permanent.

Even, or especially, in regard to the popular branch, *The Federalist* makes a point of the merits for which the people will elect their representatives. If one trusts the people, it says to the Antifederalists, one should trust their choices. Legislating is generalizing, but rather by combining various local conditions than by abstracting from them. Legislators need knowledge of their locality, the ability to communicate this knowledge to other legislators, and a capacity to combine interests to make a general law, not to mention the majority needed to pass a law. The Senate, with its longer term, is a force for stability, likely to "possess great firmness" against the evils of mutable government existing from the tendency of legislatures to legislate too frequently. The executive will have energy because he is one rather than plural, and firmness because of the length of his term and his eligibility for indefinite reelection. *Energy* is now a characteristically American term of praise; in *The Federalist* it is a scientifically neutral word free of monarchical resonance (Epstein, 1984, p. 171) and justified as a means to stability. If republican government is naturally both slow and flighty, executive energy quickens it and executive firmness solidifies it.

These descriptions of what legislative and executive powers do reveal reasoned justification for what might have seemed to be, from the negative standpoint, departures from separation of powers. Seen positively, the bicameral legislature appears not as a check irrelevant to legislation but as an aid to wise legislation, and the executive veto is seen not to violate separation of powers but to contribute to the legislative process experience and firmness that otherwise would be lacking. Even for the negative purpose of checking, the positive distinction of functions now appears necessary; for an undefined legislative power or executive power leaves encroachment undefined and thus excuses or invites it. "Parchment barriers" are not enough, but they are necessary to real barriers so that the three branches can defend themselves from defensible positions. As a whole, separation of powers creates "responsible" government in a sense now familiar but new with Madison and Hamilton (*Federalist* 63, 70) of responsible *for* rather than responsive *to*. Government with separation of powers is derived from the people but also separated from the people, responsible for the people *because* it is at a distance from them. There, government can serve the people without being servile, and the people can hold it to account without preventing it from governing.

This new notion is at its height in the judiciary, hardly mentioned in the account of separation of powers in *Federalist* 47–51; in *Federalist* 49 one learns that breaches of the Constitution should not be submitted to conventions of the people for judgment. The judiciary is the "least dangerous" branch, least able to injure or annoy the other two branches, hence not a player in the system of ambition counteracting ambition. It checks the other two branches, but not in the way that they check. It has "neither Force nor Will, but merely judgment" (*Federalist* 78). Judging, as distinct from legislating and executing, is the measuring of laws and actions against a preexisting standard, the Constitution or a law, and includes interpreting that standard. If the judiciary is to be separate, it must be independent; and if it is to be independent, its judging must reach to judicial review of the rest of the government.

Thus the judiciary passes from one power among three, and that the least dangerous, to the one above the others, the only one with its eye steadily on the whole, monitor of the separation of powers and guardian of the Constitution. So far from automatic is the working of separation that two of them must yield, when required, to the supremacy of the judiciary. To do so is not unrepublican, because it puts "the intention of the people" shown in their solemn act of establishing a constitution above the intention of their agents (that is, the other branches which have force and will) and, perhaps, even above their own "momentary inclination." But judicial review will not *seem* unrepublican, despite such high authority and lifetime tenure for judges, because it offers the possibility of relief from the injustices of government to individuals. As with Montesquieu but not in his way, government seems more tolerable with an independent judiciary, for the judiciary guarantees to each citizen not only trial by jury, but, far more valuable to Americans, the right to sue. In the American version of separation of powers, reason and republican pretensions are both satisfied, and antirepublican ambition is given its due.

To recite the history of separation of powers in the American Constitution would require a review of all American political history and an analysis of no small part of it. It would begin with the conflict that soon developed between the two principal authors of *The Federalist,* Madison (taking the side of Jefferson) and Hamilton, over presidential power; and it would continue through the recent Supreme Court case on the legislative veto, *Immigration and Naturalization Service v. Chadha et al.* (1983). Such would be a history of conflict within the system of separation of powers among partisans of the two or the three branches, defending their constitutional positions or seeking unconstitutional advantage. Apart from this history, however, critics have increasingly offered challenge to the separation of powers itself. The first, and most powerful, was Woodrow Wilson in his *Congressional Government* (1889) and *Constitutional Government in the United States* (1908). He reduced the separation of powers to its checking function, attacked it as mechanistic, Newtonian, and obsolete, and proclaimed the need for leadership to override the checks, overcome the separation, and put the system in motion toward progress. He was followed by other political scientists, E. E. Schattschneider in *Party Government* (1942) and James MacGregor Burns in *Deadlock of Democracy* (1963), who argued that party responsibility, more or less on the British model, would cure the immobility that they alleged was the aim and consequence of separation of powers. Richard E. Neustadt, in *Presidential Power* (1961), has provided a widely used definition of separation of powers—"separated institutions sharing powers" (p. 330)—which denies that the powers are separated according to function. The dislike and distrust of constitutional formalities are more systematic and more pronounced in the behavioral movement in political science led by Robert A. Dahl. In his *Preface to Democratic Theory* (1956), he maintains that the formal, institutional separation of powers presented in *The Federalist* adds nothing except confusion to the material, behavioral analysis of factions in *Federalist* 10.

In sum, whereas separation of powers in the American Constitution was above all an achievement of political science as understood and improved by the Framers, today's political science is unconvinced of that principle and, if not persuaded of any other, is yet ready to abandon it in favor of some more seemingly progressive proposal. Without attempting to judge which political science is better, one can remark that the Framers of the Constitution perhaps underestimated the risk they took when they grounded their construction on political science. But it is not easy to take account of the immutable truths of politics without relying on the fashion and fancies of political science.

Separation of Powers, Human Rights, and Constitutional Government: A Franco-American Dialogue at the Time of the Revolution[1]

Terence Marshall

THE AMERICAN CONSTITUTION'S TEXT shows separation of powers, along with federalism, to be the document's "central organizing principle."[2] Yet the chief author of that text, James Madison, designates this separation as an "invention of prudence," an "auxil-

---

[1] Portions of this article appear in modified form under the title "Human Rights and Constitutional Government: A Franco-American Dialogue at the Time of the Revolution," in *The Legacy of the French Revolution*, ed. Ralph Hancock and Gary Lambert (Lanham, Md.: Rowman and Littlefield, 1994). A French version of the latter text also appears in Jacques d'Hondt, *La Philosophie et la Révolution Française* (Paris: Librairie Vrin, 1993).

[2] The phrase comes from Glen Thurow, "Judicial Activism vs. Judicial Restraint," in *The New Federalist Papers*, ed. J. Jackson Barlow, Dennis Mahoney and John West (Lanham, Md.: University Press of America, 1988), 191. See James Madison, *Annals of Congress*, 1:604, cited in Edward J. Erler, *The American Polity: Essays on the Theory and Practice of Constitutional Government* (New York: Crane Russak, 1991), 59; William Kristol, "The Problem of the Separation of Powers: *Federalist* 47–51," in *Saving the Revolution: The Federalist Papers and the American Founding*, ed. Charles R. Kesler (New York: The Free Press, 1987), 101; Dennis Mahoney, "The Separation of Powers: A Constitutional Principle in Contemporary Perspective," in *Constitutionalism in America*, ed. Sarah B. Thurow (Lanham, Md.: University Press of America, 1988), 2:23; Harvey C. Mansfield, Jr., "Separation of Powers in the American Constitution," in this volume.

iary precaution," thus not a principle but a means for achieving the Constitution's end of justice.[3] For a century and more, however, since the writings of Woodrow Wilson, critics of this "invention" have seen it rather as a barrier than as a means to achieving this end.[4] In this respect, whereas Madison had sought to join the means with the end, the critics would separate the two.

Such a criticism of separation of powers in the name of justice was made no less sharply in the Founding period. But the form of criticism most approximating that heard today came less from the Anti-Federalists in America than from those who inspired leading members of the Constituent Assembly in France. By comparing the leading American and French arguments on separation of powers in relation to justice or rights, one might discern in Madison's design a relation between means and ends which reveals that the critics' perception of this means as a barrier is tantamount not to seeking the end more effectively but to changing it substantially.

The transatlantic character of the early debates on constitutionalism is widely recognized, but its significance for understanding the theory and practice of constitutionalism remains insufficiently appreciated.[5] Thus specialists focus on one or the other shore of "the great divide": the Federalist—Anti-Federalist debate, or else that featuring the Monarchiens, the Girondins and the Montagnards. Yet both Federalists and Anti-Federalists referred to the French philosopher Montesquieu as an "oracle" for their discussions of separation of powers.[6] At the same time

---

[3]*The Federalist*, ed. Jacob E. Cooke (Cleveland: Meridian Books, The World Publishing Co., 1965), No. 51, 349, 352.

[4]Woodrow Wilson, *Constitutional Government in the United States* (New York: Columbia University Press, 1911), 221; Lloyd Cutler, "To Form a Government," in *Separation of Powers—Does It Still Work?* ed. Robert A. Goldwin and Art Kaufman (Washington: AEI Press, 1986), 1–17; Robert Dahl, "Removing Certain Impediments to Democracy in the United States," in *The Moral Foundations of the American Republic*, 3d ed., ed. Robert H. Horwitz (Charlottesville: University Press of Virginia, 1986), 235.

[5]For a recent example, see Patrice Higonnet, *Sister Republics: The Origins of French and American Republicanism* (Cambridge: Harvard University Press, 1988). Despite the book's title, the author's focus on sociological and ideological considerations, inspired by the historiography of Bernard Bailyn and François Furet, largely abstracts from the constitutional reasoning of the American Founders and thus fails to provide a solid basis for comparing the two republican traditions.

[6]*The Federalist*, No. 47, 324ff. See James W. Muller, "The American Framers' Debt to Montesquieu," in *The Revival of Constitutionalism*, ed. James W. Muller (Lincoln: University of Nebraska Press, 1988), 87–102, which stresses the fidelity of *The Federalist* to Montesquieu. Compare Kristol, "The Problem of the Separation of Powers," which elucidates important differences between Madison and the author of *The Spirit of the Laws*. See also Mansfield, "Separation of Powers," 5, 10–11, 14.

Turgot and Condorcet, the principal founder of France's First Republic, examined and criticized the mode of separation of powers adopted in the American states. These criticisms in turn provided the occasion for John Adams' *Défense des Constitutions Américaines*, published in Paris in 1792.[7] Thomas Paine, Benjamin Franklin, St. John de Crèvecoeur, Thomas Jefferson, Lafayette, George Washington, Saint-Simon, Gouverneur Morris, Destutt de Tracy, Sieyès and Chateaubriand figured prominently in this transatlantic exchange. Indeed Morris closely advised Louis XVI on an alternate constitution to that proposed in 1791.[8] And Thomas Jefferson, who later collaborated with Destutt de Tracy's publications in America and France on Montesquieu, constitutionalism and the separation of powers, met extensively in 1789 at his home on the Avenue des Champs-Elysées, with Lafayette and other members of the Constituent Assembly preparing drafts for the Declaration of the Rights of Man.[9] As these meetings attest, the question of separation of powers was closely identified with the problem of justice or human rights. And the final version of the French Declaration specifies in its penultimate article that "Any society where the

[7]Anne-Robert-Jacques Turgot, Baron de l'Aulne, a leading French economist and administrator who was also associated with l'*Encyclopédie*, initially expressed his views on this subject in a letter sent in 1778 to Dr. Richard Price. His argument is repeated by Condorcet in *L'Influence de la Révolution de l'Amérique sur l'Europe*, in *Oeuvres*, ed. François Arago and Arthur Condorcet-O'Connor (Paris: F. Dido Frères, 1847–1849), 8:12–14. John Adams' reply, appearing in English in 1787, was published in France by the Librairie Buisson. *The Federalist* was translated into French in 1792 by Trudaine de la Sabière, and this remains the only complete translation of it in the French language.

[8]Gouverneur Morris, *Mémorial de Gouverneur Morris, Ministre Plénipotentiaire des Etats-Unis de 1792 à 1794* (Paris: Librairie Renouard, 1842). In addition, see Jared Sparks, *The Life of Gouverneur Morris with Selections from His Correspondence and Miscellaneous Papers; Detailing Events in the American Revolution, the French Revolution, and in the Political History of the United States* (Boston: Gray & Bowen, 1832), 1:348–67; 2:490–525; 3:481–500. Cf. George Anastaplo, "American Constitutionalism and the Virtue of Prudence: Philadelphia, Paris, Washington, Gettysburg," in *Abraham Lincoln, The Gettysburg Address and American Constitutionalism*, ed. Leo Paul S. de Alvarez (Irving, Texas: University of Dallas Press, 1976), 77–170; Gilbert Chinard, ed., *George Washington as the French Knew Him* (Princeton: Princeton University Press, 1940); Gilbert Chinard, ed., *The Letters of Lafayette and Jefferson* (Baltimore: Johns Hopkins University Press, 1929).

[9]*The Papers of Thomas Jefferson*, ed. Julian Boyd (Princeton: Princeton University Press, 1960), 15:107, 126–28, 230; Chinard, ed., *The Letters of Lafayette and Jefferson*, 79–80, 136–37. See also Destutt de Tracy, *Commentaire sur "L'Esprit des Lois" de Montesquieu, suivi d'Observations Inédites de Condorcet* (Paris: Librairie Delaunay, 1819) (English language edition published in Philadelphia in 1811 by Thomas Jefferson and William Duane).

guarantee of rights is not secured, nor the separation of powers determined, has no Constitution." The connection made in the French Declaration concerning separation of powers, human rights and constitutional government does not, however, amount to sharing Madison's position on the integration of the three. In *The Federalist* Madison's discussion of these questions is directed precisely against the views of Thomas Jefferson, the man in the Founding generation having most affinity with leading constitutionalists in France.[10] By contrast, in an argument closely parallel to contemporary American criticisms of "divided government," Condorcet had argued, against American institutions, that Montesquieu's doctrine of checks and balances is appropriate under a monarchy but not in a democracy. Conversely, Madison and Hamilton argue in *The Federalist* that, while a declaration of rights is suitable under a monarchy, it is of dubious merit in a popular regime.[11]

Such differences abound in French and American positions on the executive veto, bicameralism, representation, centralization and decentralization, and elections. Although the American Constitution establishes a strengthened central authority, nonetheless the maintenance of an energetic federal structure is vital to the success of Madison's design.[12] In France, on the other hand, the debate over federalism failed to result in devolving the powers concentrated in Paris since the time of Louis XIV.[13] Moreover, the vexed question of elections and representation was there debated either in terms of Sieyès' Enlightenment concern for a social division of labor guided in the legislature by elite expertise, or else in terms of the "mandat impératif" aimed at solving, in a na-

---

[10]*The Federalist*, No. 49, 338ff.

[11]Ibid., No. 84, 575ff. See No. 48, 333. Cf. Herbert Storing, "The Constitution and the Bill of Rights" and Walter Berns, "The Constitution as Bill of Rights," in *How Does the Constitution Secure Rights?* ed. Robert A. Goldwin and William A. Schambra (Washington: AEI Press, 1985), 15–35, 50–73; Robert A. Goldwin, "Congressman Madison Proposes Amendments to the Constitution," in *The Framers and Fundamental Rights*, ed. Robert Licht (Washington: AEI Press, 1991), 57–85; Jean-Claude Lamberti, "Adams et Madison, Lecteurs de Montesquieu," *Commentaire* 11 (Spring 1988): 385–93.

[12]Michael Zuckert, "Federalism and the Founding: Toward a Reinterpretation of the Constitutional Convention," *The Review of Politics* 48 (Spring 1986): 166–210; Terence Marshall, ed., *Théorie et Pratique du Gouvernement Constitutionnel: La France et les Etats-Unis* (Editions de l'Espace Européen, 1992), 168ff.; Martin Diamond et al., *The Democratic Republic* (Chicago: Rand McNally & Co., 1970), 96–103.

[13]Mona Ozouf, "Fédéralisme," in François Furet and Mona Ozouf, *Dictionnaire Critique de la Révolution Française* (Paris: Flammarion, 1988), 85–95.

tion as large as France, the problems of representation posed by Rousseau.[14]

The latter concerns differ markedly from Madison's purpose, through the mode of elections and representation, to "refine and enlarge" the electorate's opinions by promoting a deliberative disposition among the people's representatives.[15] Whereas the suspensive veto under the American project is partly conceived with a view to this purpose, the veto granted to the French king under the Constitution of 1791 was designed, not to promote the dialogical conditions of deliberation, but to ensure that the National Assembly would elaborate laws that re-present the popular will.[16] Such a concern to re-present the popular will is thus consistent with the First French Constitution's choice of a unicameral legislature unchecked by an upper chamber. Both the veto provision and the unicameral legislature of the First French Constitution confirm the very different ideas of separation of powers and human rights informing the French Declaration and the American Founding.

Indeed, if one juxtaposes, in the Declaration of the Rights of Man, Article XVI on the separation of powers and Article VI on the General Will, a revealing ambiguity appears in the French text to distinguish it sharply from the American version of separation of powers. In Article XVI alone, the doctrine of separating the legislative and the executive seems to equivocate over at least two competing grounds for the separation: the principle of independence and the principle of specialization.[17] The first principle requires, for example, that a chief executive not be appointed by the legislature, which in turn he will not be empowered to dissolve, and that members of one branch not depend on the other for

[14]See Keith Michael Baker, "Constitution," in Furet and Ozouf, *Dictionnaire Critique*, 537–52; Jacques Godechot, *Les Constitutions de la France Depuis 1789* (Paris: Garnier-Flammarion, 1979), 29–32, 71ff.; Claude Nicolet, *L'idée Républicaine en France* (Editions Gallimard, 1982), 411ff.

[15]*The Federalist*, No. 10, 62; No. 55, 374; No. 63, 424–425. Cf. Joseph Bessette, "Deliberative Democracy: The Majority Principle in Republican Government," in *How Democratic Is the Constitution?* ed. Robert A. Goldwin and William A. Schambra (Washington: AEI Press, 1980), 102–116.

[16]Baker, "Constitution," 543–51.

[17]Michel Troper, "Montesquieu and the Separation of Power in the United States," paper presented at a bicentennial conference organized by the Foundation Internationale des Sciences Humaines at the University of Virginia, November 19–22, 1987, 6. Cf. Marshall, ed., *Théorie et Pratique*, 345 ff; and Michel Troper, *La Séparation des Pouvoirs et l'Histoire Constitutionnelle Française* (Paris: Librairie Générale de Droit et de Jurisprudence, 1980).

remuneration. Under the principle of specialization all of these negative requirements are reversed. Thus, in the latter case, separation of powers means simply that members of the legislature and the executive will be concerned uniquely with their respective functions and not with those of other branches. The first principle implies the "checks and balances" derived from Montesquieu; the second, drawing from Rousseau in the *Social Contract*, anticipates the modern parliamentary system. Taken by itself, Article XVI of the French Declaration allows for either one of these principles, whereas the American Constitution seems clearly to adopt that of Montesquieu.[18]

Although remote in other respects from Rousseau's thought, Condorcet adumbrates, in his critique of American constitutionalism, a Rousseauist interpretation of Article XVI, particularly when this Article is associated with that concerning the General Will. And yet Article XVI is doubly ambiguous, since even when juxtaposed to Article VI it can also be interpreted on the basis of principles expressed in Diderot's *Encyclopedia* article, "Droit Naturel." In effect, this ambiguity accommodates the rivalry in the Constituent Assembly between the allies of Condorcet and the allies of Robespierre, the Jacobin disciple of Rousseau.[19] Nonetheless, whatever distinguishes the Encyclopedists and Condorcet from Robespierre or Rousseau over the grounds of the General Will, the idea of this Will refers to a principle of right differing radically from that inherent to the American Constitution.

This difference is clarified by examining why Madison, the principal author of the American Bill of Rights, was first opposed to having such a bill at all, and why he later opposed placing it at the head of the Constitution, as occurred in France. According to Madison, if a declaration of rights is not first grounded in a sound constitutional regime, such a declaration poses no more than a

[18]*The Federalist*, Nos. 9, 47. Cf., however, note 94 *infra;* see also Terence Marshall, "La Raison Pratique et le Constitutionnalisme Américain," *Revue Française de Science Politique* 38 (December 1988): 917–23.

[19]For the readings of Rousseau by Condorcet and Robespierre as well as by other leading members of the Constituent Assembly, see Roger Barny, *Prélude Idéologique à la Révolution Française* (Paris: Les Belles Lettres, 1985). Cf. Mona Ozouf, *L'Homme Régénéré: Essais sur la Révolution Française* (Paris Gallimard, 1989), 118, 139 ff; Baker, "Constitution," 540–51. For Rousseau's discussion of Diderot's thesis on the General Will, see *Du Contrat Social*, Première Version, in *Oeuvres Complètes* (Gallimard: Bibliothèque de la Pléïade), 3:282–89. Concerning the debates on these matters at the Constituent Assembly in 1789, see Marcel Gauchet, "La Déclaration des Droits de l'Homme et du Citoyen," *Commentaire*, no. 43 (Fall 1988): 783–90.

"parchment barrier" to despotic rule.[20] But the founding of constitutional or nondespotic government requires, beyond the imposition of effective limits on the exercise of power, also establishing suitable conditions allowing government to be not only free and popular but also stable, competent and energetic in accomplishing its tasks.[21] Liberty, says Madison, is no less imperiled by inadequate as by excessive political power.[22] But an ill-conceived bill of rights risks promoting among the people a critical spirit either so waspish as to reduce popular government to abject incompetence, or else so demanding as to undermine all proper limits on authority.

Since the American Founders sought to establish a popular regime respectful of human rights and also capable of accomplishing the quotidian tasks of politics, they aimed at integrating the principles of right with the requirements of reason. Unlike Condorcet, however, they did not consider that a synthesis of right and reason could be obtained simply by appending to a declaration of rights a distribution of constitutional authority designed separately to obtain the most efficient application of popular choices. It remains to be seen why, for the Americans, the synthesis entails the integration of constitutional ends and means.

Clearly such differences do not derive merely from the different national experiences or problems facing the two countries. Just as there were those in America who, like Jefferson and Thomas Paine, were drawn to orientations more dominant in France, there were those in France who, like Tocqueville later, were partial *mutatis mutandis* to the American practice.[23] A study of the reasons underlying these differences helps explain divergences concerning

[20]*The Federalist*, No. 48, 333. Cf. No. 25, 163 and No. 73, 494 in relation to No. 84, 575–87. Although Madison employs the expression "parchment barriers" in reference to the separation of powers, he clearly agreed with Hamilton's similar point in *Federalist* No. 84 concerning declarations of rights. See the studies by Goldwin, Berns and Storing cited above in note 11.

[21]See *Federalist* No. 37, 233–34, in comparison with Nos. 10, 48, 49, and 51.

[22]Ibid., No. 63, 428–29. Cf. *The Writings of James Madison*, ed. Gaillard Hunt (New York: G.P. Putnam's Sons, Inc., 1900–1910), 6:101.

[23]The ill-fated presidential system established by France's Second Republic, and leading to the restoration of the Empire under Louis Napoleon, is often said to have been inspired by American institutions. Tocqueville, who participated in elaborating the 1848 Constitution, corrects this view and stipulates that the failure to adopt a bicameral legislature and a system of checks and balances led within four years to the collapse of the Constitution and the establishment of a presidential dictatorship. See his *Souvenirs* (Editions Gallimard, 1978) 2:256, 263–77. Cf. Godechot, *Les Constitutions*, 261–62; François Furet, *La Révolution 1770–1880* (Hachette, 1988), 383, 402–07.

not only the separation of powers, but also the basis of rights and thus of constitutional government itself.

Indeed, if the separation of powers is conceived on either side of the Atlantic as a means for achieving justice, the different modes of separation may be governed not only by different local circumstances but also by different ideas of what justice is. All three orientations here evoked, that of Madison, of Condorcet and of Rousseau, refer the question of separation of powers to transhistorical principles of right and affirm that the latter are grounded in the principle of reason. But within the broad philosophical tradition defending the idea of transhistorical principles against those who deny them, one may discern three modes of reasoning through which political things are perceived: science, practical reason and aesthetics.[24] According to whichever mode is selected as primary, human affairs will appear under profoundly altered lights. Whereas under the aegis of the Enlightenment the perception of politics is construed through scientific method, the ensuing revolts against this construction, whether in the thought of Rousseau or in contemporary postmodernism, have led to interpreting humanity through the sensibilities of aesthetic perception.[25] And both of these determinations of political perception derive from a repudiation of the classical mode, based on practical reason.

Corresponding to the three modes of perception are, indeed, three philosophical traditions adhering to the idea of a transhistorical principle of right; and each of these traditions in turn traces a radically different path to constitutional government. To understand why this is so, one need first note what distinguishes the three modes of reason in question. For example, whereas science is concerned with things that cannot be other than they are, such as the invariable $E = mc^2$, practical reasoning and aesthetics deal with things that can be other. But despite this similitude in the objects of their thinking, practical reason and aesthetics differ with respect to the disposition requisite to their respective modes of thought. In this regard, the artist is like the scientist who can com-

---

[24]Concerning these modes, see Plato's trilogy, *The Theaetetus, The Sophist* and *The Statesman* in relation to Aristotle's *Nicomachean Ethics* VI and Kant's *Critique of Pure Reason, Critique of Practical Reason,* and *Critique of Judgment.*

[25]See Terence Marshall, "Poésie et Praxis dans l'*Emile* de Rousseau: Les Droits de l'Homme et le Sentiment de l'Humanité," *Revue des Sciences Philosophiques et Théologiques* 76 (October 1992): 589–606; Luc Ferry, *Le Droit: La Nouvelle Querelle des Anciens et des Modernes* (Presses Universitaires de France, 1984), 139, 167–68, 178–80; *Homo Aestheticus: L'Invention du Goût à l'age Démocratique* (Paris: Grasset, 1990); Hans-Georg Gadamer, *Truth and Method* (New York: The Seabury Press, 1975).

bine excellence of conception even with baseness of character. Unlike the latter, the man of practical excellence, such as a good judge, cannot accurately perceive the cases before him if his deliberation is governed by passion or interest. All the more is this true, beyond judges or policy analysts, of statesmen who must discern the common good and the means to attain it.[26] But this interpretation of practical wisdom reveals it to depend on a love of wisdom that is itself altogether rare, surpassing in the judge or statesman any other desire.[27]

Although constitutional government refers to nondespotic or limited rule, the meaning of such rule, and thus of what is rightful, alters with the employment of one or the other of these modes of reason. For example, in the classical tradition, based on practical reason, political and despotic rule are seen to differ by virtue of the disparity, which is not merely "normative" but empirical, between a free human being and a slave.[28] Unlike a servile or dependent being, one who is free, according to this tradition, possesses in addition to the capacity for deliberating well also the strength of character to obey reasoned judgment, whether in the face of another's will or against the influence of his own desires. Ancient constitutional thought therefore has as its object a paradox: how to rule human beings who are free. Achieving in practice such rightful or constitutional rule depends in some measure upon securing the requisite disposition of character (*ethika*) and of judgment, not only in citizens but especially in those who seek to perceive politics as it is.[29]

By contrast, at the origin of modernity the idea of rights developed from the machiavellian separation of ethics from politics. Partisans of the Enlightenment thus maintained that "in the state of nature, no action can be called evil" and that men have an equal

---

[26]See Aristotle *Nicomachean Ethics* 1138b18–25, 1139a1–1140b30, in relation to 1103a14–26, 1114b5–30, 1143a25, 1143b17, 1144a25–1145a12, 1176a15–17. Cf. Plato *Sophist* 254b; Jacob Klein, *Plato's Trilogy: Theaetetus, the Sophist and the Statesman* (Chicago: University of Chicago Press, 1977), 200; Leo Strauss, Letter to Helmut Kuhn (undated), *The Independent Journal of Philosophy* 2 (1978): 24–26. Cf. in this respect, Herbert Storing, "American Statesmanship: Old and New," in *Bureaucrats, Policy Analysts, Statesmen: Who Leads?* ed. Robert A. Goldwin (Washington: AEI Press, 1980), 88–113.

[27]See Aristotle *Nicomachean Ethics* 1144a24ff. (on the difference between the *phronimos* and the *deinos*) in relation to 1144a37 (that we cannot be *phronimos* without being *agathos*). Cf. the movement in the sequel, Books VII through X, examining the principle of *praxis* from *epithymia* through *philia* to *philia tes sophias*.

[28]Aristotle *Politics* 1252a7–16, 1253b1ff., 1255b16–18, 1327b19–38.

[29]Aristotle *Nicomachean Ethics* 1095b5–10, 1140b10–25; *Politics* 1254b1–1255b20, 1327b20–35.

natural right to all that their power can acquire.[30] Under this dispensation human or civil rights supersede what is moral; and constitutional government, limited to protecting such rights, has no legitimate additional concern for educating the soul. Corresponding to this view of constitutionalism, perceiving politics in terms of relations of power renders the political amenable to interpretation according to the methods of a natural science governed not by the love of wisdom, but by an acquisitive desire to master nature for the relief of man's estate.[31] The separation of rights from ethics in early modernity thus expresses a radical disseverance from the classical teaching concerning the principles of justice and of perception alike.

Well before Kant's subsequent "Copernican Revolution," Jean-Jacques Rousseau sought a principle of perception and practice reconciling anew not only "science and conscience" but morality with rights.[32] Their common quest represents, however, not a redintegration of classical ethics but an altogether novel idea of morality and of constitutional rule, grounded neither in practical reason nor in science but in an aesthetic principle: the sentiment of *humanité*.[33] This principle will be examined in the sequel. For the moment one need observe that each of the three associated sets of principles—of perception, of right and of constitutional government—is determined by a thoroughly distinct orientation. The emphasis in classical thought on measured judgment as the condition of freedom implies the concern to educate or refine the passions so that they do not dominate and thus misguide the intellect. By contrast, the emphasis on freedom in early modernity

[30]Spinoza, *Political Treatise*, 2:18; Thomas Hobbes, *Leviathan* 1.13–15; John Locke, *Essay Concerning Human Understanding* II.xxi, secs. 43–56; Helvétius, *De l'Esprit* II; D'Holbach, *Le Bon Sens*, Préface and chs. clxxi, clxxix.

[31]See Richard Kennington, "Bacon's Critique of Ancient Philosophy in *New Organon* I," in *Nature and Scientific Method*, ed. Daniel Dahlstrom (Washington: Catholic University Press, 1991), 235–51, and his "Descartes and Mastery of Nature," in *Organism, Medecine, and Metaphysics*, ed. S. F. Spicker (Dordrecht, Holland: D. Reidel Publishing Co., 1978), 201–23; Jerry Weinberger, *Science, Faith and Politics: Francis Bacon and the Utopian Roots of the Modern Age* (Ithaca: Cornell University Press, 1985); Howard B. White, *Peace Among the Willows: The Political Philosophy of Francis Bacon* (The Hague: Martinus Nijhoff, 1968); David Lachterman, *The Ethics of Geometry: A Genealogy of Modernity* (New York: Routledge, 1989).

[32]For a detailed examination of the Rousseauian roots of modern, critical philosophy, see Richard Velkley, *Freedom and the End of Reason: On the Moral Foundation of Kant's Critical Philosophy* (Chicago: The University of Chicago Press, 1989); and Susan Meld Shell, *The Rights of Reason: A Study of Kant's Philosophy and Politics* (Toronto: University of Toronto Press, 1980).

[33]Marshall, "Poésie et Praxis," 589–606.

promotes the impulse to seek liberation from taboos or constraints on the passions. Finally, the aesthetic emphasis on *humanité*, or generalized compassion, elicits indeed a moral impulse, but one now favoring the supersession of reason and passion by sentiment. The differences in 1789 among partisans of transhistoric principles of right and of constitutional government reflect the above divergent origins of these ideas in the course of their history. Uncovering the reasons informing their partisanship should thus serve to clarify contemporary convictions derived from this founding era.

At first glance, the very expression "separation of powers" suggests a modern paternity to this constitutional doctrine. Although often traced to the classical teaching of the mixed regime, the separation of powers, it seems, accentuates a modern, quantitative concept, "power," whereas the mixed regime evokes competing, partial claims to a qualitative principle of justice.[34] The very idea of modern "checks and balances" suggests, as Woodrow Wilson animadverts, a mechanistic, Newtonian vision of power balancing power. In Montesquieu's schema, liberty is thus secured not by a judgment over these competing claims but by their maintenance in perpetual tension.[35]

Madison indeed refers to Montesquieu as "the oracle who is always consulted and cited on this subject," but he does so in the dialectical context of responding to Anti-Federalist charges that the Founders deviate from the teachings of this "celebrated author."[36] It has often been observed that the doctrine of the mixed regime, defended by John Adams in his reply to Condorcet, was inapplicable to the United States, where the absence of an aristocracy and the presence of a preponderantly democratic culture made the mixed regime inconceivable. On the other hand, the doctrine of separation of powers, duly revised, does not as such question democratic precepts; and *The Federalist* could adduce this doctrine while having emphasized that the Constitution is "wholly

[34]See Martin Diamond, "The Separation of Powers and the Mixed Regime," *Publius* 8, no. 3 (Summer 1978): 33–43, esp. 35–36.

[35]Montesquieu, *De l'Esprit des Lois* (Paris: Garnier-Flammarion, 1979), 1.11.6 and 1.19.27, esp. pp. 294, 302, and 478. Cf. Pierre Manent, *Histoire Intellectuelle du Libéralisme: Dix Leçons* (Paris: Calmann-Lévy, 1987), 130–33; Thomas Pangle, *Montesquieu's Philosophy of Liberalism: A Commentary on the Spirit of the Laws* (Chicago: University of Chicago Press, 1973), 110–111, 116–135. Compare Kristol, "The Problem of the Separation of Powers."

[36]*The Federalist*, No. 47, 324, 326–27. For a meticulous analysis of this point, see Kristol, "The Problem of the Separation of Powers," 102–06. See also Mansfield, "Separation of Powers," 10–11.

popular."[37] But if, as Madison says, the separation of powers is a means for achieving justice, then designing a constitutional government enjoins confronting possible tensions between popular claims to justice and what justice in fact requires.[38]

Indeed, Madison defends the form of separation of powers under the Constitution not simply in terms of checks and balances, but for the purpose of separating the executive from the legislature as a means for obtaining stable, energetic and competent government, and also for establishing justice within a "wholly popular" regime. Says Publius:

The republican principle demands that the deliberate sense of the community should govern the conduct of those to whom they entrust the management of their affairs; but it does not require an unqualified complaisance to every sudden breeze of passion, or to every transient impulse which the people may receive from the arts of men, who flatter their prejudices to betray their interests. It is a just observation, that the people commonly *intend* the Public Good. This often applies to their very errors. But their good sense would despise the adulator, who should pretend that they always *reason right* about the *means* of promoting it.[39]

Thus, while Condorcet criticized the constraints imposed on popular will by the constitutional system of checks and balances, the American Founders were concerned with the fact that this will may issue not from a reasoned deliberation of the common good but rather from the competition of diverse ambitions and interests. The fact that a choice is widely popular or even general does not signify that it is wise or just.

"In a nation of philosophers," says Madison, "this consideration ought to be disregarded. A reverence for the laws, would be sufficiently inculcated by the voice of an enlightened reason. But a nation of philosophers is as little to be expected as the philosophical race of kings wished for by Plato."[40] Whereas in a popular government the people are sovereign, nonetheless "the aim of every

[37]*The Federalist*, No. 14, 84–85; No. 73, 497. Cf. Mansfield, "Separation of Powers," 10–13; Kristol, "The Problem of the Separation of Powers," 111ff.; David Epstein, *The Political Theory of the Federalist* (Chicago: University of Chicago Press, 1984), 146.

[38]See *The Federalist*, No. 51, 352, in relation to 59, 62, 293–97, 374, 384, 424–25 and in relation to 340–43.

[39]Ibid., No. 71, 482, emphasis original. Cf. the different formulation of this problem by Rousseau, *Du Contrat Social* 2.6, final paragraph.

[40]*The Federalist*, No. 49, 340.

political Constitution is or ought to be first to obtain for rulers, men who possess most wisdom to discern, and most virtue to pursue the common good of the society; and in the next place, to take the most effectual precautions for keeping them virtuous, whilst they continue to hold their public trust."[41]

Among these precautions, designated as such in *Federalist* 51, is the system of checks and balances under the separation of powers. But far from being conceived in the mechanistic, Newtonian terms so often ascribed to it, this "invention of prudence" is explained in terms that recall the classic problem of securing equitable judgments. Already in *Federalist* 10, Madison delineates the problem:

No man is allowed to be a judge in his own cause; because his interest would certainly bias his judgment, and, not improbably, corrupt his integrity. With equal, nay with greater reason, a body of men, are unfit to be both judges and parties, at the same time; yet, what are many of the most important acts of legislation, but so many judicial determinations, not indeed concerning the rights of single persons, but concerning the rights of large bodies of citizens; and what are the different classes of legislators, but advocates and parties to the causes which they determine? Is a law proposed concerning private debts? It is a question to which the creditors are parties on one side, and the debtors on the other. Justice ought to hold the balance between them. Yet the parties are and must be themselves the judges.[42]

The "inventions of prudence" established by the American Constitution are designed, as noted, "to refine and enlarge the public views," to render them more deliberate and just than they otherwise might be when not determined beyond passions and interests, above all by the love of wisdom.[43] The Founders' "inventions of prudence" are thus clearly distinguishable not only from the principle of *humanité* advanced by Rousseau or Kant, but also from the concept of right found in the writings of Diderot and Condorcet.[44]

In particular, while differing from Rousseau's aesthetic, the Encyclopedists' thesis on the General Will corresponds to the view

---

[41]Ibid., No. 57, 384.

[42]Ibid., No. 10, 59–60. Cf. note 38 *supra*.

[43]See ibid., No. 55, 374, No. 63, 425 and No. 71, 482–83, in comparison with No. 10, 60 and No. 49, 340. Cf. Aristotle *Nicomachean Ethics* 1144a22–1145a12.

[44]Marshall, "La Raison Pratique," 917–23. See Rousseau's critique of Diderot concerning the General Will and natural right, in *Du Contrat Social*, Première Version, 284–89, and compare *Emile* (Editions Garnier Frères, 1964), 259–60, 279, 303 and *Discours sur l'Origine de l'Inégalité*, in *Oeuvres Complètes*, 3:125–26.

that law be formulated according to the universal criteria of scientific reason. According to this view, if law is expressed in universal or noncontradictory form, it cannot err.[45] Since such a formalism corresponds to the thesis that human beings are equal in their natural freedom or their autonomous wills, the differences among human beings are thereby ignored in favor of what is universal or common among them. By dint of this universalism, whenever a law is expressed in general terms, applicable equally to all, it is "legitimate" or rational. Under such a constitutional system, therefore, nothing justifies resorting to bicameralism, or to checks and balances, to restrain the General Will. Moreover, under such a constitutionalism there is no place in the *Code Civil* for prudential considerations of equity, something at times keenly noted by those having to deal with the unvarying rules applied by the *Code*'s administrators.

Although the American Declaration of 1776 adumbrates the universalism of 1789 by affirming that "all men are created equal" and that "they are endowed by their Creator with certain unalienable rights," nonetheless the Declaration of 1776 also refers in the context to what "prudence . . . will dictate" and to what "all experience hath shown."[46] Thus, when the American Founders maintain that all men are created equal in their rights, this does not

[45]Diderot, "Droit Naturel," in *Oeuvres Politiques* (Editions Garnier Frères, 1963), 32–35; Condorcet, *Essai sur l'Application de l'Analyse à la Probabilité des Décisions Rendue à la Pluralité des Voix* (Paris: 1785); *Vie de Turgot*, in *Oeuvres*, 5:211; Rousseau, *Du Contrat Social* 2:3; Immanuel Kant, *Critique of Practical Reason*, 1.1.7.

[46]Although the principal author of the American Declaration, Thomas Jefferson, was close to the French Encyclopedists, he acknowledged that his aim in the American Declaration was to express less his own thought than "the harmonizing sentiments of the day," including those not only of the "Modern" John Locke or Algernon Sidney, but also of the "Ancients," Aristotle and Cicero. See his Letter to Henry Lee, May 8, 1825, in Thomas Jefferson, *Political Writings* (Indianapolis: Bobbs-Merrill, 1955), 8; Carl Becker, *The Declaration of Independence: A Study in the History of Ideas* (New York: Vintage Books, 1942), 24–26, 135–141. Outside of the United States and its "harmonizing sentiments" Jefferson was more explicitly "Modern," as shown by his striking out "the care of one's honor" from Lafayette's draft of the Declaration of the Rights of Man and Citizen. See Gerald Stourzh, *Alexander Hamilton and the Idea of Republican Government* (Stanford: Stanford University Press, 1970), 100, 240; and Chinard, ed., *The Letters of Lafayette and Jefferson*, 138. Following a common practice among French scholars, Claude Fohlen, former director of North American Studies at the Sorbonne, notes the difference between the two Declarations but oddly concludes that, unlike the French Declaration, the American does not refer to a universal principle. Rather, what is at issue is the nature of the universal. See Claude Fohlen, "Bills of Rights et Déclarations des Droits de l'Homme," in *Focus: Le Temps des Constitutions, 1787–1795* (Paris: Ambassade des Etats-Unis, 1988), 17–19, 22.

mean that, in establishing a regime to secure these rights, one may conveniently ignore the inequalities among men in their virtues and defects. Each, independently of birth or station, equally deserves justice; but the content of what is just varies, again independently of birth or station, according to what each in particular deserves.[47]

Unlike the scientific rationalism propounded by Condorcet, therefore, "prudence will dictate" that, when elaborating a Constitution, one take account of the virtues, weaknesses or defects found diversely among human beings. This implies that separation of powers be conceived, not simply on the basis of a functional analysis of institutions, but rather on the basis of considering human psychology or nature. And this reflection suggests that the formal logic of legal science be displaced by the dialectical logic of practical reason.[48]

Although, says Madison, there are "qualities in human nature which justify a certain portion of esteem and confidence" and "republican government presupposes the existence of these qualities in a higher degree than any other form," nonetheless the establishment of such a government does not betoken the disappearance of contrary qualities.[49]

If men were angels, no government would be necessary. If angels were to govern men, neither external nor internal controuls on government would be necessary. In framing a government which is to be administered by men over men, the great difficulty lies in this: You must first enable the government to controul the governed; and in the next place, oblige it to controul itself. A dependence on the people is no doubt the primary controul on the government; but experience has taught mankind the necessity of auxiliary precautions.[50]

---

[47]Abraham Lincoln, *Collected Works*, ed. Roy Basler (New Brunswick: Rutgers University Press, 1953), 2:405–06; *The Federalist*, No. 10, 58–59. Articles I and VI of the French Declaration of the Rights of Man remain ambiguous, in the sense that they can be accommodated as much to the Rousseauist thesis on distributive justice as to that of the classical tradition. Cf. Rousseau, *Discours sur l'Origine de l'Inégalité*, in *Oeuvres Complètes*, 3:222, in comparison to Hobbes, *Leviathan* 1.15, "Justice Commutative, and Distributive"; and to Aristotle *Nicomachean Ethics* 1130b30 et seq.

[48]*The Federalist*, No. 10, 61–62. Cf. Nos. 47–51, and particularly 332–34, 340.

[49]Ibid., No. 55, 378. Cf. 58–61, 340, 349. Although Marx advances an analogous critique of the juridical formalism of the *rechtsstaat*, his historicist rejection of the idea of a permanent human nature leads to a failure to consider in any depth the permanent problems of human nature, or psychology, such as those deriving from an ambitious or despotic will to power. Such problems were fundamental to the constitutional thought of the American Founders as well as for Rousseau.

[50]*The Federalist*, No. 51, 349.

Since ambitions and interests always bedevil political disputes, public authority must be divided so as to conserve, in the midst of such contention, the possibility for a more noble or reasonable disposition to influence events.[51] But as Martin Diamond has shown, institutional divisions alone will not prevent a disciplined majority, organized in favor of unreasonable or unjust policy, from taking simultaneous control of the legislative and executive powers. To frustate such a contingency, the American Founders separated the branches of government in such a way that the bases of the presidential and legislative majorities would always differ.[52] In addition to bicameralism, the staggered system of elections and the differing terms of office are examples of this strategy for securing what is right under majority rule. But just as unchecked power must be avoided, the checks must not be such as to render government incompetent.[53] Therefore, particularly crucial to this strategy to promote political moderation is the attempt to diminish the force of partisan passions in relation to deliberative reason by multiplying the interests to which passions are attached. And to accomplish this required diversifying the economy, then overwhelmingly agricultural, by inducements favoring the development of commerce.

From this strategy derive the constitutional protection of patent rights, promoting technological variety, and also the security granted to private property and to contracts, as well as the Constitution's elimination of tariff barriers among the states.[54] Given the aim of multiplying factions, or autonomous interest groups, the inducements promoting commerce also require maintaining multiple foci of authority, as provided by federalism in the United States. If real power were concentrated in a single place, as the only objective for ambition, then interest groups would be in-

[51]See ibid., No. 55, 374; No. 63, 424–25; No. 71, 482, in relation to 62, 378 and 488.

[52]Diamond et al., *The Democratic Republic*, 161–62.

[53]Ibid., 159–63, 321–37. Cf. James Ceaser, *Liberal Democracy and Political Science* (Baltimore: Johns Hopkins University Press, 1990), 207–10, and his *Presidential Selection: Theory and Development* (Princeton: Princeton University Press, 1979), 123–69; Michael Malbin, "Political Parties Across the Separation of Powers," in *American Political Parties and Constitutional Politics*, ed. Peter W. Schramm and Bradford P. Wilson (Lanham, Md.: Rowman & Littlefield, 1993), 75–90.

[54]Constitution of the United States, Art. I, sec. 8, para. 8. Cf. *The Federalist*, No. 10, 58–60; Robert A. Goldwin, *Why Blacks, Women, and Jews Are Not Mentioned in the Constitution, and Other Unorthodox Views* (Washington: AEI Press, 1990), 57–74; Terence Marshall, "Dissidence et Orthodoxie dans l'Interprétation de la Politique Constitutionnelle des Etats-Unis," *Revue Française de Science Politique* 38 (April 1988): 181–207.

duced to abandon their autonomy and to forge unvarying alliances mobilized to secure the sole power at hand. Conversely, the federal distribution of political authority into diverse localities contributes to maintaining the flexible autonomy of influence-seeking interests that a commercial economy begets.[55] Through these "inventions of prudence" the American Founders deemed that "in the extended republic of the United States, and among the great variety of interests, parties and sects which it embraces, a coalition of a majority of the whole society could seldom take place on any other principles than those of justice and the general good."[56]

Yet to succeed in preventing vehement, embittered conflict among large, self-interested movements or classes, this strategy clearly requires eliminating obstacles to equality of opportunity. Failure to eradicate such obstacles would, on the contrary, foster a common class consciousness among those having no hope as individuals for improving their lot. But, by the same token, this same strategy requires opposition to policies favoring equality of result, for the latter policies would no less extinguish the hope of amelioration through individual endeavor, and thus would also obstruct the multiplication of interests required by the constitutional strategy. This implies that equal human rights are consistent with social inequalities, and that the principle of equal rights ultimately depends on a political judgment capable of discerning where equality is right and where it is wrong.

Ostensibly, such an economic solution seems derivative from writings on the commercial republic published by John Locke, Montesquieu, David Hume and Adam Smith.[57] According to these authors, if the acquisitive spirit is freed from ethical constraints and channeled by well conceived institutions, it can supply "the defect of better motives" in securing human rights.[58] Yet almost from its inception, this constitutional solution to the problem of political economy elicited, forty years prior to the debates of 1789, the well known remonstrance of Jean-Jacques Rousseau: "Ancient politicians incessantly talked about morals and virtue, those of our time

---

[55]*The Federalist*, No. 10, 63–64; No. 51, 350–52.

[56]Ibid., No. 51, 349, 352–53.

[57]Douglass Adair, "The Tenth *Federalist* Revisited" and " 'That Politics May be Reduced to a Science': David Hume, James Madison and the Tenth *Federalist*," in *Fame and the Founding Fathers* (New York: W. W. Norton & Co., 1974); Diamond, "The Separation of Powers," 33–34; Thomas Pangle, *The Spirit of Modern Republicanism* (Chicago: University of Chicago Press, 1988); Ann Cohler, *Montesquieu's Comparative Politics and the Spirit of American Constitutionalism* (Lawrence: University Press of Kansas, 1988).

[58]*The Federalist*, No. 51, 349. Cf. Montesquieu, *De l'Esprit des Lois* 20.1.

talk only of business and money."[59] And this isolated voice in 1750 produced such an echo that its source would later be dubbed "The Legislator of the French Revolution."[60]

The Rousseauist critique of "bourgeois" society, mentioned above in the discussion of political perception and rights, has since had the effect of promoting the classification of Madison, together with the Encyclopedists, Condorcet and modern liberalism generally, under a common designation: defenders of a society of self-centered individualists indifferent to the exploitation or suffering of the unfortunate.[61] According to Rousseau, the Enlightenment, as defined by the foregoing perspective, undermines by its skepticism the civic spirit required for effectuating the rights it ostensibly champions. Thus, instead of adhering to the ends of scientific rationalism, the Genevan seeks, for "completing" men, "to perfect [their] reason by sentiment."[62] How this should affect the separation of powers will be seen after linking this principle of reason with that of right.

But whatever the differences separating Rousseau from the Enlightenment, his project displays an agreement with his modern

[59]Rousseau, *Discours sur les Sciences et les Arts*, in *Oeuvres Complètes*, 3:19. Cf. Montesquieu, *De l'Esprit des Lois* III.3.

[60]The expression is Edgar Quinet's, cited in Furet and Ozouf, *Dictionnaire Critique*, 872. Cf. Leo Strauss, *Liberalism Ancient and Modern* (New York: Basic Books, 1968), 5; Lucien Jaume, "Les Jacobins et Rousseau," *Commentaire*, no. 60 (Winter 1992–93): 929–36. Jaume's useful study seeks to show how the Jacobins misunderstood Rousseau; but his method, which focuses on "la logique de la déformation" (929) in the Jacobin readings of Rousseau, abstracts from Rousseau's own thought in a way that is analogous to the simplifications that Jaume attributes to the Jacobins. The result is an overemphasis on the *Contrat Social* and a misinterpretation of the question of *amour-propre* in Rousseau's teaching. Rousseau's most widely read works prior to the Revolution, the *Nouvelle Héloïse* and the *Emile*, had a more subtle influence on French thought, and extended to diverse revolutionary factions, including amply, of course, the Girondins. Cf. Marshall, "Poésie et Praxis"; also Barny, *Prélude Idéologique;* Nathalie Robisco, *Jean-Jacques Rousseau et la Révolution Française, 1792–1799* (Université Toulouse-Le Mirail, 1992); and Robert Thiéry, ed., *Rousseau, l'Emile et la Révolution* (Paris: Universitas, 1992).

[61]Applied to the American Founding, versions of this widely accepted thesis appear in such influential works as J. Allan Smith, *The Spirit of American Government: A Study of the Constitution: Its Origin, Influence and Relation to Democracy* (New York: Macmillan, 1907); Charles A. Beard, *An Economic Interpretation of the Constitution of the United States* (New York: MacMillan, 1913); Richard Hofstadter, *The American Political Tradition* (New York: Vintage Books, 1956); Louis Hartz, *The Liberal Tradition in America* (New York: Harcourt Brace & World, 1955); Gordon Wood, *The Creation of the American Republic, 1776–1787* (New York: W. W. Norton & Co., 1972); Joyce Appleby, *Capitalism and the New Social Order* (New York: New York University Press, 1984). Cf. Rousseau, *Emile*, 10, 70, 217–29, 438–43, in relation to ibid., 583–97, 600; *Discours sur l'Origine de l'Inégalité*, 164–94, 202–08, 222–23.

[62]*Emile*, 237.

predecessors, in opposition to classical prudence, with respect to subordinating reason to the nonrational. As with the Encyclopedists, for Rousseau as well, self-love and not the love of wisdom is the point of departure for establishing the ground of practice.[63] Nonetheless, the project "to perfect reason by sentiment" also proceeds from a different idea of the "function of the observer and the philosopher," redefined henceforth as he "who knows the art of sounding hearts while working to form them."[64] In Rousseau's view, the philosopher becomes a poet, and his function that of the creative founder, the Legislator. Differentiating himself thereby from the Encyclopedists, and undertaking his "sounding" among the passions and interests which divide human beings, Rousseau seeks for his principle of right a sentiment which unites them.

According to him, the primacy of moral sensibility over judgment can be achieved in political dispositions by a synthetic composition of several elements of the modern consciousness: dogmatic skepticism, utilitarianism, egalitarianism, compassion, and pride (amour propre). The first three elements constitute the intellectual horizon of the Encyclopedists. Along with a novel version of egalitarianism, Rousseau adds to his horizon of perception the elements of pity and pride. Evoking these perceptions by his literary power, Rousseau endeavors to duplicate what formerly was achieved by the Bible or the Encyclopedia, to shape the intellects of the educated who in turn would form statesmen and citizens.

Rousseau's starting point is identical to that of the Enlightenment: the rejection of philosophy, or "metaphysics," in favor of dogmatic skepticism.[65] Indeed, if wisdom is impossible, so must be its pursuit (philia tes sophias). By virtue of rejecting the quest for wisdom, the Enlightenment reveals its vision as emanating not from the light of knowledge, nor even from seeking it, but from the imagination. Yet, while wisdom is imagined to be impossible and men thus consigned to live under illusions, according to Rousseau this inference does not imply that within the Cave there can be no free regimes.[66] Popular government does not, he insists,

---

[63]Ibid., 88, 247ff. Cf. Rousseau Juge de Jean-Jacques: Dialogues, in Oeuvres Complètes, 1:805–18; Discours sur l'Origine de l'Inégalité, 125–26.

[64]Emile, 266. Cf. Du Contrat Social 2.7 in relation to Emile, 9.

[65]Emile, 324. Cf. ibid., 184, 278–79, 321–25, 344.

[66]Just as the Emile was in part conceived to replace the educational project of Plato's Republic, by the same token the Contrat Social, described by Rousseau as an appendix to the Emile, begins by an allusion to the inhabitants of the Cave. Compare Du Contrat Social 1.1 with Plato The Republic VII, 514a-c, and Du Contrat Social, Première version, 284–88, with The Republic II, 357a-367e. In what is perhaps an early draft for the Preface to his projected Institutions Politiques, Rousseau states his intention to provide there an "Examen de la Rép[ublique] de Platon." See Oeuvres

depend upon Enlightenment, and modern skepticism, far from inevitably undermining the civic spirit, might even serve it.[67]

Among the greatest number, the propagation of skepticism leads, in the first instance, to utilitarianism, or to an incapacity to take seriously ideas which do not refer to what can be perceived by the senses and which are not "useful."[68] The pretension to having an open mind with respect to the "empirical" conceals its opacity with respect to the premises of its perceptions. Like Emile, the modern citizen must have a "precise and limited" mind.[69] In the moral order, his "inductions" are indeed conducive to epicureanism. But, contrary to the vulgar epicureanism of the Enlightenment, Rousseau accentuates, with respect to the principles of practice, a distinction between those pleasures or pains associated with sensation and those associated with sentiment.[70] On the basis of this distinction, Rousseau finds in the sentiment of pity an epicurean principle unifying men beyond the interests which divide them.[71]

Consistent with the modern rejection of classical teleology, Rousseau indeed places less emphasis on pleasure than on the painful impression which images of suffering impose on popular sensibilities. The sufferings which one evades, or a negation, unify men in the sentiment of humanity, or of pity "generalized and extended to the whole of mankind."[72] Yet in fact, while founded on a negation, pity is not lacking in pleasure. "Pity is sweet because, in putting ourselves in the place of the one who suffers, we nevertheless feel the pleasure of not suffering as he does."[73] The image of suffering bestirs pity to the extent that, when not suffering oneself, one can imagine oneself suffering like the other. Thus pity, or the sentiment of humanity, represents a projection by the imagi-

---

Complètes, 3:473; also De l'Imitation Théâtrale: Essai Tiré des Dialogues de Platon, in Oeuvres de J.J. Rousseau (Paris: Librairie de L. Hachette et Cie, 1862), 1:358–70, where Rousseau restates in nondialectical form the arguments of Republic X and Laws II. Cf. Emile, 10; and Rousseau's Letter to Duchesne of May 23, 1762, in Correspondance Générale, ed. Théophile Dufour, 7:233.

[67] See Emile, 266, in comparison with Discours sur les Sciences et les Arts, 30.

[68] See Emile, 202, in comparison with ibid., 121, 201, 230, 392, 396. Cf. Alexis de Tocqueville, De la Démocratie en Amérique, 2.1.1; 2.2.8–11, 17.

[69] Emile, 177. Cf. ibid., 217, 221, 239, 295, 392, 394, 419, 422. See also Hiram Caton, "Carnap's First Philosophy," The Review of Metaphysics 23 (June 1975): 622–59.

[70] Rousseau Juge de Jean-Jacques, 805–18; Emile, 267–68, 278–79, 348–50; Notes sur "De l'Esprit" d'Helvétius, in Oeuvres Complètes, 4:1121ff.

[71] Discours sur l'Origine de l'Inégalité, 125–26; Emile, 260–66, 273, 302–03.

[72] Emile, 303. Compare ibid., 260–61, 270 with 83.

[73] Ibid., 259–60, 270.

nation of love for oneself. "Indeed, how do we allow ourselves to be moved to pity, if not by transporting ourselves outside of ourselves and identifying with the suffering animal, by leaving, as it were, our being to take on its being? We suffer only so much as we judge that it suffers. It is not in ourselves, it is in him that we suffer. Thus, no one becomes sensitive until his imagination is animated and begins to transport him outside of himself."[74] To perfect this alienation, the poet-legislator must therefore consistently express himself in tones which conjure the image of suffering humanity: "We are attached to those like us less by the sentiment of their pleasures than by the sentiment of their pains, for we see far better in the latter the identity of our natures with theirs and the guarantees of their attachment to us. If our common needs unite us by interest, our common miseries unite us by affection."[75]

To awaken this sentiment, therefore, all obstacles to the capacity for identifying with another, such as those posed by class distinctions, must be eradicated. The sentiment of humanity, as a principle of right, enjoins an egalitarian politics. But this requirement compels no less a dissimulation of the rare and specific happiness of the natural man, who alone perceives correctly. "The appearance (aspect) of a happy man inspires in others less love than envy. They would gladly accuse him of usurping a right that he does not have in giving himself an exclusive happiness; and self-love (amour propre) suffers, too, in making us feel that this man has no need of us."[76] Since the image or the idea of another's superiority stirs envy, the amour-propre of the common man thus paradoxically becomes a guardian of the egalitarian spirit. "Let us extend amour-propre over other beings. We shall transform it into a virtue, and there is no man's heart in which this virtue does not have its root."[77]

Reconciled with the sentiment of humanity by way of egalitarianism, the sentiment of amour-propre shares the pleasures accompanying the former sentiment and augments these pleasures by those based on having a "favorable witness of oneself."[78] Thus composed, the critical spirit of the democratic consciousness extinguishes simultaneously the honor of classical nobility and the in-

[74]Ibid., 261.

[75]Ibid., 259.

[76]Ibid. Cf. Rousseau's notes on pp. 93 and 99, indicating the ironic meaning of p. 442 concerning the spirit of community.

[77]Ibid., 303. Cf. ibid., 279; also Discours sur l'Origine de l'Inégalité, 189, and Discours sur l'Economie Politique, in Oeuvres Complètes, 3:254–55.

[78]Emile, 341, 351, 355–58. Cf. ibid., 279, 303, 304, 315–27, 386, 423, 440, 494–97, 567 in relation to Du Contrat Social 1.8.

terestedness which moves the Enlightenment. Unlike Madison's
prudential strategy for securing human rights, that of Rousseau
and those he inspires consists largely in the attempt to raise this
democratic consciousness. Yet, since this consciousness rests on
sentiment, its evocation requires a new rhetoric, that of "the language of signs," of images or symbols, of music. "One of the errors
of our age is to use reason in bare form, as if men were only mind.
In neglecting the language of signs that speak to the imagination,
we have lost the most energetic of languages. The word's impression is always weak, and one speaks to the heart far better through
the eyes than through the ears."[79] The poet-legislator conducts the
citizen to take pleasure in alienating his nature through the sentiment of humanity, the principle of judgment which "perfects"
political reasoning.[80]

When Kant proclaimed Rousseau "the Newton of the moral
universe," he perceived in part the revolution that Rousseau had
introduced into the judgment of good and evil.[81] This revolution
prepared the ideas on human rights later developed by Kant's critical philosophy, which by abstracting from human nature is faithful to Rousseau's premise that the citizen must forget his origins.
Abstracting from the origins, however, also obscures the composition of the critical spirit itself, while at the same time leading to a
misperception of its consequences.

Certainly, unlike the nihilistic results of the Enlightenment,
the pleasures of a "favorable witness of oneself," or of one's dignity,
provide critical philosophy with an anchor to brace the convictions
underlying its moral or political judgments. Composed of amour-
propre, refined epicureanism and dogmatic skepticism, the sentiment of humanity responds with indignation to any image of
manifest oppression or injustice. Yet, as the arche of practical judgment, this sentiment contains no measure beyond itself. Thus, under the impression caused by images of "inequality," the moral
indignation fomented by the sentiment of humanity would hardly
be disposed to seek after, or deliberate over, the veritable nature of
an apparent injustice.[82] Moreover, with respect to those who are so

[79]Emile, 398. Cf. ibid., 399–401, 406; and Essai sur l'Origine des Langues, ch. 12.
[80]Emile, 9–11, 256, 259–61, 266.
[81]Kant, Beobachtungen über das Gefühl des Schönen und Erhabenen, in Gesammelte
Schriften, herausgegeben von der Preussischen Akademie der Wissenschaften (Ber-
lin: Walter De Gruyter, 1905), 20:58.
[82]Compare, however, Discours sur l'Origine de l'Inégalité, 191, and its influence on
Tocqueville, De la Démocratie en Amérique, 2.2.1. Cf. Jean-Claude Lamberti, Tocqueville et les Deux Démocraties (Presses Universitaires de France, 1983) in relation to
John C. Koritansky, Alexis de Tocqueville and the New Science of Politics (Durham:
Carolina Academic Press, 1986).

disposed, when the results of their deliberation do not seem humane, one would be inclined not to seek after their reasoning, but to perceive them as either benighted or insensitive. In this way *amour-propre*, linked to the sentiment of humanity, conduces to a democratic version of the disdain felt by the noble towards vulgarity. "These diverse impressions," says Rousseau, "have their modifications and degrees, which depend on the particular character of each individual and his previous habits. But they are universal and no one is completely exempt from them. There exist later and less general impressions which are more appropriate to sensitive souls."[83]

Since "sensitive souls" and "bourgeois" souls do not perceive human things in the same way, there could not really be a dialogue between them.[84] The same applies to their respective exchanges with those disposed to deliberate prudently over public affairs. And from these differences derives the misunderstanding among diverse partisans of human rights. Condorcet fell victim to it. In his venture to make politics into an objective science, he ignored the power of any other sensibility than that of self-interest. Disdaining in his calculations the "inventions of prudence" which explained the separation of powers, he suffered with the Vendée the consequences of his innocence, as soon as the Assembly produced a majority ready to exercise differently its unchecked power.[85]

In this century, after so many decades of intellectual abdication of this domain, both the movements for civil rights and the vast and terrible experiences of some of the cruelest tyrannies ever known have reawakened thoughtful interest in the idea of rights. But celebrating declarations of rights while abstracting from problems of their meaning, and of their relation to the questions of means for securing them, would seem to warrant Burke's criticism that such an idea alienates the judgment of its partisans from the prudence required in practice. In addition to the war in the Vendée, where over 300,000 men, women and children were slaughtered at the behest of the French Revolutionary Assembly in the name of the Rights of Man, one need recall, in considering these problems, the plebiscitary use made by Hitler of the Wilson-

---

[83]*Emile*, 267. Cf. *Rousseau Juge de Jean-Jacques*, 672.

[84]*Emile*, 56, 110, 121, 298, 392–93. In this respect Habermas' sanguine "Theorie des kommunikativen Handelns" corresponds to the thought of Emile, as distinguished from that of Rousseau.

[85]The thought of Condorcet's admirer Destutt de Tracy, who barely escaped decapitation during the Terror, illustrates how the prejudices of the Encyclopedists could resist the lessons of experience. See Emmet Kennedy, *A Philosophe in the Age of Revolution: Destutt de Tracy and the Origins of 'Ideology'* (Philadelphia: The American Philosophical Society, 1978).

ian principle of a people's right to self-determination, or Stalin's claims of the people's right to employment, with the result of establishing the unlimited power of the people's defenders.[86] Since Kant, the distinction between principled judgment and prudence has indeed had the effect of rejoining the "normative" idea of rights to that of morality, but only to separate consideration of such disinterested "norms" from a deliberate, "empirical" attention to practice.[87]

Overcoming such a conceptual estrangement between "normative" and "empirical" thought reveals it was not interestedness that led Madison to support the separation of powers by creating the commercial republic. Rather, it was the concern to attenuate the force of passions which differences provoke among human beings.[88] Conceived by another moderation than that cultivated by Rousseau or Kant against vulgar epicureanism, Madison's commercial republic is not an end in itself, but a prudential means for securing justice or the common good. It remains to be seen, however, whether this different moderation can still attenuate the hostility it provokes among the partisans of humanity, the "new class" anticipated by Rousseau. Moved to focus on suffering where it can be found, including in the best of times, such a perspective, ab-

---

[86]See Goldwin, "Three Human Rights Are Enough," in *Why Blacks, Women, and Jews Are Not Mentioned in the Constitution*, 89ff. Cf. the Constitution of the U.S.S.R. of December 5, 1936, in Maurice Duverger, *Constitutions et Documents Politiques* (Presses Universitaires de France, 1974), 655–57; Marc Plattner, ed., *Human Rights in Our Time* (Boulder: Westview Press, 1984), 119–20; Marshall, ed., *Théorie et Pratique*, 263. Concerning the suppression of the counter-revolution in the Vendée (1793–1796), even scholarly estimates vary considerably on the number of those killed, in part because of disagreement as to whether the suppression in Normandy and in northern Brittany should be associated with that in the Vendée proper, and in part because population records were destroyed with the destruction of parish churches in the region. Chateaubriand's early estimate of 300,000 killed was widely held to be exaggerated until recent demographic studies, carefully correlated with casualty lists, supported his claim. Today estimates range from a low of 200,000 to as high as 600,000 when including the republican troops who perished. To this day there remain villages in the Vendée region that refuse to observe the July 14 Bastille Day holiday. Even Simon Schambra's excellent book *Citizens*, which antedates the more recent studies, relies on understated figures. Cf. Daniel Amson, *Carnot* (Perrin, 1992); and Reynald Secher, *Le Génocide Franco-Français: La Vendée-Vengé* (Presses Universitaires de France), 1986.

[87]See Immanuel Kant, *Perpetual Peace*, App. 1; Pierre Hassner, "Immanuel Kant," in *History of Political Philosophy*, 3d ed., ed. Leo Strauss and Joseph Cropsey (Chicago: University of Chicago Press, 1987), 589, 594, 602, 608, 610, 616–20; Jeremy Rabkin, "Bureaucratic Idealism and Executive Power," in *Saving the Revolution*, ed. Kesler, 191.

[88]Marshall, "Dissidence et Orthodoxie," 181–206; and "La Raison Pratique," 917–23.

stracting from constitutionalism, risks judging peremptorily the commercial economy as the cause of such results, while insisting that proposed reforms be judged in terms of their humane intent. Though their indignation seldom leads to revolutionary fervor, disciples of this view tend to sympathize with such fervor while overlooking how their own disposition undermines constitutionalism as such.[89]

To be sure, whether in the United Kingdom or generally in Western Europe since the Second World War, the parliamentary system has avoided the catastrophes it encountered in France following 1789. Commentators such as Robert Badinter have thus sometimes perceived the modern parliamentary system as vindicating Condorcet's constitutional purpose. But while parliaments, when properly designed, can provide stable, energetic, democratic government, they do so under unchecked conditions that still lead such governments to ignore the interests of electoral minorities. Once having lost, minorities have, until the next election perhaps five years hence, no further legitimate power from which to negotiate their concerns. Given the party discipline of parliamentary systems, the result sharpens divisions, diminishes consensus, and injects more bitterness in electoral contests. Although elections under these circumstances produce more sharply defined party programs, rarely does the program selected by a plurality of voters correspond totally to the plurality's preferred policies. Yet, unimpeded by the compulsory bargaining of divided power, the government's program will be effectively applied unchecked.[90] Majority will thus prevails over deliberative prudence except to the chance extent, without constitutional support, that the moral disposition of prudence persists within the ruling party itself.

By comparison, the Madisonian design compels negotiation and compromise, the very feature often most despised by its critics. But the apparently most deplorable instance thereof, Madison's

[89]See Joseph Knippenberg, "From Kant to Marx: The Perils of Liberal Idealism," *The Political Science Reviewer* 20 (Spring 1991): 118–19.

[90]See the comments, applying these considerations to the constitutional problem of European Union, by René Rémond, President of the Fondation Nationale des Sciences Politiques, in Marshall, ed., *Théorie et Pratique*, 181. Cf. ibid., 18–19, 171–74, 183–84, 199. See David Brady, "The Causes and Consequences of Divided Government: Toward a New Theory of American Politics?" *The American Political Science Review* 87 (March 1993): 189–94, in comparison with James Ceaser, "In Defense of Separation of Powers," in *Separation of Powers—Does It Still Work?* ed. Goldwin and Kaufman, 168–93. Concerning the relation of these questions to the larger problem of political perception and political science, see Ceaser, *Liberal Democracy*, and Harvey C. Mansfield, Jr., *America's Constitutional Soul* (Baltimore: Johns Hopkins University Press, 1991), 1–17, 137–63, 209–19.

compromises with slavery in the constitutional design, is instructive in several respects. As indicated in *Federalist* 54, these compromises do not betoken abandonment of the principles of right the Constitution was designed to establish. Rather, the compromises were so conceived as to induce the slave states to adopt, against their interests, a regime dedicated to securing these rights and destined, through commercial diversification of the economy, to place despotism, then established in the South, "in course of ultimate extinction."[91] Deferring on such a question neither to epicurean complaisance nor to puritanical harshness, Madison's complex design interweaves prudence and the principles of right. "Inventions of prudence," such as the separation of powers and encouragements to equality of opportunity combined with barriers to equality of results, correspond to the constitutional protection within the regime of the practical reason which founded it.

But precisely because the Constitution is not "a machine that would go of itself," Madison well knew there was no inevitability of success. The provisional failure of his project in the early nineteenth century, culminating in the tragedy of civil war, reveals that the constitutional protection of political virtues does not suffice to produce them. That Madison harbored no illusions thereon is shown by the significance he attached to a liberal, civic education, under the police powers reserved to the states.[92] Although

---

[91]See Herbert J. Storing, "Slavery and the Moral Foundations of the American Republic," and W. B. Allen, "A New Birth of Freedom: Fulfillment or Derailment?" in *Slavery and Its Consequences: The Constitution, Equality, and Race*, ed. Robert A. Goldwin and Art Kaufman (Washington: AEI Press, 1988), 45–63 and 64–92; and Harry V. Jaffa, *Crisis of the House Divided* (Seattle: University of Washington Press, 1973), 308–29. Among the causes for the temporary frustration of this strategy, Jaffa mentions particularly the inventions of the cotton gin and of the British power loom, transforming the textile industry, and also the additions of the vast territories of Louisiana, Florida, and Texas after the disappearance of the Federalist Party to increase the representation of Southern interests in the Senate. See Harry V. Jaffa, *Equality and Liberty: Theory and Practice in American Politics* (New York: Oxford University Press, 1965), 62–63; also Michael Zuckert, "Completing the Constitution: The Fourteenth Amendment and Constitutional Rights," *Publius* 22 (Spring 1992): 69–91.

[92]Jonathan Elliot, *The Debates of the State Conventions on the Adoption of the Federal Constitution, as Recommended by the General Convention at Philadelphia in 1787*, 2d ed. (Philadelphia: J.B. Lippincott, 1866), 3:536–37. Cf. Marvin Meyers, ed., *The Mind of the Founder: Sources of the Political Thought of James Madison* (Hanover: University Press of New England, 1981), 347ff.; Thomas G. West, "The Classical Spirit and the Founding," in *The American Founding: Essays on the Formation of the Constitution*, ed. J. Jackson Barlow, Leonard Levy and Ken Masugi (New York: Greenwood Press, 1988), 42–43.

through the federal design the Founders anticipated "a general assimilation of [the] manners and laws" of the states in the Union, the courts have since eroded the states' police powers to regulate and promote such "manners" in a way far exceeding the Founders' intent.[93] Indeed, taking account of these reserved powers as originally conceived reveals that the Madisonian integration of rights and prudence, or of ends and means, derives from a more remote source than Montesquieu or Hume, Locke or Voltaire. An attentive reading of *The Federalist* reveals in the first place that the practical reason it manifests is founded not on a passion for security, but on a concern for the measured disposition of soul requisite to a just or reasonable deliberation of public affairs.[94]

The support Madison gave to the Revolution of 1789 is epitomized by his acceptance of honorary French citizenship. He thereby indicated that the Declarations of 1776 and of 1789 illustrate the same, universal principle: that rights are not based on class or birth, but on the particular merit of each individual.[95] But his idea of this universal principle, associated to that of practical reason, derives from a mode of thought antecedent to that which determined the Enlightenment and the Revolution in France. Contrary to the modern view, according to which wisdom and thus philosophy are impossible, Madison merely emphasized their probable absence among those involved with practical affairs. This absence, however, does not signify their irrelevance, or that one may forget the permanent need for qualities which are wanting. On the contrary, as indicated in *Federalist* 49, this signifies that when elaborating the institutions of a nondespotic regime, one

[93]See *The Federalist*, No. 53, 364; No. 41, 276–77; and No. 56, 381–82. Cf. Zuckert, "Completing the Constitution"; Walter Berns, *Taking the Constitution Seriously* (New York: Simon and Schuster, 1987), 209–41; and Walter Berns, *The First Amendment and the Future of American Democracy* (Chicago: Gateway Editions, 1985).

[94]See *The Federalist*, Nos. 10 and 51 in relation to Nos. 49, 55, 57, 63, 71, 78, 84, esp. pp. 59–60, 62, 340–43, 349–53, 374, 384, 424–25, 482–83, 521–30, and 581, in comparison with Montesquieu, *De l'Esprit des Lois* 6.5, 11.6, 19.11, and with Aristotle *Nicomachean Ethics* VI, 1140b8–30, 1141b25–1142b34, 1144a11–1145a12.

[95]Meyers, ed., *The Mind of the Founder*, 195. Cf. however, *Selected Writings and Speeches of Alexander Hamilton*, ed. Morton J. Frisch (Washington: AEI Press, 1985), 413–16, 467–68, 470; Mackubin Thomas Owens, Jr., "Alexander Hamilton on Natural Rights and Prudence," *Interpretation* 14 (May & September, 1986): 331–51; Harvey Flaumenhaft, "Concluding Essay: Americanism Abroad," in *Constitutionalism in America*, ed. Thurow, 3:246.

need take thoughtful account of the absence of such qualities, with a view to obtaining them to the degree that is plausible.[96]

Such a synthesis of prudence and right indicates a different political science from that inspiring the principles of 1789, and which since has prevailed in American and European universities alike. For the Founders meeting in Philadelphia, the best guarantee for the rights of man, or for liberty and equality properly understood, depends less on the formulation of lists thereof, than on the sound establishment of constitutional government. In this sense, the separation of powers, though a means, is inseparable from its end. In its teaching on these matters, *The Federalist* reminds its readers that nondespotic rule depends, not on a science of politics or of law, nor on an unchecked, humanistic *amour-propre* expressed as a general will lacking a superseding measure, but first on the recognition that ordinary men, while invested with rights, are neither angels nor gods.[97] Beyond the confines of history,

---

[96]*The Federalist*, No. 49, 340–43. Compare Madison's reference there to Platonic wisdom, and the need for a substitute thereof in veneration for a prudent regime, and Aristotle's silence in *Politics* II concerning Plato's philosopher king, in contrast to his praise in this book for the commercial republic of Carthage. Cf. Aristotle's later discussion, at 1295b25–1296a20, of the benefits in establishing a regime based on the middle class in a large *polis* as a substitute for a regime based on true virtue. Aristotle concludes this discussion with a reference to the "best legislators," including Solon, who figures in Plutarch's *Parallel Lives* as the parallel to Publius. In addition to Hamilton's attachment to Plutarch's writings, the future secretary of the treasury had read Aristotle's *Politics* during the Revolutionary War, as aide de camp to General Washington. In 1776, coincidentally with Adam Smith's *Wealth of Nations*, appeared the first English translation of Aristotle's *Politics* made directly from the Greek. Hamilton preferred the economic arguments of Hume and Smith to that of Aristotle in Book I of the *Politics*; but in his 1783 list presented to the Continental Congress for the purpose of constituting a library for political education, Madison included Aristotle's *Politics*. See Dennis Thompson, "The Education of a Founding Father," *Political Theory* 4 (November 1976): 509. Cf. Abram Shulsky, "The 'Infrastructure' of Aristotle's *Politics*: Aristotle on Economics and Politics," in *Essays on the Foundations of Aristotelian Political Science*, ed. Carnes Lord and David O'Connor (Berkeley: University of California Press, 1990), 74–111. On this question, the contemporary academic debate concerning the tension between the virtues of "civic humanism" and the requirements of the commercial republic frequently overlooks the difference between a republican virtue with and without *phronesis*. Whereas disciples of John Pocock, following Machiavelli, interpret the question of civic virtue in abstraction from *phronesis*, for Aristotle's republicanism and for that of the Founders, the problem of practical reason is crucial. See John Pocock, *The Machiavellian Moment* (Princeton: Princeton University Press, 1975), 525–26, 534, 537–39, 550–52, in relation to ibid., 20–21, 24–25, where prudence is reduced to "intuition" and "experience" in abstraction from the disposition of soul requisite to sound deliberation.

[97] See *The Federalist*, No. 51, 349, compared to the first two paragraphs of the Declaration of Independence, and in contrast with the thesis of *vox populi vox dei*.

the rational grounds for constitutional government and human rights depend, it seems, on recollecting the wisdom men lack and need, and on a recognition of the unpredictability of its presence in politics.[98]

[98] See *The Federalist*, No. 10, 60, and No. 49, 340, in comparison with Hegel, *Grundlinien der Philosophie des Rechts* § 272–81 and addendum to § 272; *Phänomenologie des Geistes* VIII; and with Aristotle *Nicomachean Ethics* 1134b28–31, 1139a3–15, 1140b25–30.

Executive Power and the American Founding

Joseph M. Bessette
Gary J. Schmitt

In 1960, in what became an influential text on the American presidency, Richard Neustadt wrote, "The constitutional convention of 1787 is supposed to have created a government of 'separated powers.' It did nothing of the sort. Rather, it created a government of separated institutions *sharing* powers."[1] Dozens, perhaps hundreds, of times since Neustadt's book was written, students of American political institutions have cited Neustadt's formulation with approval. Indeed, this view has become a kind of dogma: the Constitution did not separate the powers or functions of government; it separated institutions. And those institutions—a bicameral Congress, the presidency, and the Supreme Court—share the powers of government. Or, as many would now say, these separated institutions share the power to make public policy.

At one level, the Neustadt view is obviously correct: the separated institutions do share *some* powers. The president, for example, through his qualified veto shares in the legislative power. The Senate, through its authority to pass on the appointment of high-level executive officers, shares in the executive power. But in its fullest sense, the Neustadt view says more than this. By denying that the Framers created a government of "separated powers" (indeed, he says that "it did nothing of the sort"), Neustadt calls into question the formal distinction of governmental power into three main types—legislative, executive, and judicial—and the assignment of the *bulk* of each type of power to one of the three branches. Those who embrace Neustadt's view tend, instead, to think of governmental power as a kind of undifferentiated mass, a

---

[1] Richard E. Neustadt, *Presidential Power: The Politics of Leadership* (New York: John Wiley & Sons, 1960), 33, emphasis in original.

policy-making mass, over which the separated institutions of American government compete for control.

This understanding of American separation of powers has done much to obscure the nature of executive power written into the Constitution of 1787 and the way it promotes good government in the United States. Despite the views of Neustadt and his intellectual progeny, the Framers very much believed in a formal separation of the powers, or functions, of government and expressly designed each of the governing institutions to carry out effectively the category of powers assigned to it. As we will show, those who wrote this nation's fundamental law possessed a well-formed understanding of the nature of executive power, of the importance of a strong executive for effective government, and of the tensions inherent in accommodating an energetic executive to republican institutional forms. We will begin with the Framers' constitutional understanding of separation of powers more generally and then turn to the central features of their understanding of executive power.

THE CONSTITUTION AND SEPARATION OF POWERS

In assessing the evidence as to whether the Constitution of the United States rests upon an understanding of a principled distinction between the legislative, executive, and judicial powers, there is no more important place to begin than the Constitution itself, which, as we will see, is surprisingly revealing on this matter.

In examining our fundamental law, what is most obvious is that the document is structured according to the separation of powers model: Article I is on the Congress, Article II on the presidency, and Article III on the judiciary. (The remaining Articles IV-VII on miscellaneous topics take up only about one-fifth of the document.) So the institutional design of the new government is the first thing that strikes the reader. (Many of the state constitutions, by contrast, had a quite different structure.) Moreover, each of the first three articles begins with a statement about power.

Article I begins: "All legislative Powers herein granted shall be vested in a Congress. . . . " Note that the Constitution does not say, "All the *following* powers shall be vested in Congress" but rather "All the legislative Powers herein granted. . . ." Certain kinds of powers that are by nature legislative are granted to the legislative institution of the new government.

Similarly, Article II, on the president, begins: "The executive Power shall be vested in a President. . . . " Again, it does not say, as it certainly could have, "The *following* powers shall be vested" but rather, "The executive Power shall be vested. . . . " The very language implies that this thing, executive power, exists independently of the Constitution itself and through the Constitution is vested in the executive agency of the new government. (As we shall see below, this is exactly how the leading Framers understood the vesting clause of Article II.)

Finally, Article III, on the judiciary, begins: "The judicial Power of the United States, shall be vested in one supreme Court, and in such inferior Courts as the Congress may from time to time ordain and establish." Again, the presumption is that there is such a thing as judicial power in itself, and this judicial power is vested in the federal courts by the Constitution.

Thus, the vesting clauses of the first three articles join three distinct formal powers with three distinct governing institutions. Because the phrase "separation of powers" is sometimes used to refer to a separation of institutions and other times to a separation of powers, or functions, of government, there is a tendency to confuse the two meanings. Although many modern commentators accept the institutional separation—the Congress, presidency, and federal courts are obviously distinct governing institutions—but not the functional distinction of governing power into three main types, those who wrote the Constitution clearly embraced *both* notions of separation of powers.

We can see this, for example, in the placement of several specific powers within the Constitution. Where, for example, do we find the president's veto power—clearly a legislative authority—listed in the Constitution? Not in Article II, which lists the president's other powers, but in Article I, on the Congress, where the "legislative Powers" are granted. Similarly, the Senate's authority to pass on presidential appointments to high executive office—which would seem to be an executive function—is listed not in Article I, where the bulk of the Senate's powers are found, but in Article II, on the presidency, where the "executive Power" is vested. These two examples reflect the Framers' understanding that Article I lists powers that are *by nature* legislative, even if shared in part with the president; and Article II lists powers that are *by nature* executive, even if shared in part with the Senate.

We can see this same understanding of a formal distinction of powers in James Madison's and Alexander Hamilton's contributions to *The Federalist,* written in the months after the Constitution was completed and called by no less an authority than Thomas Jefferson "the best commentary on the principles of government, which ever was written." Here, for example, are a few sentences from the beginning of *Federalist* 48, written by Madison: "It is agreed on all sides that the powers *properly belonging* to one of the departments ought not to be directly and completely administered by either of the other departments. . . . After discriminating, therefore, in theory, the several classes of power, as they may *in their nature* be legislative, executive, or judiciary, the next and most difficult task is to provide some practical security for each, against the invasion of the others."[2] Or consider what Hamilton says on the presidency in *Federalist* 75: "The essence of the legislative authority is to enact laws, or, in other words, to prescribe rules for the regulation of the society; while the execution of the laws and employment of the common strength, either for this purpose or for the common defense, seem to comprise all the functions of the executive magistrate."[3] Clearly, both Madison and Hamilton believed that legislative power and executive power were fundamentally different things and that the bulk of each power was vested in the legislative and executive institutions, respectively, of the new federal government.

Less than two years after the Constitution was written the meaning of "the executive Power" vested in the president became the subject of an important debate in the First Congress. The issue was whether the Congress had the authority through legislation to regulate the president's power to remove cabinet-level officials. Although the Constitution carefully specified the means by which department heads would be appointed, it was silent on removals. Some maintained that given the silence of the Constitution, Congress could regulate removals as it saw fit. Others argued that because the approval of the Senate was required to appoint, so should its approval be required to remove. Still another view was that removals could take place only through the constitutionally prescribed impeachment process. Contrary to these interpretations, however, Madison forcefully maintained that the removal of a high-level executive appointee was the exercise of intrinsically executive authority and thus was vested in the president *by implication* through the opening words of Article II: "The executive Power shall be vested in a President. . . . "

After lengthy and serious debate about both constitutional and prudential aspects of regulating removals, the majority in the House adopted the Madisonian view. As Madison described the opinion that "prevailed" in the First Congress in a letter to a

---

[2]Alexander Hamilton, James Madison, and John Jay, *The Federalist Papers*, introduction by Clinton Rossiter (New York: New American Library, 1961) 308, emphasis added.
[3]Ibid., 450.

friend, "the Executive power being in general terms vested in the President, all power of an Executive nature not particularly taken away must belong to that department. . . . "[4]

Another clear illustration of this way of thinking about governmental power as naturally falling into several distinct types, each of which should be assigned to a separate branch of government, occurred several decades later when Jefferson criticized the Virginia practice of the state legislature nominating state judges: "Nomination to office is an executive function. To give it to the legislature, as we do, is a violation of the principle of separation of powers. . . . By leaving nomination in its *proper place*, among executive functions, the principle of the distribution of power is preserved."[5]

From this brief survey of the Constitution and its early interpretations we can conclude with some confidence that the document itself and the words of the leading Founding Fathers demonstrate a clear and consistent belief (1) that the powers of government by their very nature fall into three distinct types: legislative, executive, and judicial, and (2) that the cause of good government is best served when the bulk of each type of power is assigned to a distinct institution structured in a way to promote the effective exercise of the power in question.

With this background on separation of powers, we can back up a bit to the first years of American independence to explore more fully the development of executive power in the new republic.

THE IDEA OF EXECUTIVE POWER IN REVOLUTIONARY AMERICA

What was the Founding generation's attitude toward executive power? Did the first Americans fear it as dangerous to human freedom or embrace it as necessary for good government? Did they look to popularly elected legislatures to check the power of the sword, or did they create powerful executive institutions to counterbalance legislative aggrandizement?

Many commentators are struck by the contrast between the grand authorities and prestige of the modern American presidency and what they take to be the Founding generation's animus toward powerful chief executives. The American Revolution, after all, was fought against a tyrannical king; and this had followed de-

---

[4]James Madison, Letter to Edmund Pendleton, June 21, 1789, *Letters and Other Writings of James Madison*, vol. I (New York: R. Worthington, 1884), 478.

[5]Thomas Jefferson, Letter to Samuel Kercheval, July 12, 1816, *The Portable Thomas Jefferson*, ed. Merrill D. Peterson (New York: The Viking Press, 1975), 556.

cades of conflict throughout the colonies between royal governors and popularly elected assemblies. Although modern Americans have come to accept "presidential government" and to view a relatively strong presidency as necessary for the safety and well-being of the nation, the notion that the Founders would have countenanced the creation of such a "princely" office only a decade after having ridded themselves of a king seems to many to be dubious on its face.

Typically, those who embrace this view cite the language of the Declaration of Independence and the creation of weak governors in the early state constitutions for evidence that the last thing the Founding generation wanted was a powerful and energetic executive. Nonetheless, a fair examination of the Declaration, the state constitutions, and the history surrounding their creation leads to the conclusion that this understanding of the Founders' position on executive power is overstated and, in key particulars, simply wrong.

The Declaration of Independence does, of course, contain a lengthy and serious list of charges against King George III. It was this "long train of abuses and usurpations" that justified breaking with Great Britain. By his actions the monarch had evinced "a design" to set over the Americans an "absolute despotism" and deny them, as a result, the exercise of their "unalienable rights." In short, the king had become a despot or, as Thomas Paine put it, "the royal brute of Britain." Is it possible, many scholars ask, that a people so incensed with the behavior of their king (and, for years before, his royal governors) that they were willing to cut all ties to their homeland would put in place a new and powerful chief executive in the Constitution a short eleven years later?

Recalling Paine's words, however, should remind us that the Declaration of Independence does not, as did Paine's famous pamphlet *Common Sense,* condemn kingship simply. While there is an implicit preference for some form of representative government underlying the Declaration's argument, the document does not, strictly speaking, attack George III for being a king, but rather for being an *unjust* king. Following the argument of Jefferson and his colleagues in the Second Continental Congress, as expressed in the Declaration, the revolution would not have been necessary, nor justified, if the British crown had not undertaken actions inimical to the colonists' fundamental human rights. "A prince," the Declaration tells us, "whose character is thus marked by every act that may define a tyrant, is unfit to be the ruler of a free people." It would seem to follow that a prince who did *not* act the tyrant could indeed be fit to be the ruler of a free people.

Moreover, the Declaration's indictment of the king is somewhat misleading in that no direct mention is made of the British Parliament. Yet this legislative body had as much to do with British imperial and colonial policy as the king did. Indeed, it was Parliament's insistence that it had the right to tax and regulate the internal affairs of the North American colonies that forced the colonists back to the first principles of all just government: natural rights and the consent of the governed. If government failed to secure rights, then the consent of the governed could legitimately be withdrawn, or, to put it more forcefully, the people could legitimately revolt against the established authority. However, because the Americans did not accept the legal argument that they owed any obedience at all to the "acts of pretended legislation" of the British Parliament (in which they were not represented) and because they maintained instead that their legal tie to the motherland was through the king alone, the Declaration specifically addressed only the unjust acts of the king. If Jefferson and the Congress had formally attacked Parliament as well, they would have indirectly recognized that body's legal authority over them, thereby suggesting that if the Parliament had behaved more moderately it would still have had the right to tax and govern the internal affairs of the colonies without their representation or consent.

It follows, then, that the bearing of the indictment of the British monarchy in the Declaration of Independence on the Founders' understanding of executive power is more complex than some have suggested. The Declaration does not, as noted, condemn monarchy or kingship or strong executive power per se, but only the unjust exercise of such ruling power. Moreover, as the history surrounding the Declaration indicates, the Founders were well aware that legislatures could display the same despotic intent as executives.

That said, however, it must be acknowledged that the decades-long struggle within each of the colonies to expand political liberty and self-rule—which institutionally took the form of a contest between the locally-elected colonial assemblies and the royal governors appointed by London—obviously had its effect on how the Americans thought about executive power. This was perhaps most evident in the constitutions adopted by the states after independence in which the governor was typically given very circumscribed powers and was made largely subordinate to the state legislature. It is not surprising that these early state constitutions are often taken as evidence for the Founding generation's animus toward strong executives.

Here again, however, the picture has been overdrawn. In the first place, not all the states wrote constitutions with weak executives. And here the exceptions are important. In two key states, New York and Massachusetts, the constitutions created relatively powerful executive posts. In both instances those elected to be governor became the state's preeminent political figure and dominant political force.

Moreover, even in the states where the executive was *formally* weak, they were not weak simply and always. Specifically, at various times during the Revolutionary War a significant number of the governors were either delegated extraordinary, prerogative-like powers to deal with the necessities of statecraft involved in prosecuting the war or they exercised those authorities unilaterally, which is to say extra-constitutionally. For example, in May of 1780 the Virginia assembly passed a measure vesting "the Executive with extraordinary powers for a limited time," noting in the law's preamble that "in this time of public danger . . . [it was] highly expedient" to do so. Perhaps the most extreme instance of such a delegation occurred in British-occupied South Carolina. There the state legislature made the governor a virtual dictator, authorizing him "to do anything necessary for the public good except taking the life of a citizen without public trial." (More on the state governors below.)

Furthermore, the idea that there were times when a powerful executive was needed was not confined to extraordinary circumstances, such as fighting a war. For example, under the Northwest Ordinance of 1787 (the law enacted by the Congress of the Articles of Confederation for governing the territories not yet incorporated into the new nation as states), the territorial governors were given an expansive range of powers, such as commander-in-chief of the militia, an extensive appointment power, an absolute veto over statutes passed by the territorial legislature, and the power to convene, prorogue, or dissolve the legislature, as they saw fit. The executive, in this instance, was intentionally made the preeminent political branch. In fact, it appears that James Monroe, the chief draftsman of the bill, modeled the office and authorities of the governors in large part on the formal commissions given the former British governors of North America.

In summary, the Founding generation's view of executive power was more complex than is usually recognized. In spite of the Americans' struggle with the crown, even the most whiggish among them retained an appreciation for the fact that at times a strong executive capacity was needed if a government was to be effective. The real issue, then, was not whether a strong or a weak executive was to be preferred but, rather, when and how the executive's great potential was to be utilized. Was a powerful executive needed more or less often, and would the decision to employ that power rest, under a constitution, largely with the legislature or with the executive itself? For example, during the debate in the Virginia Convention (June 9, 1788) over the ratification of the Constitution, Anti-Federalist leader Patrick Henry offered the "illustrious example" of Rome in which dictators were pulled from the ranks of the great and virtuous. In contrast, those who supported the Constitution's adoption argued the advantages of institutionalizing executive energy in a way that would not require periodic resorts to extraordinary, extra-constitutional powers.

As the debates of the Constitutional Convention of 1787 and the subsequent contest for ratification in the states demonstrate, there were important principled disagreements in the Founding era about how to establish the executive power in a republican government. Yet at a fundamental level these differences rested on a shared understanding that all governments at some time required the capabilities of a powerful chief executive. Like Patrick Henry in the Virginia ratifying convention, Publius noted quite pointedly in *Federalist* 6: "Every man the least conversant in Roman history, knows how often that republic was obliged to take refuge in the absolute power of a single man under the formidable title of dictator."[6] In short, the real issue for the Founders was not whether this potentially fearsome aspect of government could be avoided but, instead, how it might best be called on, put to use, and, when necessary, regulated or checked.

STRUCTURING EXECUTIVE POWER IN THE STATES AND CONFEDERATION

The decade after independence saw executive power in the new nation exercised by a melange of governmental entities that were not institutionally executive in character. Assemblies, committees, and congresses were all in the business of performing functions that previously had been reserved to the king and his ministers. On its face the mix of legal and constitutional arrangements that developed in the United States in the wake of independence seems to imply that there was no one paradigm for thinking about and arranging the executive powers of government. Ironically, the historical inadequacy of the "conventionalist" view of

[6]*The Federalist Papers*, 423.

executive power can be shown through a closer examination of those various committees, congresses, and assemblies that wielded authorities that traditionally had been the prerogative of the executive.

In the wake of independence in 1776, most of the royal governors left or were removed from office, leaving the colonial assemblies as the only effective authorities capable of governing the states. Because the legislatures were either too busy when in session to do everything or unable to act when out of session, however, they regularly created committees of the house to carry on the government's business. Named Committees (or Councils) of Safety, these ad hoc boards—despite their institutional lineage and make-up—were nevertheless understood by others and themselves as exercising executive powers. Whether organizing the war effort in their state, conducting negotiations with Indian tribes, running secret operations, or simply making sure the laws passed by the assembly were enforced, the committees saw themselves as conducting the executive business of the state in the absence of a governor. As each state normalized its governmental arrangements by adopting a new constitution, and with it, an executive office, the committees were disbanded. Revealing in this respect is the statement made by New York's Council of Safety to the head of the continental forces, General George Washington. The council informed Washington that General George Clinton had been elected governor of New York and that therefore "on the governor's admission to Office, all the executive powers of the state are to be surrendered by the council to him."

A second example of this sort is the Continental Congress and, its successor, the Congress of the Articles of Confederation. While both bodies exercised a variety of powers—some clearly legislative in character—the significant bulk of their authorities was concerned with the new country's defense and foreign affairs. In effect, the Congress replaced the king in these areas.[7] Moreover, by Congress assuming these functions, it was also understood that the state governors had been essentially shorn of the like responsibilities. What is important to note here is that these authorities were not thought of as being any less executive in nature because they were exercised by a plural representative body.

Evidence of this can be found in any number of letters or commentaries of the time. An especially interesting illustration of this

---

[7]For a useful analysis of this point, see Jerrilyn Green Marston, *King and Congress: The Transfer of Political Legitimacy, 1774–1776* (Princeton: Princeton University Press, 1987).

point is found in an exchange of letters written in 1785 between James Madison and a friend in the territory of Kentucky. In the letter addressed to Madison, the Kentuckian asked Madison for his thoughts on the principles that might guide the territory's efforts at organizing a new government. In his reply, Madison admitted to some perplexity when it came to establishing the post of governor; for in his view "all the great powers which are properly executive" had already been "transferred to the foederal Government."[8] He meant, of course, the great powers over national defense and foreign affairs that the Articles of Confederation vested in the national congress.

The apparent confidence, however, with which Madison and others could describe certain authorities as executive by nature—despite the fact that they were exercised by bodies whose forms were far from traditionally executive in character—seems belied by the great variety of types of governors' offices established in the new state constitutions: no one governor matched another exactly in institutional design or formal powers. Again, the impression left is that there was no consensus about what powers were properly the executive's.

Yet, as before, this view is overdrawn, as can be seen by comparing the most powerful of the state chief executives (New York's governor created in 1777) with the weakest (Pennsylvania's executive council created in 1776). While the former was specifically fashioned to avoid the latter's perceived defects, it is noteworthy that, with only one important exception, New York's governor was given virtually the same set of formal authorities as Pennsylvania's executive council.[9] Yet the two executives, seen in the context of the early state constitutions, could not have been less alike. In learning from the failures of Pennsylvania's notoriously weak plural executive, New Yorkers had created a significantly different constitutional animal. In contrast to Pennsylvania's committee of twelve, whose members could serve no longer than three years in a row and whose president was annually elected by the legislature, the New York governor was a single chief executive elected by the people for a three-year term with no limits on eligibility for reelection. These constitutional features gave the New York executive a

---

[8]James Madison, Letter to Caleb Wallace, August 23, 1785, *The Mind of the Founder: Sources of the Political Thought of James Madison*, ed. Marvin Meyers (Indianapolis: Bobbs-Merrill, 1973), 47.

[9]Unlike Pennsylvania's executive, New York's governor was given (in conjunction with a committee consisting of a small number of justices) the qualified power to veto legislation.

continuity (the first governor, George Clinton, served eighteen years), popular support, and energy that were all lacking in its Pennsylvania counterpart. As a result New York state was much more effectively governed during the revolutionary period— indeed, so well governed that the New York governor became in many respects the model for the American presidency.

As this comparison and the preceding analysis suggest, behind the great variety of institutional forms for exercising executive power that characterized the first decade of American indepen- dence stood a far more coherent view of the essential elements of executive power than is often thought to be the case. What the in- stitutional variety—committees of safety, the national congress, and the first state governors—reflects is not confusion about the nature of executive power but rather uncertainty about how to in- stitutionalize the executive function within a nation both federal and republican.

Consequently, the key question that faced the members of the Constitutional Convention in Philadelphia in 1787 when they came to creating the presidency was not how to define executive power, but rather how to structure, or institutionalize, the exercise of that authority in their new republican government.[10] The Vir- ginia Plan—which was put forward within the Convention's first days and was the basic outline for what became the Constitution— had begun clearly enough: the new executive was to administer the laws and exercise the "Executive Rights vested in the Con- gress" of the Confederation. The difficulty (and one that plagued the members throughout the summer of 1787) was that no one had a clear idea of how to establish an executive office capable of exercising those authorities without creating in fact, if not in name, a monarch. Understood in this light, the real story of the Convention with respect to the presidency is how the delegates came to square that circle and create an executive office that was both a comfortable home to what Madison had called "the great powers" and fundamentally republican as well.[11]

[10]A key exception to this generalization was the extent to which the president would control decisions of "war and peace." See the debates in the Constitutional Convention on June 1, July 17, and August 17.

[11]Interestingly enough, the Convention's decision to address federal and repub- lican concerns by having the Senate share in the treaty-making power came under attack by the opponents of the Constitution for violating the principle of separa- tion of powers. Repeatedly, the Anti-Federalists complained that this mixing of the branches was a problem not only because it created a potentially dangerous "aris- tocratic" alliance between the president and the Senate but also because it involved the latter in what was properly "executive" business. The solution most often put

EXECUTIVE POWER AND THE AMERICAN CONSTITUTIONAL ORDER

How, then, can we characterize the essential elements of the Framers' understanding of executive power as incorporated into the Constitution through the language of Article II? Drawing upon the materials discussed above as well as the more detailed provisions of Article II such as commander-in-chief, pardoning power, treaty power, appointment power, etc., we can identify the following key features: the conduct of war, the superintendence of our relations with foreign nations, the execution of the laws and therefore the direction of the administrative apparatus of the government, the appointment and removal of high-level executive officials, and the guiding of the legislative process through information and proposed measures. Throughout all the governmental turmoil and institutional experimentation of the revolutionary years, the Founders' understanding of "the great powers . . . properly executive" remained constant. And these are the great responsibilities that were placed on the president of the United States by the Constitution of 1787.

In its details the Constitution required some sharing of these executive powers with the Senate (e.g., confirmation of high-level appointments and treaty ratification), as it also clarified the reach of some of these powers (e.g., the president as commander-in-chief would direct the operations of war once authorized or begun, but only Congress could legitimately move the nation from a state of peace to a state of war). Moreover, as is well known, by 1793 Hamilton and Madison found themselves in a very public disagreement over the president's constitutional authority in foreign affairs. Their debate in the Pacificus and Helvidius Letters, written in the wake of President Washington's proclamation of American neutrality in the European war, confronted the issue of just how far the executive power reached in matters of war and peace and foreign relations. Although Madison adamantly denied Hamilton's contention that the powers to declare war and make treaties were in their nature executive, he did not dispute the intrinsically executive nature of the power to conduct war once authorized or

---

forward was to remove the Senate from the treaty-making process altogether and create a permanent and distinct privy council whose job it would be to advise the president on treaties and the making of appointments. This criticism of the Constitution, of course, reinforces the notion that there was general agreement among the Founders about the character and extent of "the executive power." The criticism also helps to explain the somewhat defensive tone of Publius in *The Federalist* in trying to justify the Senate's role in treaty making with the argument that this power may not be simply executive in nature.

the power to carry out foreign negotiations. Nor, for that matter, did he dispute the executive nature of the other central elements of executive power outlined here.

Two other points about Madison's argument should be noted. First, contrary to some contemporary interpretations of his position, at no point did he deny that the vesting clause of Article II actually vests power. That is, Madison did not take the position in his Helvidius Letters that the president possessed only the *specific* powers, such as commander-in-chief, bestowed in Article II. Thus, his dispute with Hamilton was not over the concept of implied powers (which he had strongly endorsed in the removal power debate in the First Congress) but rather over the interpretation of the furthest reaches of those implied powers. Second, Madison's whole mode of analysis in his five Helvidius essays presumed a formal distinction of the powers of government into three main types: legislative, executive, and judicial. In this, those moderns who deny that the Framers meant to formally separate not just the institutions but also the powers, or functions, of government could not be further from the understanding that animated the man who has rightly earned the title "father of the Constitution."

More than half a century later, Abraham Lincoln's Civil War presidency revealed the fullest dimensions of the constitutional presidency. Drawing particularly upon the Take Care Clause ("he shall take Care that the Laws be faithfully executed") and the presidential oath ("I . . . will to the best of my Ability, preserve, protect and defend the Constitution of the United States"), Lincoln argued that the chief executive had a special responsibility for ensuring obedience to national law and for preserving the integrity of the nation. Though obedient to the laws passed by Congress to confront the nation's greatest crisis, Lincoln acted vigorously on his own authority when Congress was not in session and when necessary before the slower, more deliberative body could act. In Lincoln's view, his extraordinary exercise of emergency powers was well grounded in the words of the nation's fundamental law. As he said near the close of his First Inaugural Address in words specifically directed to the South: "In *your* hands, my dissatisfied fellow countrymen, and not in *mine*, is the momentous issue of civil war. The government will not assail *you*. You can have no conflict, without being yourselves the aggressors. *You* have no oath registered in Heaven to destroy the government, while *I* shall have the most solemn one to 'preserve, protect and defend' it."[12]

---

[12]Roy P. Basler, ed., *The Collected Works of Abraham Lincoln* (New Brunswick, NJ: Rutgers University Press, 1953), 4:271.

CONCLUSION: A HOUSE BEFITTING THE OFFICE

Lest the words and deeds of the Founding generation leave us uncertain as to the full dimensions of the powers vested by the Constitution in the chief magistrate, those who invented presidential government have left us in the stone, brick, and mortar that became the president's home a monument to their understanding of executive power as anything but weak or subordinate. While advances in engineering since the Founding have made gigantic structures a routine feature of nearly every major city's skyline and, thus, have altered our sense of scale for what constitutes a grand building, the fact is that the president's home (whose core remains essentially as designed in the early 1790s) was, for its time, an enormous residence. Indeed, the records suggest that the White House was until the 1850s or so the largest home built in North America. It is no wonder then that the residence was at times—and not, at least initially, pejoratively—referred to as the "president's palace." The only home built for a government official, the White House is solid testimony to the fact that in setting up the presidency the Founders had in mind a potentially powerful executive office.

Moreover, the president's constitutional stature and independence were reaffirmed by the plan for the capital city drafted by the French-born artist and engineer, Pierre L'Enfant. As the plan makes clear, the president's home and the Capitol were to serve as geographically distinct and equal anchors around which the city was expected to grow and revolve. Separated by what at the time was a fair distance, the president's residence and the Capitol were also built so that they did not face each other directly. Connected by a single, large avenue, neither structure's main vista was of the other. The White House looked south, down the Potomac, and north. The Capitol looked east, where its front steps faced a part of the city designated for commercial and residential development, and west down the mall. While the exact placement of the two principal government buildings was, in part, a matter of local topography and of placating local landowners, the plan's effect was to reinforce the idea that the two political branches were essentially separate and sovereign in their own areas and in their own ways.

Of course, the Capitol was built on the heights of what was then known as Jenkins' Hill. This gave the Congress a preeminent position within the federal district's core, reflecting no doubt its high, public responsibility of passing laws for the republic as a whole. Yet counterbalancing this was the decision made soon thereafter to locate the buildings housing the departments of war, state, and treasury on the grounds reserved for the executive's mansion. Congress was placed on a pedestal, but the weight of the government's day-to-day business was adjoined to the presidency. The placement of these departments, designed to correspond architecturally with the White House, generally reflected the view that these functions belonged more to the executive sphere than the legislative.

In constituting the city, then, as they had constituted the new government, the Founding generation had a clear idea of what they wanted, despite some later disagreements over the precise meaning of "the executive Power." Indeed, at the time the president's mansion was being planned and its place in the city fixed, Washington's chief aide on these matters was not his powerful secretary of the treasury, Alexander Hamilton, but his secretary of state, Thomas Jefferson. This same Jefferson, who would later accuse the Federalists of monarchical tendencies, showed no inclination to house the president in anything but a large and impressive residence. Thus, whatever the nature of the eventual split between the Federalists and Republicans, the leading Founders initially shared a vision of the presidency that was anything but modest.

Separation of Powers and Judicial Review

Bradford P. Wilson

TWENTIETH CENTURY SCHOLARSHIP on the power of American federal courts has always been shadowed by a debate over the constitutional legitimacy of judicial review.[1] Recent interpretations of the historical sources are raising new questions as to the adequacy of prevailing doctrines on the subject.[2] With this scholarly ferment in mind, I propose to reconstruct the classic account of the constitutional purpose of judicial review. As that account is essentially theoretical, it is necessary first to place it in its proper and peculiar theoretical context. My procedure then is to discuss the more fundamental principles and characteristics of modern republican constitutionalism before taking up the derivative question of judicial power.

LIBERAL PRINCIPLES

Today it is commonplace to identify liberalism and democracy, no doubt in part because of the more than 200 year history of

The author is grateful to the Earhart Foundation for its support in his writing of this article.

[1] By judicial review, I mean the power of a court of law, in a case or controversy properly before it, to judge the constitutionality of an act of a coordinate branch of government, and to refuse to give effect to the act if it is judged to be contrary to the law of the Constitution.

[2] See Robert Lowry Clinton, *Marbury v. Madison and Judicial Review* (Lawrence: University Press of Kansas, 1989), 1, which argues that *Marbury* v. *Madison* reflected "a generally agreed-upon notion of the reach of judicial power in constitutional matters: that federal courts are entitled to invalidate acts of coordinate branches of government only when to allow such acts to stand would violate constitutional restrictions on judicial power, not on legislative or executive power." See also James R. Stoner, Jr., *Common Law & Liberal Theory: Coke, Hobbes, & the Origins of American Constitutionalism* (Lawrence: University Press of Kansas, 1992), 205–10, which argues that judicial review is best seen as a consequence of the common law background of the judiciary.

American devotion both to liberty and to popular government or majority rule. To appreciate the underlying causes of the specific institutional arrangements of the American constitutional order, however, it is helpful to step back from those arrangements and to reflect on the fact that the identification of liberalism and democracy is alien to liberal political philosophy as it was understood by its chief architects. A strong case has been made that the founder of the fundamental principles of liberal thought and government was Thomas Hobbes,[3] who regarded the best regime to be rule by a monarch wielding unqualifiedly absolute power. The liberal debate in political philosophy that followed Hobbes, and which eventually shifted the regime question to the plane of democratic thought, was a debate which revolved, not around the fundamental principles themselves, but around alternative ways to deal with the problems generated by those principles.

What are those principles and what problems do they raise? The principles in Hobbes's presentation can be briefly summarized: Hobbes resolves civil society into its constituent elements— the individual wills. Those wills are reducible to and in the service of the most fundamental, because the most powerful and ineluctable, of man's passions—the desire for self-preservation. Because that desire is the most powerful universal spring of men's actions and is ineradicable, it is beyond blame and is thus the source of all right.[4] All men have a natural right to self-preservation.

A right to an end implies a right to the means to that end. Therefore men have a right by nature to the liberty necessary for their pursuit of preservation. Because all men are equal in their ability to deny one another's natural right through violence, it is in their interest to turn this natural equality, which is to their disadvantage in the state of nature, to their mutual advantage. This is done by all men acknowledging their respective equality by nature, which acknowledgement provides the rock of their political salvation. Because men are equal, all have an equal right to consent. Each man covenants with every other man to constitute civil society with a sovereign authority, and to regard the will of the sovereign as representative of his own will. The sovereign authority

---

[3]See Leo Strauss, *Natural Right and History* (Chicago: University of Chicago Press, 1953), 181–82.

[4]See Thomas Hobbes, *Leviathan* (London: Oxford University Press, 1909), ch. xiii, 97. What is even more fundamental in Hobbes's account than the desire for self-preservation is its negative counterpart, the fear of violent death. It is the passion Hobbes first mentions in his list of those passions which "incline men to peace." Ibid., 98.

retains the absolute power possessed by each person in the state of nature, while every party to the covenant gives up his natural right to all things into the hands of the sovereign.

Men perform this authorization for the sake of providing for their preservation, which is their due by nature. This fact creates a certain paradox in Hobbes's thought: "It is true that when one considers the end of authorization, the formula of authorization seems to require a limitation for the sake of the end: not absolute power but power 'in those things which concern the common peace and safety.' But when men aim at this end, they cannot achieve it. Accordingly, the formula of authorization achieves the end by absolutizing the means, that is, the sovereign."[5] By insisting on the necessity of absolute or unlimited means to achieve a specific end, Hobbes endows liberal thought with a tension that provides the horizon within which the regime question is raised and from which it takes its bearings. That tension is one inherent in the coexistence of individual right and governmental sovereignty,[6] which in turn is the resurrection of the perennial question of the relationship between nature and convention in its new and characteristically modern form.

However great and original have been subsequent contributions to liberal thought, there has been universal liberal acceptance of the Hobbesian doctrine that limits the ends of government to securing individual rights. And, in that subsequent history, there has been widespread recognition with Hobbes of the social contract as the origin of political society along with acceptance of the original equality of men and the radical artificiality of civil society (as owing its being to human will).

The distinctive differences within liberal thinking, then, are not over the issue of what government is for. The significant disagreements, which account for a rather clear movement or development in the liberal tradition, address the question of the form, as distinct from the origin or end, of government. Breaking from the premodern tradition in which the debate over the proper form of government was part and parcel of the debate over the proper ends of government, modern liberalism treats the regime question as only becoming meaningful or legitimate once the question of ends has been settled. The kinds of regimes are no longer under-

---

[5]Harvey C. Mansfield, Jr., "Hobbes and the Science of Indirect Government," *American Political Science Review* 65 (1971): 102.

[6]Strauss calls this tension an "insoluble conflict" in Hobbes. *Natural Right and History*, 197.

stood as intrinsically connected with peculiar ways of life, but rather are seen as different means to the same end, viz., the liberal way of life.

For Hobbes, the natural equality of men, while necessarily implying the equal right of all to participate in the generation of the commonwealth through their consent, in no way implies the right of any man to a share in rule. Man's nature determines the origin and end of government but is silent on the question of who should rule. For Hobbes, the primary institutional problem is to provide for a form of government which will best maintain the advantages deriving from absolute sovereignty—peace, modesty, and property.[7] The regime least conducive to that task is democracy, which is characterized by contention, vanity, and avarice. What is crucial in the doctrine of sovereignty is the unification of the multiplicity of wills found in the state of nature. That unification is best represented by one man.

Hobbes's resolution of the political problem sets in high relief the tension between individual natural right and absolute government. This tension is the point of departure for Locke and the subsequent liberal tradition. Locke argues that the protection of the natural right of the individual demands not absolute government, but rather limited government.

While Locke's alternative to Hobbes's absolutism is complex, he proposes in essence three solutions, or more precisely, mitigations of the Hobbesian tension. One is in manifest opposition to Hobbes: an insistence that citizens be governed only by "promulgated standing Laws" from which "[n]o Man in Civil Society can be exempted"[8]—the primary meaning of the rule of law. Second, Locke removes the stigma imposed by Hobbes on the provision of some form of popular participation, not only in the original constituting act, but also in the operation of government.[9] This takes place through a broadening of the notion of representation found in Hobbes. Locke's third major contribution to the practical resolution of the tension is his expansion of the private sphere in a manner consistent both with governmental sovereignty and individual right. Hobbes's criticism of all previous political thinkers was that, by considering those things which men take most seri-

---

[7]See De Cive, Ep. ded.; Leviathan, ch. xv. Hobbes says of the Leviathan that it is "[j]ustitiae mensura, atque ambitionis elenchus." Opera Latina, vol. 1, xciv.

[8]John Locke, Two Treatises of Government, ed. Peter Laslett (Cambridge: Cambridge University Press, 1988), II, §§ 136, 94.

[9]See ibid., II, §§ 142, 143, 154, 157, 158.

ously to be subject to political controversy and, through that controversy, to political determination, they encouraged ambition and vanity which can only lead to strife, the worst of all civic evils. Locke capitalizes on the Hobbesian insight by withdrawing, as far as is compatible with civil society, the contentious goods—primarily property and religion—from public determination.

From Hobbes's perspective, such a significant reversion to the private is a step back towards the state of nature. But Hobbes's absolute monarch is beyond contention and thus is singularly qualified to make judgments of good and bad. Because of his rejection of Hobbes's monarchical solution, however, Locke allows controversy back into the public realm. It thus was necessary to remove the *objects* of controversy from the political arena by falling back on the private realm, the source of all human difficulties in the first place. In the final analysis, Locke's optimism regarding the success of liberal reliance on private judgment and popular participation in politics rests on his estimation of the character of the people as more "slow" than it is "unsteady."[10]

AMERICAN REPUBLICANISM

The American Founding stands firmly on liberal principles of equality and liberty. It takes the primary purpose of government to be securing individual rights, and, accepting the Lockean contribution, sees the central task of liberal politics to be the preservation of private, or civil, liberty. It departs from the older view, however, by holding that the form of government best fitted to achieve that end is a species of popular government, with popular government understood as one in which the people rule, either directly or through representatives of their own choosing.

The shifts in liberal thinking from Hobbes's advocacy of absolute monarchy, to Locke's openness to and Montesquieu's argument for a mixture of hereditary and popular elements, to the wholly popular regime of the United States are stages in the liberal struggle with the fundamental intractable problem found in Hobbes. With the Americans, a certain "realism" begun by Locke reaches its fruition: Hobbes was right in recognizing a theory of representation as the key to the prevention of separate interests of ruler and ruled. He was wrong in thinking that its virtue lay in its abstractness. The way to provide for a harmony of interests be-

---

[10]See ibid., II, § 223. See also Strauss, *Natural Right and History*, 233, n. 104.

tween ruler and ruled, thereby preventing the theoretical tension between rights and sovereignty, nature and convention, from becoming an ever present practical crisis, is through a representative mechanism which links rulers to ruled not only formally but materially. Through working out the requirements of this representative mechanism, the Americans committed themselves to a wholly popular government.

REPUBLICAN LIBERTY AND THE REPRESENTATIVE PRINCIPLE

In what sense should government be popular, or "by the people"? In *The Federalist*, which is the most comprehensive and illuminating exposition of the design and intention of the American Constitution, a clear distinction is made between free government and republican government.[11] Free government is government that secures individual rights. Republican government, and thus *political* freedom, as distinct from civil liberty, is valued chiefly (though certainly not exclusively) as a means to the end of securing private rights. *The Federalist*'s defense of republican government is based on a judgment that political freedom best perfects the protection of civil liberty or individual rights.[12]

Yet we must be careful about labeling the American Founders as "democrats." They were democrats if by that we mean those who maintain that governments "deriv[e] their just Powers from the Consent of the Governed"[13] and, in addition, that "the deliberate sense of the community [in practice, of the majority] should govern the conduct of those to whom they entrust the manage-

[11]See *The Federalist*, ed. Jacob E. Cooke (Middletown: Wesleyan University Press, 1961), No. 9, 51, where Alexander Hamilton indicates that there have been successful free governments that were not republican. See also ibid., No. 26, 165–66, where Hamilton identifies the Glorious Revolution and the elevation of the Prince of Orange as the moment that "English liberty was completely triumphant." *Federalist* 39 clarifies the unrepublican nature of the post-1688 British government. Ibid., 251.

[12]James Madison points to "that honorable determination, which animates every votary of freedom, to rest all our political experiments on the capacity of mankind for self-government." *Federalist* No. 39, 250. Martin Diamond has argued that this is "the very heart of the matter: As votaries of freedom, *individual liberty was to the Founders the comprehensive, unproblematic good; and they were determined to secure that good by an experiment in democracy.*" "The Declaration and the Constitution: Liberty, Democracy, and the Founders," in *As Far as Republican Principles Will Admit: Essays by Martin Diamond*, ed. William A. Schambra (Washington: The AEI Press, 1992), 237, emphasis original.

[13]Declaration of Independence, ¶ 2.

ment of their affairs."[14] Consider the argument of the authors of
The Federalist, however, that the principle of representation, while
not unknown to the ancients, was not "well understood"[15] by them
because of their failure to recognize its proper virtue: The true
difference between the ancient governments and the American
governments lies "*in the total exclusion of the people in their collective
capacity*, from any share in the *latter*, and not in the *total exclusion of
the representatives of the people* from the administration of the
former."[16] American republicanism differs from premodern republicanism because of the use to which representation is put. The system of representation is the means for keeping the people as a
collective body *out* of government—letting the people in at the
point of choosing representatives, and keeping them out at the
point of the actual operation of government. The effect of the representative principle is to "refine and enlarge the public views, by
passing them through the medium of a chosen body of citizens,
whose wisdom may best discern the true interest of their country,
and whose patriotism and love of justice, will be least likely to sacrifice it to temporary or partial considerations."[17]

Representation is not, then, a substitute for direct popular
rule, as though the latter were superior in principle but had been
rendered impossible by the increased population and extensive
territory of the modern nation state. It does, of course, provide
the key to bringing a greater number of citizens and a greater extent of territory within the compass of popular government. But
the enlargement of the orbit of popular government through republican representation is not so that "[w]hat Athens was in min-
iature, America will be in magnitude."[18] It is instead to guard

---

[14]*Federalist* No. 71, 482. For a discussion of why calling the defenders of the Constitution "democrats" "does [not] foster analytical clarity," see Herbert J. Storing,
What the Anti-Federalists Were For (Chicago: University of Chicago Press, 1981), 90, n.
19.
[15]*Federalist* No. 9, 51.
[16]*Federalist* No. 63, 428, emphasis original.
[17]*Federalist* No. 10, 62.
[18]Thomas Paine, *The Rights of Man* (England: Penguin Books, 1969), 202. Paine
did not understand the principle of representation as in any way a refinement or
filtration of the popular will. Rather, he saw representation as a principle that is
merely "ingrafted" upon democracy. The "original simple democracy . . . affords
the true data from which government on a large scale can begin." The representative system "retains democracy as the ground." Ibid. On the basis of his understanding that man is by nature good, Paine could argue, as he did, for the sheer
naturalness of *political* liberty, in addition to civil liberty. (But see Paine's *Common
Sense* in *Tracts of the American Revolution*, ed. Merrill Jensen [Indianapolis: Bobbs-
Merrill Co., Inc., 1967], 404: "As nothing but Heaven is impregnable to vice,

against the danger of the vice peculiar to popular government, whatever its specific form, which is its propensity to factious combinations of a majority. The traditional republican teaching held that the larger the society, the greater the threat to republican liberty. James Madison recognized that the opposite was true, that republican liberty was most vulnerable in small societies because of the greater likelihood of the appearance of a homogeneous majority with the motive and opportunity to oppress the rights of the minority. The representative principle makes possible the reconciliation of the popular principle with the requirement of free, nonoppressive government.[19]

At the root of the Framers' rejection of the simple democratic standard or ideal is their acceptance of the defectiveness of man's natural condition. Although popular government is desirable, it must be formed in such a way as to avoid as much as possible the undesirable consequences of human imperfection. That is done in the first place by rejecting simple democracy and the overly sanguine view of human nature upon which it rests. At the same time, we must keep in mind that a tyranny of the majority, which was identified by Madison as the most critical problem facing the Founders,[20] only becomes a problem after the principle of majority rule has been rendered legitimate.

The representative principle solves some problems, but not others, and may even create a few. In choosing to limit themselves, the people acknowledge the limits of their capacity to govern themselves directly.[21] But the representative principle, though it

---

[individuals, after entering society,] will begin to relax in their duty and attachment to each other: and this remissness will point out the necessity of establishing some form of government to supply the defect of moral virtue.")

[19]See *Federalist* No. 10, 63–64. See also Madison's restatement of this argument in *Federalist* 51, where he asserts the common security for civil and religious liberty (assuming them both to be rights of the individual): "In a free government, the security for civil rights must be the same as for religious rights. It consists in the one case in the multiplicity of interests, and in the other, in the multiplicity of sects. The degree of security in both cases will depend on the number of interests and sects; and this may be presumed to depend on the extent of country and number of people comprehended under the same government." *Federalist* No. 51, 351–52.

[20]*Federalist* No. 10, 60–61: "When a majority is included in a faction, the form of popular government . . . enables it to sacrifice to its ruling passion or interest, both the public good and the rights of other citizens. To secure the public good, and private rights, against the danger of such a faction, and at the same time to preserve the spirit and the form of popular government, is then the great object to which our enquiries are directed."

[21]See Harvey C. Mansfield, Jr., *Taming the Prince* (New York: The Free Press, 1989), 254.

does guarantee popular government, and makes possible free government, does not guarantee popular *and* free government. For that, a certain internal structure for the working of government is needed.

THE SEPARATION OF POWERS

But what is government itself but the greatest of all reflections on human nature? If men were angels, no government would be necessary. If angels were to govern men, neither external nor internal controuls on government would be necessary. In framing a government which is to be administered by men over men, the great difficulty lies in this: You must first enable government to controul the governed; and in the next place, oblige it to controul itself. A dependence on the people is no doubt the primary controul on the government; but experience has taught mankind the necessity of auxiliary precautions.[22]

This famous statement from *The Federalist* occurs in the context of an explanation and defense of the principle of separation of powers as it appears in the plan of the Constitution. The first task of founding is to supply government with sufficient power to accomplish the ends for which governments are instituted among men—securing the unalienable rights of life, liberty, and the pursuit of happiness. Power ought not to be granted sparingly, for "[e]nergy in Government is essential to that security against external and internal danger, and to that prompt and salutary execution of the laws, which enter into the very definition of good Government."[23] Good government, government able to provide secure liberty, must be powerful government. It will also be administered by men, and men are not angels. Sobriety about human nature leads immediately to considerations of limiting governmental power in the name of liberty and security. The "primary controul" is supplied by the republican principle, which links the policies of the government to the will of the people through the scheme of representation. But, as we have seen, representation is as much a reflection on the limits of self-government as it is a means to self-government. Furthermore, it is by itself an insufficient foil to the danger of uncontrolled power. "Auxiliary precautions" are necessary, in particular, an effectual separation of powers, even if we may finally conclude that the principle of separation of powers is nonrepublican in character.

[22]*Federalist* No. 51, 349.
[23]*Federalist* No. 37, 233.

Locke and Montesquieu promoted the separation of powers as a response to the Hobbesian problem inherent in the coexistence of individual rights and governmental sovereignty. Hobbes's solution to the insecurity of human rights was a unitary and indivisible sovereign power, creating the "frightful dilemma"[24] of a government jeopardizing the very rights it was established to secure. As suggested above, Lockean innovations in the rule of law, representation, and privatization are of massive significance in the development of modern liberalism from its Hobbesian beginnings. But the auxiliary precaution of the separation of powers, as republicanized by the American Framers, provides the American Constitution with its own signal contribution to meeting the Hobbesian dilemma.

Recent scholarship has traced the historical development of separation of powers theory and considered its sometimes confusing relationship with theories of mixed or balanced government.[25] For our purposes, it is only necessary to observe that neither Locke's nor Montesquieu's analysis of the separation of powers is republican in character.

Montesquieu's discussion of the separation in Book XI of *The Spirit of the Laws* served as the common authority for Americans debating the proper internal structure of the national government at the time of the Founding. When Madison begins the discussion in *The Federalist* of "the particular structure of this government, and the distribution of [the general mass of power allotted to it] among its constituent parts,"[26] he immediately turns to ascertaining the meaning of "the celebrated Montesquieu," who is "[t]he oracle who is always consulted and cited"[27] when the subject is the separation of powers. Madison is silent about the weight Montesquieu places in his analysis on the executive's person being sacred and his conduct unimpeachable, or on the necessity of one house of the legislature consisting of a hereditary nobility "distinguished by birth, wealth, or honors."[28] The phenomenon of separation of

[24]James W. Ceaser, *Liberal Democracy and Political Science* (Baltimore: The Johns Hopkins University Press, 1990), 189.

[25]See M. J. C. Vile, *Constitutionalism and the Separation of Powers* (London: Oxford University press, 1967); W. B. Gwyn, *The Meaning of the Separation of Powers* (New Orleans: Tulane University, 1965); and Harvey C. Mansfield, "Separation of Powers in the American Constitution," in this volume.

[26]*Federalist* No. 47, 323.

[27]Ibid., 324.

[28]Montesquieu, *The Spirit of the Laws* (Cambridge: Cambridge University Press, 1989), 160. See William Kristol, "The Problem of the Separation of Powers: *Federalist* 47–51," in *Saving the Revolution*, ed. Charles R. Kesler (New York: The Free Press, 1987), 105.

powers is treated by Montesquieu, then, in the context of an understanding of balanced government, deriving from Aristotle's mixed regime, in which the "separate views and interests"[29] of the nobility and the people are separated within the legislature with sufficient power (not only legislative) to guard against class oppression.[30]

This context is replaced in the thought of the American Framers by a wholly republican one. Their affirmation of republican government leads them to a new appreciation both of the necessity for Montesquieu's principle and of the need to integrate it into a new constitutional balance that is consistent with the republican principle. The result is a balanced government more complex in its constitutional organization, powers, and operation than even the traditional mixed governments of Europe. Abandoning the social differentiations, natural or conventional, that gave the different parts of government their weight and authority in the tradition of mixed government, the Framers replaced them with what they regarded as a new and better kind of complex and balanced government.

The government of the Constitution is a "balance of *constitutional* orders or powers, blended with a constitutional differentiation of functions."[31] Constitutional orders, orders which have no existence outside of or apart from the Constitution, replace social orders or estates, with the balance of the Constitution no longer finding its primary locus in the legislature[32] but now in the internal structure of powers organized and delegated by the sovereign Constitution—with two of the three "supreme powers of the state"[33] standing independent of the legislative body. The weight of each of the various parts in the constitutional balance depends

[29]Montesquieu, *The Spirit of the Laws*, 160.

[30]See Martin Diamond, "The Separation of Powers and the Mixed Regime," in *As Far as Republican Principles Admit*, 58–67.

[31]Storing, *What the Anti-Federalists Were For*, 62, emphasis original.

[32]For a contrary view, see Ann Stuart Anderson, "A 1787 Perspective on Separation of Powers," in *Separation of Powers—Does It Still Work?* ed. Robert A. Goldwin and Art Kaufman (Washington: The AEI Press, 1986), where it is argued that the Senate "is the only true balancing device to be found in the American constitutional system" (157). This claim has its premise in the assertion that "the Senate was *the* device relied on by the framers to prevent the abuse of legislative power." (Ibid., 158, emphasis original.) This is entirely consistent with, and seems to be derivative from, the writer's assumption of legislative supremacy. That assumption, however, is difficult to maintain in the face of a constitution that makes all the branches and powers of government its mere creatures, and all of whom participate in the sovereignty of the government.

[33]*Federalist* No. 51, 349.

on what the Constitution delegates to it and not on what the participants in government bring with them when they enter.

The implications of this arrangement for Lockean legislative supremacy are of fundamental significance. As all governmental power flows from the Constitution, which itself flows from the people, no particular constitutional power can claim to be sovereign. Each body wielding constitutional power can legitimately claim to be representative because it represents the popular will embodied in the Constitution. And the argument from the supremacy of law-giving to the supremacy of the legislative power gets derailed by the supremacy of the higher law of the Constitution, which gives law to all the rest. In this manner, the Framers were able to replace legislative sovereignty with a constitutional balance of powers.

Raising the question of why the Framers chose to deny sovereignty to the legislature brings us back to a consideration of republicanism and the problems it creates for liberty and good government. Previous championing of legislative sovereignty tended to be accompanied by an argument for or assumption of a governmental balance, primarily legislative, that depended on the representation of class interest. The Madisonian system of multiplying interests by means of the extended republic and the protection of liberty destroys the social materials upon which the traditional balance depended, and which the spirit of republican equality would not in any case support. The effect of legislative sovereignty in republican circumstances, as many of the American states in the period between 1776 and 1787 discovered, is a dangerously feeble executive.[34] The delegation and separation of powers would have to come to the aid of balanced government.

The Framers' debt to Montesquieu is paid early in Madison's discussion of the separation of powers in *The Federalist:* "The accumulation of all powers legislative, executive and judiciary in the same hands, whether of one, a few or many, and whether hereditary, self appointed, or elective, may justly be pronounced the very definition of tyranny." The strength of this "political truth" is so great, writes Madison, that, were there any "dangerous tendency to such an accumulation in the federal constitution,"[35] that constitution would have to be abandoned. Earlier arguments in *The Federalist* had established the republican credentials of the

[34]See Charles C. Thach, Jr., *The Creation of the Presidency, 1775–1789* (Baltimore: The Johns Hopkins Press, 1969), Ch. II; and Gordon S. Wood, *The Creation of the American Republic, 1776–1787* (New York: W. W. Norton & Co., 1969), 132–143.
[35]*Federalist* No. 47, 324.

Constitution.[36] But the republican principle, which is that of "a dependence on the people," is an insufficient security against tyranny. A structural principle of "separate and distinct" powers is required. That principle seems to belong to no particular form—monarchical, aristocratic, or republican—but is necessary if any form is to secure liberty. Thus, the modernity of the principle of separate and distinct powers is revealed—its end is the "preservation of liberty"[37]—at the same time as is its nonrepublican character.

Legislative sovereignty would be compatible with separation of powers if the legislative body were in need of no external advice for the justice of its laws, which is to say, if the balance within the legislature were all the balance that was needed to protect liberty. Indeed, as W. B. Gwyn has shown,[38] the origination of separation of powers theory in the writings of the 17th century British republicans had as its purpose the subordination of the executive to the rule of law, which meant to the legislature, by denying the executive the authority of law-making. The Framers' recognition of the need to extend the constitutional balance beyond the legislature reflects their judgment that in a republic, the legislature, however arranged, would constitute that branch of government most dangerous to individual security and liberty. As Madison puts it in *Federalist* 51, "In republican government the legislative authority, necessarily, predominates."[39] This, however, is not an acknowledgement of "legislative sovereignty," with its baggage of juridical claims. Rather, it is a facing up to a necessary effect of republicanism, an "inconveniency"[40] to be remedied by artificially strengthening the weaker departments of government through placing additional powers, understood as constitutional checks, in their hands.

It is not enough "to mark with precision the boundaries of [the legislative, executive, and judicial] departments in the Constitution of the government,"[41] for "[p]ower is of an encroaching

[36]See ibid., No. 39, 250–53, which demonstrates the republican character of all three branches, though they vary in their proximity to the people.

[37]Ibid., No. 47, 324.

[38]See Gwyn, *The Meaning of the Separation of Powers*, ch. IV.

[39]*Federalist* No. 51, 350.

[40]Ibid. Madison explores the reasons for legislative predominance in *Federalist* 48, warning that, in a "representative republic," it is "against the enterprising ambition of this department, that the people ought to indulge all their jealousy and exhaust all their precautions." Ibid., 334.

[41]Ibid., No. 48, 332–33.

nature."[42] And the most potent power in a republican government is the legislative. There are certain precautions that can contribute to a sound foundation for the separate and distinct exercise of the different powers of government by supporting a separate will in each department.[43]

But the greatest security against a gradual concentration of the several powers in the same department, consists in giving to those who administer each department, the necessary constitutional means, and personal motives, to resist encroachments of the others. The provision for defence must in this, as in all other cases, be made commensurate to the danger of attack. Ambition must be made to counteract ambition. The interest of the man must be connected with the constitutional rights of the place.[44]

Here we have the argument for the necessity of checks and balances as the primary means of securing the separation of powers, thereby preserving liberty. It thus appears that the connecting and blending of powers or functions that can be found in the Constitution—e.g., the qualified executive veto of legislative acts—are measures of departmental self-defense against the encroachments of the stronger into the sphere of the weaker. Without such constitutional controls, "the degree of separation which the maxim [linking separation with liberty] requires as essential to a free government, can never in practice, be duly maintained."[45]

There is an obvious alternative for "keeping the several departments of power within their constitutional limits," and which would be "strictly consonant to the republican theory": an "appeal to the people themselves." After all, "the people are the only legitimate fountain of power, and it is from them that the constitutional charter, under which the several branches of government hold their power, is derived."[46]

In *Federalist* 49, Madison raises this alternative and rejects it because of "insuperable objections" to involving the people, except for "certain great and extraordinary occasions,"[47] in constitutional controversies among the branches. "A frequent reference of constitutional questions, to the decision of the whole society"

---

[42]Ibid., 332.
[43]See ibid., No. 51, 348–49.
[44]Ibid., 349.
[45]Ibid., No. 48, 332.
[46]Ibid., No. 49, 339.
[47]Ibid. For these occasions, the Constitution provides the exceedingly difficult amendment process, which requires a super-majority for success.

will (1) undermine popular confidence in the government and its laws because of the implication of some defect and thus create instability and so insecurity; (2) promote disorder and discord "by interesting too strongly the public passions" in the reconsideration of "established forms of government," experiments in constitutional revision being "of too ticklish a nature to be unnecessarily multiplied";[48] and (3) result, in most cases, in "an aggrandizement of the legislative, at the expense of the other departments"[49] because of the superior influence with the people enjoyed by the legislature due to its numbers and the nature of its public trust. In any event, the decision would never "turn on the true merits of the question,"[50] for the spirit of party and personal influence would dictate the result. "The *passions* therefore not *the reason,* of the public, would sit in judgment. But it is the reason of the public alone that ought to controul and regulate the government. The passions ought to be controuled and regulated by the government."[51]

We are now able to see more fully the implications of Madison's remark that, while "[a] dependence on the people is no doubt the primary controul on the government,"[52] auxiliary precautions are necessary. The republican principle alone is incapable of sustaining a separation of the functional distribution of power. A republican legislature, because of its closer connection and superior influence with the people, will predominate in a republic and must be prevented from "drawing all power into its impetuous vortex."[53] The republican principle must be moderated in light of the nonrepublican principle of separation of powers, a "nonrepublican auxiliary to republicanism."[54]

The modern principle of representation does not itself succeed in squelching the danger of majority tyranny in a republic, despite its vast superiority in this regard to direct rule by the people. For "the legislature at once has the mantle of popular authority and is capable, unlike the people, of rationally pursuing the objects of its passions,"[55] which are likely to be reflections of the objects of the people's passions. Or perhaps it is better to say that the republican principle of representation, though not by itself solving the republican problem of majoritarian injustice, contrib-

---

[48]Ibid., 340–41.
[49]Ibid., 341.
[50]Ibid., 342.
[51]Ibid., 343, emphasis original.
[52]Ibid., No. 51, 349.
[53]Ibid., No. 48, 333.
[54]Mansfield, "Separation of Powers," 3.
[55]Kristol, "The Problem of the Separation of Powers," 110.

utes mightily to its solution by being extended, as it is in the American Constitution, to all three branches of government. For only then can the republican form embrace a separation of powers directed against the republican legislature.

JUDICIAL REVIEW

A proper appreciation of the novel aspect of the judicial power of the United States, the right of judicial review, depends on approaching the question in terms of its relation to the larger purposes of the separation of powers. The text to which scholars most often repair when inquiring into the justification for the judiciary's power of judicial review is John Marshall's opinion in *Marbury* v. *Madison*.[56] Marshall's argument is there directed at the limits of the legislative power and is compelling in its simplicity.

The "original and supreme will" of the people, Marshall explains, "organizes the government, and assigns to different departments their respective powers." If it chooses, that original will may "proceed further and establish certain limits not to be transcended by those departments," as was done with the government of the United States. The Constitution is written so that "those limits may not be mistaken or forgotten." If judges are obliged equally to enforce acts prohibited and acts allowed by the Constitution, "[t]he distinction between a government with limited and unlimited powers is abolished":

The constitution is either a superior paramount law, unchangeable by ordinary means, or it is on a level with ordinary legislative acts, and, like other acts, alterable when the legislature shall please to alter it. If the former part of the alternative be true, then a legislative act, contrary to the constitution, is not law: if the latter part be true, then written constitutions are absurd attempts, on the part of the people, to limit a power, in its own nature, illimitable.

Written constitutions are framed to serve as "the fundamental and paramount law of the nation." Thus, "the theory of every such government must be, that an act of the legislature, repugnant to the constitution, is void." No other theory, according to Marshall, can be compatible with a written constitution.

But what are the obligations of courts when confronted with an act of the legislature that is repugnant to the Constitution?

---

[56] 1 Cranch 137 (1803). *Marbury* is the first case in which an act of Congress was declared unconstitutional by the Supreme Court.

Must judges give effect to such an act despite its invalidity? Can a legislative act that is not really a law nonetheless "constitute a rule as operative as if it was a law?" Marshall answers that it cannot, consistently with the judicial duty. For "[i]t is, emphatically, the province and duty of the judicial department, to say what the law is." When two conflicting rules apply to a case, and one is the Constitution and the other an ordinary act of the legislature, the Constitution must necessarily govern the case. For the courts to act otherwise and "close their eyes on the constitution and see only law" would "subvert the very foundation of all written constitutions, . . . giving to the legislature a practical and real omnipotence." In this way, "[w]hat we have deemed the greatest improvement on political institutions, a written constitution," would be "reduce[d] to nothing."[57]

Does Marshall's argument succeed in establishing a necessary connection between judicial review and limited government? While it was sufficiently powerful to erect the practice of judicial review as a permanent institution in American constitutional government, it has had over the years its fair share of critics. What has appeared unpersuasive to them is Marshall's claim that it is the judicial department's province to say what the law is, when the "law" at issue is the Constitution. In the words of Marshall's most respected modern critic, Marshall's argument "begged the question-in-chief, which was not whether an act repugnant to the Constitution could stand, but who should be empowered to decide that the act is repugnant."[58]

Those in our as well as in Marshall's time who would deny this power to the courts would instead find it in the legislature, in accordance with strict republican principle.[59] That understanding, however, does not do justice to the sense in which the doctrine of judicial review is the positive complement to the negative teaching of *Federalist* 49. An insurmountable obstacle to referring constitutional questions to the people was the likelihood that the decision would turn on the passions and not the reason of the public. Such is the nature of republican legislatures, moreover, that the ordinary ambition of their members, their sharing in the

---

[57]Ibid., at 176–178.

[58]Alexander M. Bickel, *The Least Dangerous Branch*, 2d ed. (New Haven: Yale University Press, 1986), 3.

[59]Bickel did not deny the constitutional propriety of judicial review. Others have and do. See, e.g., *Eakin v. Raub* (Gibson, J., dissenting), 12 Sergeant and Rawle (Supreme Court of Pennsylvania) 330 (1825); Anderson, "A 1787 Perspective," especially 139–40, 154–55; and George Anastaplo, *The Constitution of 1787: A Commentary* (Baltimore: The Johns Hopkins University Press, 1989).

"prepossessions"[60] of the people, and the strength of their bonds with their constituents, infuse into the legislative body the same dangers to constitutional limits that reside in the people themselves. Judicial review by independent courts serves as an institutional replacement for a recurrence to the people (and, by implication, their legislators) when constitutional limits are threatened. Courts, and ultimately the Supreme Court, are meant to represent the "reason of the public [which] alone . . . ought to controul and regulate the government."[61] They do so by enforcing, by means of the judicious exercise of the reviewing power, the reason of the Constitution, which is the fixed and permanent reason of the people, preserving the separation of powers and the written limits of the Constitution.

Marshall's argument in *Marbury* leads us to these reflections because it tacitly invokes the thought and method of *Federalist* 49. After Marshall asserts the original right of the people to establish a constitution, he observes that

[t]he exercise of this original right is a very great exertion; nor can it, nor ought it, to be frequently repeated. The principles, therefore, so established, are deemed fundamental: and as the authority from which they proceed is supreme, and can seldom act, they are designed to be permanent.[62]

Seen in that light, judicial review is connected with the fading away of the here and now of the original will or the original right. The principles of the Constitution are *deemed* fundamental, though what is truly fundamental is the original right of the people. And the Constitution's principles are designed to be permanent, though the truly permanent principles are those of natural justice.

As argued by Hamilton in *Federalist* 78, the judiciary's power of judicial review comes first to sight as an "excellent barrier [in a republic] to the encroachments and oppressions of the representative body" against the "will . . . of their constituents." By transforming their original will into the written law of the Constitution, the people make it possible for the judiciary whose "proper and peculiar province [is] the interpretation of the laws" to be designed as "an intermediate body between the people and the legislature, in order, among other things, to keep the latter within the limits assigned to their authority."[63]

---

[60]*Federalist* No. 49, 341.
[61]Ibid., 343.
[62]*Marbury*, 1 Cranch at 176, emphasis added.
[63]*Federalist* No. 78, 525.

This view might seem to indicate that the sole purpose of judicial review—and of the separation of powers that makes it possible—is "to guard the society against the oppression of its rulers"[64] when the representative principle fails to prevent the formation of separate interests of ruler and ruled. A look at Hamilton's full discussion of judicial review shows the inadequacy of that interpretation, however.

Hamilton anchors the power of judicial review in the argument from the theory of a limited constitution in the manner adopted by Marshall in *Marbury,* concluding that the courts of justice are "the bulwarks of a limited constitution against legislative encroachments."[65] Courts, "whose duty it must be to declare all acts contrary to the manifest tenor of the constitution void," must have "complete independence" and therefore a "permanent tenure"[66] to be able to stand firmly against legislative attempts to commit unconstitutional acts against the interests of the people. But the judiciary is also enlisted in the fight against what Madison referred to as the most fearsome of the "diseases most incident to Republican Government,"[67] unjust combinations of the majority.

Hamilton proceeds to reveal the role that the courts (armed with judicial review)—and by implication the separation of powers—are meant to play in the critical work of "guard[ing] one part of the society against the injustice of the other part,"[68] which in a republic will mean guarding the minority against the factious designs of a majority:

This independence of the judges is equally requisite to guard the constitution and the rights of individuals from the effects of those ill humours which the arts of designing men, or the influence of particular conjunctures, sometimes disseminate among the people themselves, and which, though they speedily give place to better information and more deliberate reflection, have a tendency in the mean time to occasion dangerous innovations in the government, and serious oppressions of the minor party in the community. . . . Until the people have by some solemn and authoritative act annulled or changed the established form, it is binding upon themselves collectively as well as individually;

[64]Ibid., No. 51, 351.
[65]Ibid., No. 78, 526.
[66]Ibid., 524. Compare Hamilton's obscuring of the constitutional standard of tenure during good behavior, which he had previously declared, in favor of permanence to Marshall's obscuring in *Marbury* of original right in favor of the "permanent" principles of the Constitution.
[67]Ibid., No. 10, 65.
[68]Ibid., No. 51, 351.

and no presumption, or even knowledge of their sentiments, can warrant their representatives in a departure from it, prior to such an act.[69]

Judicial independence is not only the "best expedient which can be devised in any government, to secure a steady, upright and impartial administration of the laws."[70] It also gives to judges that "uncommon portion of fortitude" they will need to guard the Constitution "where legislative invasions of it have been instigated by the major voice of the community."[71]

The power of judicial review, then, is not properly understood as an artificial power added to the natural power of the courts for purposes of self-defense. It is instead "deducible . . . from the general theory of a limited constitution," which constitution "attempts to set bounds to the legislative discretion."[72] The right of judicial review is therefore not limited to guarding the judicial power against encroachment, or even to guarding the separation of powers, but rather extends to guarding the Constitution as a whole,[73] for it is the Constitution in all of its parts that is the foundation of security for the individual and his rights.

It may seem paradoxical that a constitution that is formulated in order to represent the supreme will of the people also serves the purpose of making recurrence to that first principle infrequent. We must recognize, however, that the judiciary, whose members are "the choice, though a remote choice, of the people themselves,"[74] in the ordinary exercise of its powers performs the extraordinary function of speaking for and defending the reason of the public as it finds expression in the Constitution. The republican principle of "a dependence on the people"[75] is modified and moderated in the direction of "a *due* dependence on the people."[76] A due dependence permits attention to the dangers of an undue dependence. The republican principle can then be supplemented with constitutional arrangements that are chosen because of their contributions to the proper end of government—the securing of rights—without undue concern for the source of authority for

[69]Ibid., No. 78, 527–28.
[70]Ibid., 522.
[71]Ibid., 528.
[72]Ibid., No. 81, 543.
[73]Of the three powers, the judiciary is "the only one with its eye steadily on the whole, monitor of the separation of powers and guardian of the Constitution." Mansfield, "Separation of Powers," 14.
[74]Ibid., No. 39, 252.
[75]Ibid., No. 51, 349.
[76]Ibid., No. 77, 520, emphasis added.

those arrangements.[77] The structure of the separation of powers is derived from the same source as is the right of judicial review, which is "the general theory of a limited constitution."[78]

The balance of the American Constitution is a balance between the stronger—which in most circumstances is the legislative—and the weaker departments, and more fundamentally, is a balance between a dependence on the people and the auxiliary precautions, the chief one of which is the separation of powers. The argument of *Marbury* and of *The Federalist* invites us to hold that the balance in either case cannot be maintained in the absence of the power of judicial review.

CONCLUSION: WHAT THE FRAMERS CAN TEACH US ABOUT LIMITS

The Framers were responsible for an extension of the crucial constitutional balance from the sphere of the legislature to that of the whole government, which implied a decisive downgrading of the status of the legislature, compelling it to take its place alongside the other agencies of government as one element in a complex equilibrium. Including the right of judicial review in the judicial power was, together with a bolstering of the executive power, a critical feature in saving limited government from the danger of legislative domination.

But the right of judicial review was derived from the threat posed to the rule of the Constitution. It finds its genesis in the rule of the law of the Constitution and is entirely confined to and enclosed by that law. For this reason, courts cannot be understood as licensed to look beyond the Constitution either to expand the catalogue of constitutionally protected rights or to expand the catalogue of constitutionally authorized power. To do so would be to replace the "reason of the public" embodied in the Constitution and put into motion by the authority of the people with the direct rule of judges—a profoundly anti-republican idea.

The Constitution, which is both higher law and the command of the sovereign people, cannot authorize any departure from the law of the Constitution without ceding its own sovereignty to the sovereignty of an agency of its own creation. As our discussion of legislative sovereignty was meant to indicate, any such result would

---

[77]"[T]he structure [of the separation of powers] is not derived from the authority of the people, though it is implemented by authority of the people." Kristol, "The Problem of the Separation of Powers," 112.

[78]*Federalist* No. 81, 543.

destroy the constitutional balance of the Framers, which they regarded as the perfection of constitutional government.[79]

A second cautionary teaching for the judiciary deriving from the Framers' institutional analysis begins with the fact that the first task of founding is to "enable the government to controul the governed."[80] "Justice is the end of government,"[81] understood as the security of rights. And "liberty may be endangered by the abuses of liberty, as well as by the abuses of power."[82] This observation reasonably suggests a wariness of novel doctrines that attempt to advance the cause of individual freedom by erecting jurisprudential obstacles to the ability of society's institutions, guided by the consent of the governed,[83] to support habits of civility and moderation.

This leads to a final point: Liberal republican constitutionalism counsels a certain moderation in what one expects from life and government. This requires that republican citizens not confuse wants and needs that government can satisfy tolerably well for

[79]In the context of American constitutional politics, the implications of this argument are unfriendly to the powerful contemporary currents of "transformative" constitutional jurisprudence. For example, the silence of the Constitution on the general and abstract right to "equal dignity" or "equal concern and respect" necessarily implies a judicial silence as well. To hold otherwise would be to abolish the "distinction between a government with limited and unlimited powers." *Marbury*, 1 Cranch at 176. See the text of Justice Brennan's widely noted speech at Georgetown University ("The Constitution of the United States: Contemporary Ratification," in *Interpreting the Constitution*, ed. Jack N. Rakove [Boston: Northeastern University Press, 1990], 23–34), in which, according to one commentator, "the term 'dignity' is employed thirty-four times and explicated very little if at all." Harry M. Clor, "Constitutional Interpretation and Regime Principles," in *The Constitution, the Courts, and the Quest for Justice*, ed. Robert A. Goldwin and William A. Schambra (Washington, D.C.: American Enterprise Institute, 1989), 134, n. 31. "Equal concern and respect" is advanced as a juridical concept in Ronald Dworkin, *Taking Rights Seriously* (Cambridge, MA: Harvard University Press, 1978), xii.

[80]*Federalist* No. 51, 349.

[81]Ibid., 352.

[82]Ibid., No. 63, 428.

[83]The lack of concern for the republican requirement of consent in the work of theoreticians and practitioners of contemporary "transformative" jurisprudence has been remarked, in the case of John Rawls, by Harvey C. Mansfield, Jr., in *The Spirit of Modern Liberalism* (Cambridge: Harvard University Press, 1978), 89–101; in the case of Rawls and Ronald Dworkin, by Clifford Orwin and James R. Stoner, Jr., "Neoconstitutionalism? Rawls, Dworkin, and Nozick," in *Confronting the Constitution*, ed. Allan Bloom (Washington: The AEI Press, 1990), 437–56; and in the case of Laurence Tribe by Stanley C. Brubaker, Review of *American Constitution Law*, 2d ed., by Laurence M. Tribe, in *Constitutional Commentary*, vol. 6, no. 2 (Summer 1989), 469–94. See also Susan Shell, "Idealism," in *Confronting the Constitution*, 269, for the roots of this phenomenon in Kant's thought.

all members of society with those that no government can satisfy for all, and which the attempt to satisfy for some leads to mischief and injustice for many.[84] A constitutional republic has its limits; it cannot do everything. In particular, it cannot guarantee, and therefore does not promise, personal happiness. But it can provide for what the founding generation called public happiness, by which they understood the security of every citizen's equal right to consent to government and to pursue his happiness free from irrational and arbitrary restraint. A written constitution, representation, separation of powers, and judicial review are meant to serve that end and, in the Framers' view, are limited by that end. As the human cost of the more radical 20th century alternatives to the Framers' constitutionalism continues to be tallied, we are justified in asking whether far-reaching criticisms of the Framers' handiwork are not built on utopian expectations of both human nature and political life.

[84]"While rights, properly understood, can be secured, not all wants can be satisfied. As our history attests, however, when those rights are secured, many wants are satisfied. Their satisfaction depends on their not being seen as rights." Walter Berns, "The Constitution As Bill of Rights," in *In Defense of Liberal Democracy* (Chicago: Gateway Editions, 1984), 28.

PART II

On Developments after the Founding

Doctrines of Presidential-Congressional Relations

James W. Ceaser

Introduction

Since the time of the Founding, four major constitutional doc-trines have been introduced in an effort to define the proper al-location of institutional powers and responsibilities among the president, Congress, and Court: the Jeffersonian Republican idea, the Jacksonian idea, the Whig party theory, and the "idea of the modern presidency." There have, of course, been other important statements bearing on the relations among the institutions, such as the views expressed by Presidents Abraham Lincoln and The-odore Roosevelt and the positions argued in the Supreme Court opinions of *Myers* v. *United States*[1] and *United States* v. *Curtiss-Wright*.[2] But none of these, I would contend, qualifies as a major doctrine, by which I mean here a view articulated by a significant political force (a political party or a body of opinion leaders) that has been formulated with the aim of establishing a settled opinion or consensus about the proper workings of our institutions.

This essay looks at the development of these four doctrines and at their connection to the original constitutional view of presidential-congressional relations.[3] To remind the reader briefly of these doctrines, the Jeffersonian republicans emerged in the 1790s in reaction to the alleged "monarchism" of the administra-tions of Washington and Adams. The party sought to rein in the president's powers and establish the Congress as the central insti-tution of leadership and policy. Jacksonian doctrine, which was the

---

[1] 272 U.S. 52 (1926).
[2] 299 U.S. 304 (1936).
[3] Due to limitations of space I will not be able to treat the judicial branch.

89

most short-lived of the four, developed in opposition to efforts to impose the strict letter of Jeffersonian Republican doctrine on the presidency. President Jackson and elements of the new Democratic party rallied to protect the presidency and to maintain fundamental constitutional powers. The Whig theory, which its adherents presented as the heir to Jeffersonian Republican doctrine, grew up in reaction to Jackson's alleged "popular dictatorship" and sought to place the strictest limitations on presidential authority. It became the dominant doctrine of the nineteenth century and was adopted by large elements of the Republican party. Finally, the doctrine of the modern presidency, formulated by Woodrow Wilson and supported by most progressives, sought directly to counter the weak presidency that had become the accepted norm and to make the presidency and presidential leadership the "center of action" in the American political system. This doctrine was supported by Democratic party liberals and by large parts of the academic community from Wilson's day up until the end of the 1960s. It survives in a few quarters today.

As there is a large amount of ground to be covered in this essay, it may be helpful to note at the outset the principal themes and assumptions that underlie the argument. First, all four of these doctrines (although the Jacksonian idea far less than the other three) deviate in important ways from the original constitutional design. Adherents of the Jeffersonian Republican and the Whig doctrines generally denied this fact and represented their positions as true interpretations of the Constitution and the theory of the separation of powers. In the case of the doctrine of the modern presidency, many of its proponents concede that it is in tension with the original design, in particular with the theory of the separation of powers. They have tended to argue, however, that their theory can be grafted onto the Constitution by a series of "creative" interpretations, without the need of any formal amendments.

Second, these constitutional deviations—let us call them simply distortions—managed by the 1850s to obscure the original constitutional view. Although people continued to refer to an original constitutional view, its content had been appropriated by a series of unfaithful glosses. Above all, during the nineteenth century the Jeffersonian Republican idea and its successor, the Whig theory, shaped the dominant understanding of the Constitution, with the effect that a weak presidency came to be regarded as the embodiment of the original constitutional view. This fact explains the paradoxical result that important elements of the idea of the modern presidency—which is the only doctrine defined explicitly against the constitutional view—are not nearly as much in tension with the original constitutional design as many of its own adherents have supposed.

Third, these successive acts of misinterpretation and appropriation have had the effect of making it more difficult to conceive of a sound view of the relations among the branches. This statement assumes, of course, that the original constitutional view is superior to any of the four subsequent doctrines.[4] The obscuring of the original constitutional view has diminished our capacity to think clearly about the relations between the president and Congress. It is only recently, thanks to a new wave of scholarship, that students of American politics have begun to recapture the original view and with it a standard by which to help guide and regulate presidential-congressional relations.[5]

Fourth, the practical consequences of the doctrinal confusion have not been as dire as the preceding argument might lead one to think. The reason is that practice has not always been dictated by these doctrines. The words of the Constitution and the institutions the Constitution established have built systems of incentives and a body of precedent that have had a great influence on conduct, often in spite of what doctrine has taught. Institutions, to a far greater degree than many imagine, shape behavior. Whig presidents, for example, never allowed themselves to be subjected to the full measure of humiliation that the party's doctrine required. The Constitution has thus managed to survive its own doctrinal misinterpretations. Still, I cannot claim all the irrelevance for my subject that I would wish, as these doctrines have had, and continue to have, important negative effects. While we therefore do well just to live under the Constitution, we would do better if we could understand the Constitution under which we live.

THE THEORY OF THE SEPARATION OF POWERS AND THE ORIGINAL VIEW OF THE ALLOCATION OF POWER BETWEEN PRESIDENT AND CONGRESS

All four of the doctrines, as noted, make reference to the theory of the separation of powers and have treated it as the key to

---

[4]I adopt this position not because the original position came first, which has no particular bearing on its merits, but because it in fact embodies the best theoretical understanding.

[5]See Joseph Bessette and Jeffrey K. Tulis, eds., *The Presidency and the Constitutional Order* (Baton Rouge: Louisiana State University Press, 1981); Harvey C. Mansfield, Jr., *Taming the Prince* (New York: Free Press, 1989); and David K. Nichols, *The Myth of the Modern Presidency* (Pennsylvania State University Press, 1994).

interpreting the Constitution, whether for good or, as in the case of the doctrine of the modern presidency, for ill. But even where the theory has been praised, there is an important ambiguity in how it has been used. Adherents of the Republican and Whig doctrines argued that the theory did indeed inform the original constitutional design, but that the authors of the Constitution itself did not *fully* apply or respect it. Whigs and Republicans contended that to interpret the Constitution in the way most beneficial to the nation meant to interpret it in the light of the real theory of the separation of powers, i.e., the theory as they understood it. The problem, however, is that the meaning of the theory of the separation of powers was in dispute from the very outset. The Founders had one view, the Anti-Federalists had another.

Let us first try to restate the way in which the Founders used the theory of the separation of powers. They applied this theory, which they also helped to develop and refine, to the question of how to allocate power inside the federal government. The Founders never claimed that this theory, even with their own elaborations on it, accounted fully for the constitutional scheme of allocating powers.[6] The theory informed that scheme. It provided the basic concept for the design of the foundation of the federal government. On this foundation, however, the Founders built an edifice that drew on other ideas and themes. To interpret the Constitution properly, therefore, one must understand both the theory of the separation of powers *and* the other theoretical principles that the Founders employed in determining the constitutional allocation of powers.

The theory of the separation of powers consists of two major elements. First, it holds that power can be conceived as powers, i.e., as a few distinct categories defined according to general functions. It had always been recognized, of course, that the exercise of power consists in performing different discrete tasks (war making, legislating, taxing, etc.). The theory of the separation of powers goes on, however, to group these discrete tasks by reference to certain categories. In the evolution of the theory, there were debates on exactly what these categories were. But by the time the theory had come to America, it was accepted on all sides—working mostly from Montesquieu's design—that there were three basic powers: a legislative power, meaning a power to make laws; a judicial power, meaning a power to apply penalties (criminal or civil) and to have

[6]See, for example, Alexander Hamilton, James Madison, and John Jay, *The Federalist Papers*, introduction by Clinton Rossiter (New York: New American Library, 1961), Nos. 37, 47, 48, 66, and 71.

a role in applying law (including constitutional law); and an executive power, meaning in a strict sense a power to execute or carry out laws and, more broadly, a discretionary power to act in behalf of the nation, especially in crisis or foreign affairs, when laws either could not apply or when they might conflict with the national interest.

At the time of the Founding, the content of the executive power was the least well understood of the three powers, and was embroiled in partisan dispute. Many opponents of the Constitution, out of fear of monarchy, defined the executive power to include only the ministerial power of carrying out the law. By contrast, the Founders understood the executive power in its broader sense as well. It is not too much to say that the dispute over whether to recognize the executive power in this broader sense—meaning an admission of its existence, of its importance for any government worthy of the name, and of the need for its being exercised effectively—was the central question in the debate over the Constitution.

The second element of the theory of the separation of powers holds that there are important advantages to be achieved from housing the main part of each power in a separate institution. Each of these institutions, moreover, should possess a certain independence and a capacity to proceed in some measure on its own. This element of the theory, outlined by the first sentence of each of the first three articles of the Constitution, is responsible for the basic structure of the national government, which is unique among the major democratic systems in the world.

The advantages deriving from this allocation of power are two-fold. First, dividing power among different institutions provides safety for liberty and freedom from despotism. It does so by avoiding a concentration of power in the hands of one person or institution. Admittedly, this purpose might be served by any division of power among two or three institutions, whatever the principle of the allocation. But the theory of the separation of powers, precisely because it delineates three *important* categories, ensures that a division will not only spread power out broadly, but will also supply a rough logic to the boundaries. Moreover, experience shows that in one vital respect this particular allocation of power provides an essential guarantee of liberty: the separation of the judicial power of punishment from the powers of making and executing laws gives citizens the feeling that their rights are secure from arbitrary power.

Second, the allocation of power according to the principle of the separation of powers promotes efficiency, at least in one respect. Because these functions are different in character, their effective performance demands different qualities. Each institution can be structured to carry out its own function in an effective way. Thus the executive power can be housed in an institution headed by one individual in order to be able to act quickly and secretly, while the legislative power can be placed in an institution that provides for broad representation and ensures deliberation.

To sum up, then, the theory of the separation of powers informed the Founders in regard to two fundamental points. First, it provided them with an understanding of the nature of each power, its distinctness and importance; and second, it provided them with an understanding of why it is advantageous to build a structure of government that allocates political power on a foundation that takes account of the basic distinction among the powers. But the theory did not exhaust the question of how all powers should be allocated.

Before turning to the other considerations that guided the constitutional allocation of powers, we must take note of another view of the theory of separation of powers current at the time. This view held that the theory demanded a pure separation, meaning that all of each power and only each power had to be placed in its "home" institution. One may note also that under this understanding, the theory of the separation of powers goes much further: it offers a complete scheme for the allocation of powers and leaves no room for further considerations. It provides all one knows and all one needs to know.

The Founders emphatically rejected this view. They argued that there had never been anything in the theory itself or in human experience that justified demanding this kind of "logical" precision. Powers, the Founders contended, could be shared in some measure without violating the theory, although such sharing could not go too far without vitiating the basic structure. Between a pure separation of powers and a consolidation of powers, there was room for further inquiry guided by other elements of theory and lessons of experience.[7]

Which powers should be shared, to what degree, and for what reasons? The Founders advanced four considerations to justify deviating from a strict separation and permitting a sharing of certain powers among two or more of the institutions:

1. Powers can be shared with a view to helping assure that each branch will be better able to maintain its independence. This reason for sharing certain powers flows from the theory of the

[7]See *Federalist* Nos. 47–51.

separation of powers and is thus an annex to it. Guaranteeing a separation of powers in practice requires institutions that can maintain their independence over time. This objective is best achieved not always by following a strict separation, but sometimes by judiciously mixing certain powers. The veto, which gives the president a part of the legislative power, is a case in point, as it allows the president to protect his powers from the designs of a legislature bent on usurping his authority.

2. Powers can be shared to assure that a certain standard of republican legitimacy is met. For example, placing a large part of the war power—which is part of the executive power—into the legislature insures conformity of the government to the spirit of republican or popular government. No popular government, it was thought, could afford to vest a decision as basic as that of war and peace in one individual.

3. Powers may be shared to promote better governmental decisions (usually, in fact, to avoid bad decisions) by requiring concurrence by more than one branch. For example, the naming of administrative officers and judges, an executive function, is shared with the Senate to minimize the possibility of incompetent appointments. Or again, the existence of the president's veto power enables him to prevent ill-conceived legislation. The idea here is to share certain powers with a view to adding a "check" on their exercise.

4. Powers can be shared in a way that adds efficiency or energy to governing. The main instance is found in the grant to the president of an important role in what we would call today "providing leadership" in the legislative process. Through his powers to report on the state of the union, recommend measures to Congress, and use his veto positively, the president, as the only unitary force inside the government, is placed in a position to supply the government *as a whole* with more energy and direction. The nature of the powers granted to the president does not, of course, assure success, but rather provides the president an opportunity to "lead." It is, however, an important opportunity.

Some scholars have tried to group these four considerations into a single theory of "checks and balances," which can then be added to the theory of the separation of powers to give us a complete account of the constitutional allocation of powers. While no one can quarrel with the fact that the Founders introduced "checks and balances" into the constitutional design, not all of the checks derive from instances in which powers are shared. Nor does every instance in which powers are shared aim at a checking or balancing. Let us examine each of these points.

The checking and balancing in our system is based as much on the scheme of separating powers as it is on sharing them. It is true, of course, that insofar as the powers are separated, different powers are assigned to different branches. This division means in many cases that each institution can proceed on its own without a check (as, for example, when a president decides to grant a pardon). Yet in other instances, while the powers remain distinct juridically, the accomplishment of any significant objective requires the concurrence or cooperation of more than one branch. This frequent situation is exemplified by instances where a president's strategic or diplomatic strategy requires a vote of funds. For example, President Reagan's support for the Nicaraguan Contras was constantly opposed and thwarted by Congress. In this kind of situation, we have two distinct powers being exercised, but in a way in which one institution is in a position indirectly to check and balance the other. This characteristic of the separation of powers was understood from the moment the theory was advanced in England. The king, exercising his executive prerogative, might commit the nation to war; but the conduct of a significant war might require certain large expenditures, which would necessitate an action on taxing by the Parliament.

These indirect checks deriving from the separation of powers, as well as the more explicit checks deriving from instances of sharing certain powers, do have the general effect of retarding or slowing down governmental action. The Founders were of course aware of this characteristic of their plan. If the Constitution, as noted, promotes efficiency in one sense (by assigning powers designed to exercise them well and granting them exclusively to one institution), it also can impede efficiency in another (in cases where the conduct of any policy requires concurrence of more than one institution). The Founders were willing to purchase the benefits—the safety of greater protection of liberty and the avoidance of policy errors—at the cost of a certain degree of efficiency.

This characteristic of inefficiency, it is worth noting, is the central criticism made by adherents of the doctrine of the modern presidency. They argue that the Constitution leads to policy stalemate and deadlock, preventing majorities from having their way. Interestingly, this criticism was almost never heard until this century. Earlier critics attacked the constitutional plan on the grounds that it provided the federal government not with too little, but with too much, capacity for action. It was the Founders themselves, not their contemporary critics, who worried about how to make the government energetic enough.

This brings us to the other point, which is that not all instances of mixing or sharing of power were intended as checks. Granting the president a role in the legislative process was, as noted, intended to endow the government as a whole with a greater capacity for the effective exercise of power. Adding a positive legislative role to the president's existing executive powers was understood to provide a capacity of government to "administer" in the broadest sense, meaning to establish a general direction or policy and to assemble the power to put that policy into effect.

This positive aspect of the president's powers is frequently overlooked in general treatments of the Founding because it does not fit into either of the two basic theoretical categories that many advance to explain the Constitution. It is not part of the separation of powers, and it is not in any usual sense a check or a balance. Even some of those who have acknowledged this "leadership" quality in the Constitution seek to marginalize it by attributing it to Alexander Hamilton, as if this fact alone makes it suspect. But Hamilton, while he was surely the most eloquent spokesmen of the view that effective government needs to be able to assemble power, was scarcely alone in this judgment. Morris, Wilson, Washington, and Jay, among others, joined him in citing the need of an officer in the government who would be able to set in motion the mechanism of government.

To emphasize a concern for leadership as part of the constitutional design is accordingly not to read back into it an alien element, but to emphasize an important characteristic that was present in the original plan and that has been obscured by subsequent doctrines. The proof for this claim is found in two simple points. First, the potential for strong leadership was widely recognized in the ratification debates and in fact formed one of the principal grounds of opposition to the Constitution. Opponents claimed time and again that the Constitution was creating a president whose powers differed scarcely from those of a monarch. (Given this criticism, proponents of the Constitution sought, if anything, to play down the potential of the office.) Second, this leadership potential was immediately put into effect under Washington's presidency in a way that left Jefferson and Madison dismayed and overawed. They began to oppose the presidency on the grounds that it was a "monarchic" institution.

THE ANTI-FEDERALISTS ON THE ALLOCATION OF CONSTITUTIONAL POWERS

Having sketched the ideas governing the allocation of powers in the Constitution, I must now add a word about the position of the Anti-Federalists, as their views served as the inspiration for the Jeffersonian Republicans and the Whigs. The connection among these three parties is indicated by the fact that the term "whig," the central connotation of which was a strong suspicion of executive power, was the label preferred by many of the Anti-Federalists. The term was then adopted by a major faction inside the Jeffersonian Republican party (the "old whigs," headed by John Randolph) before the Whig party, claiming its Jeffersonian origins, took over the name.

The Anti-Federalists' position can be summarized in four points. First, the Anti-Federalists were reluctant to give the central government full discretion with respect to certain powers connected to the executive power. Thus, they sought to regulate the size of the armed forces by *constitutional* provision, i.e., to keep this power from the hands of any governmental institution, largely for fear that the executive officer might use a standing army to establish a despotism. To the extent some of these powers of national security were granted to the government, they thought they should be largely under the control of the legislative branch.

Second, the legislative branch, in their view, was the supreme and only true representative of the people. More generally, all "motion" in government should derive from the legislature. Such discretionary power as the president might exercise must come from explicit and narrowly drawn constitutional provisions or from grants accorded to him by statutes.

Third, the executive power itself was narrowly conceived as a ministerial power to carry out the legislature's will. The executive branch should possess only this executive power. The president surely had no claim to any share of power that was not executive, such as a role in the legislative process. At most, if the president was to have a veto of some kind, it should serve only to protect his office, not to influence government policy. Endowing the president with responsibilities as a "leader" was out of the question.

Finally, the executive branch should be structured internally to guard against its being too energetic and too independent. Anti-Federalists favored a plural executive, and many preferred a selection of the president by Congress in order to eliminate any presidential claim to a direct connection to the people. The president, Anti-Federalists argued, had the powers of a king, and, as one writer put it, "a king of the worst kind: an elective king."[8] A popular connection through election, far from being seen as a

---

[8]Letter of an "Old Whig," published in the *Philadelphia Independent Gazetteer*, December 4, 1787; reprinted in *The Power of the Presidency*, 3d ed., ed. Robert Hirschfield (New York: Adeline, 1982), 28–29.

check on the president, was considered by many Anti-Federalists to present new dangers.

The Anti-Federalists saw themselves as champions of the theory of the separation of powers, which they interpreted to require a pure separation. If separation was good, they argued, then strict separation must be better. As they invoked this argument mostly to suit their notion of legislative supremacy, one may question how much they really respected even their own principle. Nevertheless, one can grant them a kind of cramped internal consistency, provided one accepts their initial premise about the limited character of the executive power. The Anti-Federalists used their argument on the separation of powers to the greatest rhetorical effect in those instances in which the Constitution—by the Founders' own admission—rejected a strict separation and granted certain *additional* powers to the president. This assignment of powers, Anti-Federalists maintained, was the clearest sign of the Founders' monarchist leanings.

THE JEFFERSONIAN REPUBLICAN DOCTRINE OF PRESIDENTIAL-CONGRESSIONAL RELATIONS

The Jeffersonian Republican party had as its main objective the elimination of "monarchism," meaning a reduction or moderation of the president's powers. The Republicans presented this position as a return to the original Constitution—or to the spirit that lay behind it—which they maintained had been subverted by the Federalist party under Washington and Adams.

Exactly what this reduction or moderation of presidential power should entail was a matter of dispute inside the party. One group, known as the "old whigs," defended the faith of full legislative supremacy, at times against the party's mainstream, under the guidance of Jefferson. But the difference in doctrine between the old whigs and the mainstream was not great. In fact, Jefferson tended to support publicly their views of the Constitution, often redoubling his concessions at just those moments when he was acting contrary to their principles. Public professions of orthodoxy, he seemed to believe, would absolve him of any of his sins.

Republican doctrine began by renouncing a good part of the president's executive or discretionary powers. Thus Jefferson, as Gary Schmitt has shown, went out of his way in the actions involving the Barbary pirates to deny the presidency certain defensive war powers that he had exercised. He also went out of his way in the Louisiana Purchase to renounce the diplomatic and discretionary powers that he had just employed.[9] More generally, the presidency, in the Republican view, was not the source of its own motion in most areas, but must await direction from the legislature.

In regard to the president's role in the legislative process, Republicans, relying on their view of the proper understanding of the separation of powers, continually preached the theme of denial. The mainstream, while never completely renouncing the use of the veto as an instrument of policy, came very close to adopting this position. Republican presidents also renounced any formal claim to a leadership role in the legislative process. Jefferson ended the practice of delivering the state of the union address in person, and he professed—or let others declare—the dominance of Congress in the initiation of policy. Jefferson himself, of course, exercised tremendous personal influence over the legislative process, which he accomplished secretly and informally through meetings with congressional members of his party. John Marshall foresaw exactly this result: "By weakening the office of the President, he will increase his personal power. He will diminish his responsibility, [and] sap the fundamental principles of government."[10]

The effects of Republican doctrine became evident, as time went on, in the administrations of Madison and Monroe. Both presidencies are conspicuous for their virtual absence of policy leadership. One student of Madison remarked, exaggerating of course, that "Madison could hardly have played a less important part during those eight uncomfortable years if he had remained in Virginia."[11] Henry Clay is reported to have said: "Mr. Monroe has just been re-elected with apparent unanimity, but he has not the slightest influence on Congress. . . . Henceforth there was and would not be a man in the United States possessing less *personal* influence over them than the President."[12] Perhaps the most telling fact about this whole situation was that this lack of influence in no way disturbed Monroe; he believed he was only doing what Republican doctrine required. And he was correct.

[9]See Gary J. Schmitt, "Thomas Jefferson and the Presidency," in *Inventing the American Presidency*, ed. Thomas Cronin (Lawrence: Kansas University Press, 1989), 326–347.

[10]Cited in Wilfred E. Binkley, *President and Congress*, 3d ed. (New York: Random House, 1962), 63.

[11]Richard Harlow, *The History of Legislative Methods in the Period Before 1825* (New Haven: Yale University Press, 1917), 196

[12]Binkley, *President and Congress*, 74.

It is important here also to point to the connection between Republican doctrine on the presidency and the party's position on the powers of the federal government. The Jeffersonian Republican party, it is well known, favored a strict construction of federal powers and a states' rights orientation. While Republicans adopted this position in large part on it own merits, many of them at the outset also supported it because they deemed it instrumental to limiting the president's power. A national government that had little to do did not need—in fact could not tolerate—any kind of strong leader. According to Ralph Ketchum, Madison woke up to the danger of monarchism in the 1790s and, in an effort to halt it, "stepped back from his ardent nationalism of the 1780s to favor both limited federal power in general vis-à-vis the states and a stricter interpretation of the powers of Congress and the executive."[13] The Jeffersonian Republicans' position of limited federal power was thus at the party's origins part and parcel of its efforts to establish a milder presidential power.

The one element of the stronger constitutional presidency that Jefferson himself did not renounce—and on which Republican doctrine would remain unclear—is the connection of the president to the public. Jefferson approached this question in 1800 not from the traditional whig perspective, which is fear of a popular base to executive authority (because it strengthens it), but from a different angle. Dating back to his early writings, Jefferson had wondered how a separation-of-powers system could be maintained in practice without one branch coming to dominate the others. Jefferson's solution was to mandate a constitutional convention every generation (eighteen years), whereupon the people could correct any imbalances that had grown up in the interim, as well as make improvements in their constitution as a whole. (The Founders rejected this solution in *Federalist* 49 as dangerous and proposed instead protecting the separation by providing each branch with the means and will to protect its own powers.) Jefferson believed that the Founders' solution had proved to be ineffective because, by the time of Washington's second administration, a real institutional imbalance had grown up in favor of the presidency ("monarchism"). Although Jefferson's plan for a constitutional convention had been dismissed, he saw the election of 1800 as the functional equivalent of a constitutional convention. It settled—through a kind of indirect popular referendum—the question of the proper relationship among the branches of the government. As the

[13]Ralph Ketcham, "James Madison and the Presidency," in *Inventing the American Presidency*, ed. Cronin, 351.

president-elect and head of the party that waged the battle for this "second revolution," Jefferson claimed a degree of authority deriving from his election.

Yet two points should be borne in mind about Jefferson's apparent deviation from whig doctrine in his "use" of the election of 1800. First, Republicans sought a mandate in 1800 to endorse a *lesser* role for the presidency. Electoral authority was employed to curtail presidential authority. Second, this function of the election was, by Jefferson's own account, exceptional ("a revolution"). In fact, Republicans did not generally assert, as a matter of constitutional doctrine, a popular base for the presidency. Although practice confirmed a more direct popular control of presidential electors in the selection process, the mainstream of the Republican party went so far by 1812 as to allow, through its caucus nominating system, what amounted to *congressional* control of presidential selection. Republicans were thus not the friends of a popular presidency that many have supposed.

Republican doctrine taken as a whole not only moved in the direction of the Anti-Federalists' positions, but was also very clearly inspired by Anti-Federalist theory, above all by the Anti-Federalists' ideas of the executive power and the separation of powers. This said, it is essential also to note that the Republicans did not call for any constitutional amendments to institute the Anti-Federalists' positions. For Republicans, it was sufficient that the Constitution be "interpreted" in the right way. Nothing is more important, in retrospect, than the Republicans' acceptance of the basic governmental design: this meant that the Constitution was left intact, not just to be called on at a later day—as it of course would be by Jackson and Lincoln—but occasionally to be used even by Republican presidents themselves when they found it necessary to deviate from their own doctrines.

It is interesting to speculate about whether and in what sense Republicans believed that their doctrine changed the constitutional view. All elements of the party, it is clear, thought that Republican doctrine was beneficial for the nation; that it was consistent with the Constitution (i.e., represented *a* legitimate interpretation of it); and that, if there was a slight tension with the original design, the new doctrine was truer to the theory of the separation of powers. To some degree, therefore, Republicans appealed to the "true" theory of the separation of powers to correct or purify the Constitution; and because it was somehow believed that Americans had meant to ratify that theory in their act of ratifying the Constitution, Republicans in a sense could claim to be standing with the Founding. Finally, many Republicans saw their doctrine as representing what they had in mind all along. Their fears of a strong executive were only vindicated by the "monarchism" of the Federalist administrations.

But these responses do not apply fully to two most important Republicans: Jefferson and Madison. Not only did both of these men clearly understand that Republican doctrine modified the original constitutional view, but they also had once endorsed the constitutional view of the strong executive. Jefferson and Madison were thus *choosing* to put into effect a new or different interpretation of the Constitution than they themselves once held. They began to change their minds when they realized what the president could actually do *under* the Constitution—how much influence he could exercise, both in the realm of the general executive power and in the realm of policy leadership. Even if they had once signed off on these powers, even if they had once acknowledged that a discretionary power in the chief executive was necessary, they now saw that these same powers could allow the president to play a much greater role than they were prepared to accept. The problem was not just the particular program of commercial development that Hamilton and the Federalists put into effect, although that was clearly part of it; it was mostly the amount of power and influence in the presidential office. The issue was one of constitutional powers more than of policy, and the best way to resolve the crisis was to devise a new doctrine to interpret the Constitution.

This new doctrine left an important question unanswered. If, as Jefferson and Madison once acknowledged, government needs certain discretionary powers and needs them to be exercised by an executive officer, then their own doctrine is defective, for it obscures that truth. Jefferson and Madison, it appears, justified this theoretical cover-up on the grounds that no doctrine that admits the full truth can be helpful; for the view that contained the truth—the constitutional view—proved in practice to be dangerous. Republican doctrine, though theoretically defective, was superior to any alternative view as a guide to practice. Whatever one may think of this argument, it is important to note that Republican doctrine is responsible for covering up a theoretical truth. All subsequent doctrines have fallen victim to this original deception.

By the logic of Jefferson and Madison, Republican doctrine leaves the problem of how to deal with what we can call a deficit of executive power—a gap between the power that the executive legitimately needs to operate for the national interest and the far more limited power that Republicans granted to the president. The efforts of Republicans to deal with this deficit tell a most interesting story of their period in power. First, Jefferson desperately sought to reduce or eliminate the need for discretionary executive powers by changing the whole nature of political life. The need for executive discretion is justified in one respect by the harsh character of international affairs and the need for speed, secrecy, and the use of force in the conduct of policy. The Jeffersonian policy during the embargo was based on nothing less than the premise that America's policy might forever alter the character of international affairs and reduce much of the need for discretionary presidential action.[14]

Second, the deficit of executive power could be dealt with (or hidden) simply by doing one thing while saying nothing or doing something quite different. This often seemed to be Jefferson's policy. The legacy of the Jeffersonian presidency is one of fairly bold examples of the use of presidential power backed by disclaimers that the president ever had such powers in the first place. The problem with this solution is not its hypocrisy, but the fact that it made future exercises of the same kind of hypocrisy more difficult. The disclaimers end up carrying more weight than the examples.

Third, to the extent Jefferson developed a coherent theoretical answer to deal with this deficit, it was—as Gary Schmitt has shown—the idea of claiming an executive prerogative *outside* the Constitution, rather than a discretionary power *inside* it: "Jefferson presumably believed that if one could revise and scale down the formal, constitutional powers of the president while at the same time granting him, as circumstances warranted, the right to exercise extra-constitutional powers, one would make the use of such powers less likely."[15] Jefferson might have thought that this novel doctrine was the answer because it would restrain presidential power most of the time while allowing it when absolutely necessary. But it is just as likely, as Schmitt argues, that this doctrine creates a precedent for the exercise of a more dangerous power beyond the Constitution, with the added unhealthy effect of putting in peril the whole idea of the rule of law.

Finally, the deficit of executive power could be "dealt with" by accepting it and its consequences. This, according to Ralph Ketcham, seems to have been the conclusion to which James Madison came, as he preferred to see Washington burn and the nation risk losing a war than do anything that might compromise his scruples about a Republican presidency. Yet Ketchum pulls back from

---

[14]The fact that this effort to reduce discretionary power required an extraordinary kind of discretionary power only repeats a familiar story of the effects of similar utopian projects.

[15]Schmitt, "Thomas Jefferson and the Presidency," 342.

taking this argument to its conclusion by suggesting that Madison "probably would also have approved of Lincoln's understanding and defense of the Union in 1861."[16] Perhaps. But the question Ketcham avoids is whether such an approval could best be based on Republican doctrine or on the constitutional doctrine it was supposed to supersede.

The Jacksonians and the Whigs

Republican doctrine evoked little if any opposition inside the nation in the early nineteenth century. A few voices here and there were heard to grumble about a weak president and governmental paralysis, but none of this discontent ever crystallized into a full-blown opposition to the party's understanding of presidential-executive relations. Jefferson's statement in his first inaugural address, "we are all Republicans, we are all Federalists," meant, in terms of institutional doctrine, that all were Republicans.

The nineteenth century doctrine in defense of a strong presidency—to the extent one exists—is the product of the presidencies of Andrew Jackson and of James K. Polk and of the Democratic party at that time. This defense emerged as a reaction to the effort to apply pure Republican institutional doctrine against the president. The Whigs, who identified themselves as the followers of Jefferson (and of the Constitution) in the realm of the allocation of powers, believed they had the *right* fully to dictate policy from Congress. Any presidential attempt to deny or interfere with this right constituted a violation of accepted constitutional principles.

Jackson, and later Polk, would have none of this. They defended the prerogatives of their office, using the clear and manifest powers granted by the Constitution. Neither president said very much about abstract theories, except occasionally to remind Americans that the theory of the separation of powers had been adopted to assure a strong and independent executive officer. They made their case largely on legal—i.e. constitutional—grounds appealing to the language and plain meaning of the text itself. Thus, after Jackson was attacked by a Senate resolution for allegedly going beyond his constitutional powers, he responded: "Knowing [the constitutional rights] of the Executive, I shall at all times endeavor to maintain them agreeably to the provisions of the

---

[16]Ketcham, "James Madison and the Presidency," 360.

Constitution and the oath I have taken to support and defend it."[17] Some scholars pretend that Andrew Jackson saved the American presidency. If this is true, it is still more correct to say that the *Constitution* saved Andrew Jackson. Time and again, Jackson was able to prevail because he had on his side broad powers contained in the document.

Jackson's defense of some of the constitutional powers of the office involved the following three points. First, against the Whig's theory that Congress could devolve a power on a cabinet minister and then by law prevent a president from exercising administrative discretion, Jackson asserted the president's authority to control the executive branch. The president could press his views on a cabinet officer and, if need be, proceed to the extreme of dismissal in order to obtain compliance. Jackson argued: "Upon [the president] has been devolved by the Constitution and the suffrages of the American people the duty of superintending the operation of the Executive Departments of the government and seeing that the laws are faithfully executed."[18]

Second, against the Whigs' claim that the veto could not be used to thwart the will of Congress, Jackson asserted the president's authority to avail himself of this constitutionally sanctioned power. In his famous veto of the Bank bill in 1832, he took his case to the American public to garner support, using the constitutional instrument of the veto message to communicate with the people. In this message, Jackson did not assert a presidential power to use the veto as a policy tool. He was concerned with arguing the legitimacy of the veto as an instrument to be used by the president to protect the Constitution as interpreted by the president.[19] Jackson's defense of the veto, however, was so powerful that it served subsequently to lay a foundation for its broader use as an instrument to promote the president's policy goals.

Jackson's own leadership was, by and large, quite limited. He saw himself as the heir to the Jeffersonian Republicans in regard to the policies of the federal government and thus sought mostly to *deny* the use of further legislative powers to the national government, which the Whigs favored. The only nineteenth century

---

[17]Cited in Binkley, "President and Congress," 97.
[18]Ibid., 96.
[19]The Whigs, by contrast, argued not only that the veto could not be used as a mere instrument of policy, but also that, in matters of constitutional judgment, the president was obliged to accept the interpretations of the Congress and the Court.

president before Lincoln who sought openly to assemble power to use it to direct an entire policy of government was the masterful James Polk.

Third, Jackson affirmed the president's popular base of support, both in the conduct of his office and in his claim of the meaning of presidential elections. Polk built on this idea and argued that the president's claim to the representation of the American people was no less than that of Congress: "The President represents in the executive department the whole people of the United States, as each member of the legislative department represents portions of them."[20] This assertion, in the Whigs' view, marked perhaps the supreme heresy, as it echoed the old Anti-Federalist fear of an "elective monarch" and challenged the whole principle that supposedly supported legislative supremacy. The Jacksonian assertion of a popular foundation for the presidency appears to have been a reaction against the dominant view of most Jeffersonian Republicans, who favored keeping the president under the shackles of the congressional caucus. David Nichols is the first to argue that this step should be seen in substantial part as a step *back* in the direction of the original constitutional view. While there clearly are new elements in the Jacksonian idea and new democratic effects connected to changes in the suffrage requirements and in the mechanics of presidential nomination and election, Nichols's thesis forces a reconsideration of the standard historical idea of a steady democratization of the presidency from the Founding through Jackson. We can now see the sense in which the original constitutional view of an executive with a popular base was actually obscured from 1800 until after 1828.

Whig doctrine was accepted not only by the Whig party itself, but also by important leaders of the Republican party after 1860. (President Lincoln's presidency clearly violated most of his party's doctrinal orthodoxies.) Whig doctrine, as we noted, claimed its roots in Jeffersonian Republican doctrine and purported to be based on the Constitution. Yet its animus against presidential power went so far that in the end it was often impossible even for the Whigs themselves to maintain the fiction that they were supporting the original constitutional design. By proposed statutes and amendments, as well as by tortured interpretations of the Constitution, the Whigs, and later some of the Republicans, assaulted the very core of the president's powers.

[20]Leonard D. White, *The Jacksonians: A Study in Administrative History, 1829–1861* (New York: The Macmillan Company, 1954), 24.

The Whigs attacked the president's executive power to run his own administration through proposals to make the secretary of treasury dependent on Congress, through a Tenure of Office Act that prevented presidents from dismissing executive officers, and through efforts to establish the precedent of executive decision by cabinet vote. They also sought to reduce dramatically the president's legislative and policy-making powers through a narrow interpretation of the legitimate uses of the presidential veto, through a proposed amendment to overturn a veto by a mere majority in each house of the Congress, and through presidential pronouncements of noninterference in legislative affairs. When it came to the technical independence of the presidency, the Whigs were sometimes content to leave the presidency alone and intact in its weakness and misery, provided presidents would renounce the Jacksonian heresy of claiming in any sense to represent the people. But in fact, they twice sought to use techniques to divest the president of his office and force compliance with Congress. One was a scheme to make John Tyler resign by denying him any cabinet officers to run the government; the other was the impeachment of President Andrew Johnson.

During the nineteenth century, the party that comes closest to defending the constitutional view of the executive is the Democratic party. Still, what is striking is the relative weakness of that defense, which can be expressed in the following two points. First, as the party of states' rights, the Democratic party had—except under President Polk—no major open national program or agenda. (The party's de facto pro-slavery program was often pursued by indirection.) Thus we have the conspicuous paradox that the party that had no legislative program—and that could have none, given its view of the powers of the national government—was the only defender of the strong presidency. Conversely, the party that had a legislative agenda, and a view of federal power that would support such a program, was militantly against a strong president. This paradox is more than a curiosity. Given the connection between limited federal power and the plan to curb presidential leadership, it becomes clear that even the party of the strong presidency began its argument on a foundation that conceded a great deal to the opposition. It could never develop a positive idea of presidential leadership, for it had defined the task of government in general in such a way as to make any kind of leadership almost impossible.

Second, the Democratic party after Polk in fact began to move away from even this limited defense of a strong presidency. The Democratic presidents who followed Polk before the Civil War were notable for their personal weakness. After the Civil War, Democrats found opportunities for a time in attacking the "dictatorship" of President Lincoln. What this development indicates is that the "strong presidency" views of the early Democrats did not survive even inside the Democratic party—perhaps a not so surprising development, given the Democratic party's origin in Jeffersonian Republican thought. In any case, the content of Democratic party doctrine after 1860 was of little direct consequence, since between Buchanan and Wilson, only one Democrat was elected president: Grover Cleveland.

What is clear, then, is that during the nineteenth century, no party really kept alive the "original" constitutional view. This view was first deliberately obscured, then appropriated, and finally lost sight of. Although the Democratic party for a moment came to the defense of certain of the constitutional prerogatives of the president, it never offered the complete defense and cut itself off from the sorts of thinkers who might have provided a deeper reason for its views. It defended a great part of the Constitution, but it never could restate the ideas and theory on which it was grounded, as these were the products of the discredited "monarchists." The dominant doctrinal view, in any case, became that of the Jeffersonian Republicans and the Whigs. Most remarkably of all, this view became widely considered as the one based on the Constitution.

THE IDEA OF THE MODERN PRESIDENCY

The idea of the modern presidency, inaugurated by Woodrow Wilson and then carried forward by a great part of the scholarly community earlier in this century, was established on the argument that the American political system vitally needs strong political leadership in the executive, but that the Constitution was constructed on a theory that denies that need. The Founding, according to Wilson, was Whig in inspiration: "The government of the United States was constructed upon the Whig theory of political dynamics, which was sort of an unconscious copy of the Newtonian theory of the Universe."[21] Wilson thus accepted the nineteenth century Whig interpretation of the Constitution as the correct one, only he rejected that design as the one that should guide us.

In Wilson's view, what should be done? If a strong presidency capable of a dynamic kind of leadership is to be constructed, it

[21] Woodrow Wilson, *Constitutional Government in the United States* (New York: Columbia University Press, 1961), 126.

must be done in some sense against the letter or spirit of the Constitution. One way, which seems to be the frankest and most open one, would be to alter radically the Constitution and build a new system on correct principles. Wilson proposed this idea early on, and it has remained the project of many reformers ever since. They argue that to create the strong executive the system needs, we must somehow eliminate the system of separation of powers and provide the president, through his party, with a legislative majority. Another way is to encourage, without any fundamental amendments, the grafting of the doctrine of the modern presidency onto the Constitution. This strategy involves building up presidential power and leadership by relying on what adherents of this doctrine regard as extra-constitutional sources of presidential power (elections, public opinion leadership, and the like). Indeed, according to Wilson in some of his later writings, these extra-constitutional developments might even be brought "inside" the Constitution. For, despite the Founders' "Whig theory," they were "practical statesmen with an experienced eye for affairs" and therefore saw the need for something more. In any case, argued Wilson, we can choose to interpret the Constitution in this light, because it is a "vehicle of life" and "no mere lawyer's document."[22] Everyone, so to speak, can agree to wink together and interpret the Constitution in a new way that includes what it was meant to exclude.

The structure of argument that lies behind this doctrine is a most curious one. In its view of the Founding, it is more Whig in character than the position espoused by the Whigs themselves, who after all conceded that the Founders unfortunately deviated from a true understanding of the separation of powers. Having started down this path, proponents of the doctrine of the modern presidency have developed a vested interest in making it appear as if the Founders rejected every idea of leadership in the presidency. Had proponents of the "modern presidency" bothered to look, they could of course have found a foundation for a strong presidency *inside* the Constitution and the Founding, albeit a presidency somewhat more modest and balanced than the one they wanted.

But they did not look to the Founders, perhaps because the Founders did not go as far as they wanted. Instead, they sought to establish their strong presidency on a new and entirely informal foundation: on the idea of the president as a "popular leader" or

---

[22]Ibid., 55, 157 and 192. See Christopher Wolfe, "Woodrow Wilson: Interpreting the Constitution," *Review of Politics* 41, no.1 (January 1979): 121–135.

"popular spokesmen." Even if one were to accept their view of a strong presidency, their own notion of how to construct it would never be able to support their own pretensions. But there are, of course, strong reasons not to support their idea of a strong presidency, for it is a presidency without sufficient checks or limits, one that evokes genuine whig fears of an institution that has consolidated all power. The Founders' idea of presidential leadership, it must be remembered, took place in a system that did in fact separate powers and provide for limiting checks and balances.

The greatest problem with this doctrine may not, however, lie in what it wants, but in the effects resulting from its understanding of the Founding. Proponents of the idea of the modern presidency argue that it is not in fact based on the Constitution, but on a pact among progressive intellectuals about how "we" should creatively interpret the Constitution. The whole idea of the modern presidency is thus built on a foundation of sand. That foundation has not held, and was abandoned by many of its advocates when it no longer supported their politics, beginning roughly during the Vietnam war. And when they turned on it, they did so with a particular vengeance. They suddenly became supporters of what they took to be the real Constitution, which they had come to believe was a whig document. The ironic consequence of the doctrine of the modern presidency has thus been the rise of a new Whiggism, which has been the dominant institutional doctrine among congressional Democrats and many intellectuals during the past twenty years.

If we wish to develop a sound doctrine to defend a strong, but still limited, presidency, there is no better place to begin than with the Constitution. The theoretical understanding on which the Constitution is based offers the fullest account in American political thought of the character of the powers of government and the best guide for determining the basic division of authority between the president and Congress.

Congressional Dominance and the Emergence of the Modern Presidency: Was Congress Ever the First Branch of Government?

David K. Nichols

WHEN COMMENTATORS LOOK BACK on the development of the separation of powers in the United States, they usually identify the nineteenth century as a period of legislative dominance and presidential weakness. The powerful modern presidency, it is argued, did not emerge until Franklin Roosevelt took office. In the most systematic treatment of the "modern presidency" to date, Fred Greenstein claims that there were variations in the exercise of presidential power in the pre-FDR presidency.[1] Jackson, Polk, Lincoln, Cleveland, Theodore Roosevelt, and Wilson exhibited many of the attributes of the modern activist presidency, but Greenstein concludes that they were the exceptions rather than the rule. Before 1932, presidential power was generally weak. The twin crises of the Depression and World War II converged with the "long incumbency of perhaps the most giftedly entrepreneurial President in American history" to permanently transform the office.[2]

Under Franklin Roosevelt "the presidency began to undergo not a shift but rather a metamorphosis."[3] Greenstein identifies

---

[1]Fred I. Greenstein, "Change and Continuity in the Modern Presidency," in *The New American Political System*, ed. Anthony King (Washington D.C.: American Enterprise Institute, 1978), 45-85.

[2]Ibid., 47.

[3]Ibid., 45.

four areas in which this metamorphosis took place. First, the president became actively involved in initiating and seeking congressional support for legislation, and consistently used the veto as a means to pursue his legislative agenda. Second, "a President that normally exercised few unilateral powers" became one who makes policy "through executive orders and other actions not formally ratified by Congress." Third, the president created an extensive bureaucracy in the executive office to support his legislative agenda and independent policy making. Finally, the office of the presidency was personalized. "Presidents are expected to be symbols of reassurance, possessing extraordinary 'nonpolitical' personal qualities that were traditionally associated with long deceased 'hero presidents'. . . ."[4]

Did the president need to be released from his constitutional shackles in order to provide unity, energy and direction for government? Was there another tradition of presidential leadership already available in the constitutional presidency? If so, that tradition has been obscured by our belief that the nineteenth century was a century of congressional dominance. As long as we accept that idea, it is difficult to take as seriously as we should the arguments about presidential strength in the Constitution. If the nineteenth century presidency was merely a weak servant of Congress, then it is only common sense to conclude that the real source of presidential strength must have come from outside the Constitution. Otherwise, we would not have had to wait over a hundred years for the emergence of a strong modern presidency.

We have already seen that Greenstein offers a long list of premodern quasi-"modern presidents" including Jackson, Polk, Lincoln, Cleveland, Theodore Roosevelt, and Wilson. Washington, Jefferson, and McKinley could easily be added to this list. The terms of these presidents would cover sixty of the first one hundred and twenty years of the American presidency. There were, to say the least, some serious gaps in the congressional dominance of the nineteenth and early twentieth centuries.

But what may be even more revealing is to examine those periods when the presidency was clearly the weaker and Congress the stronger. In particular, we should examine the post-Civil War presidency in order to see the extent to which Congress was ever dominant under the constitutional separation of powers. We should then look at the theoretical origins of the "modern presidency" in the Progressive movement to better understand why

[4]Ibid., 46.

we assume today that a strong presidency must be an extra-constitutional presidency. Finally, we should look at those early twentieth century presidents who rejected the Progressive or modern presidency to see if they in fact favored or encouraged a weak presidency and congressional dominance.

Such an examination will show that Congress has never exercised the powers associated with the modern presidency. The modern presidency has not usurped traditional congressional authority. To the extent that we have seen periods of presidential weakness, these periods have been characterized not by congressional dominance but by political drift.

EXECUTIVE-LEGISLATIVE RELATIONS IN THE POST-CIVIL WAR PERIOD

It would be difficult to find a period better exemplifying presidential weakness and congressional assertiveness than the presidency of Andrew Johnson.[5] Andrew Johnson's presidency could easily be identified as the low point of presidential power and peak of congressional dominance. Johnson's policies initially appeared to be a continuation of those of Lincoln. Johnson did not want to punish the South for the Civil War; he wanted to restore the Union as quickly as possible. He began his presidency by attempting to continue Lincoln's moderate policy toward the South and by asserting presidential control over Reconstruction. He was met by stiff resistance in Congress, but in some respects it was no worse than that met by Lincoln—and no better.

What tipped the balance in Johnson's case was that he rejected Lincoln's moderation and adopted a simple states' rights position in his opposition to the extension of the Freedmen's Bureau and the Civil Rights Bill. Because Johnson came from a Jacksonian democratic tradition of states' rights, he believed that, short of secession, the states should be given relative freedom to pursue their own policies. Thus he was unwilling to sanction any effort by the federal government to insure that the states would guarantee the equal protection of the laws to former slaves. When Johnson vetoed the Civil Rights Bill, he lost the support of even the moderate Republicans in Congress and thereby lost the ability to influence the debate on Reconstruction policy. When Johnson later

[5]For an account of the significant events in Andrew Johnson's presidency and other presidencies treated in the remainder of this paper, see Sidney M. Milkis and Michael Nelson, *The American Presidency: Origins and Development, 1776-1990* (Washington, D.C.: Congressional Quarterly Press, 1990).

encouraged some southern states to reject the Fourteenth Amendment, Congress proceeded to strip Johnson of his power over the military commanders directing Reconstruction. He thereby lost any long-term control over Reconstruction.

Having lost control over the policy arena, the remaining question was whether he would lose control over the office of the presidency itself. The early returns on this issue were not favorable. Almost immediately after Johnson took office, the Radical Republicans sought to have their opponents in the cabinet removed by Johnson. But Johnson rejected the Radicals' suggestion, and they were not able to name their own Cabinet. By 1867 relations had deteriorated to the point that Congress passed the Tenure of Office Act forbidding Johnson to remove his cabinet officers without Senate approval. This was clearly one of the greatest threats to executive independence in the history of the nation. The Radical Republicans wanted to hold on to their supporters in the Cabinet in order to thwart Johnson's control of even the executive branch. Johnson's refusal to accept such restrictions became the core of the impeachment proceedings that followed.

Johnson briefly seemed like a modern president. He toured the country trying to build popular support, going over the heads of congressional and party leaders. This turned out to be a disaster. Some have claimed that the failure of such an appeal was preordained in the anti-rhetorical political tradition of the nineteenth century.[6] Jackson and Lincoln, however, had both appealed to the people over the heads of Congress and party leaders and had done so quite successfully. The difference between them and Johnson was that, first of all, Johnson did not do it well. He did not understand how to appeal to the people without demeaning the office. In addition, he was defending a policy that could make no moral claim on the nation. The retreat to states' rights eliminated the possibility of any such claim, particularly in the aftermath of the Civil War.

Ultimately Johnson won on the impeachment issue—a narrow victory, but a victory nonetheless. It was a victory that was made possible at least in part by the constitutional provision requiring a two thirds majority for removal in the Senate, and in part by a recognition on the part of some Republican Senators that removal was not to be undertaken merely as a means of resolving policy disputes. The president was not intended to serve at the pleasure of Congress.

---

[6]Jeffrey K. Tulis, *The Rhetorical Presidency* (Princeton: Princeton University Press, 1987), 87-93.

Johnson could never be described as a successful president, but the success of the Congress in usurping executive authority was at best mixed. The Tenure of Office Act remained on the books and played an important role in postwar politics. But Johnson did remove his Secretary of the War and he was not forced to accept a cabinet that was in effect appointed by the Senate. No Whiggish version of cabinet government was established during his tenure. Other weak presidents such as Grant made at least some attempt to defend executive power in this area. The Tenure of Office Act was revised under Grant, although his ineptitude led him to settle for much less than he could have gotten.

The real irony, however, is that Congress's attempt to gain control over the administration as a means of controlling the postwar policy agenda backfired for the most part. By the end of Grant's administration, the point in American history when Congress should have had the strongest hand, the major congressional policy initiative of the postwar period, Radical Reconstruction, was ended. It ended because long before 1876, the primary concern of Congress had ceased to be policy. Its primary concern had become patronage.

This should not be a major surprise if one understands the institutional character of Congress. As a diverse body concerned with representing the various interests of its constituents, Congress could never take control over administration in such a way as to direct or unify policy. Congress was never able to dominate the senior administrative appointments. Presidents from Hayes forward resisted such attempts. Congressional dominance of administrative appointments remained at the sub-cabinet level. Being forced to work from the bottom up, Congress lost sight of the broader policy issues. They also discovered the potential benefit of using the administration not as a source of policy but as a source of spoils. The spoils system became a way of insuring continuation in office for themselves and for their party.

The end of Reconstruction illustrates this transformation. The election of 1876 was hotly contested. Although Samuel Tilden, the Democrat, had won a majority of the popular vote, the electoral vote was very close. Charges of fraud and corruption were rampant, and in some states the Governor forwarded to Congress the votes of one slate of electors while the legislature forwarded the votes of another set of electors. An electoral commission was created to decide which of the disputed slates of electors would be accepted as legitimate. The commission sided with the Republicans in every case, giving Rutherford B. Hayes the presidency. Had one of the disputed electoral votes gone to Tilden, he would have become president.

Many thought a constitutional crisis might be at hand, but the Democrats surprisingly acquiesced in the decision. The price, however, was that the Republicans be willing to withdraw all federal troops from the South, thereby ending Reconstruction. The Republicans were faced with a choice: give up Reconstruction or face the potential loss of the presidency. But by 1876 the choice had become easy. The moral fervor over Reconstruction had died, and the party's primary concern had become the protection of its control over the spoils system. What Johnson could not accomplish out of his prudent belief in moderation and imprudent allegiance to state's rights was eventually accomplished by an appeal to the greed and self-interest that had been generated by congressional involvement in the appointment process.

This fact gave rise to the moral issue that was to begin to replace slavery as the agenda-setting issue of the postwar period— the issue of civil service reform. It was on this issue that presidents began to recapture the ground of moral leadership, and it was on this ground that they began to reassert the doctrine of an independent executive branch.

The president's failure to dominate the legislative agenda in this period is not surprising, nor is his failure to exercise many unilateral powers. Relative world peace and American prosperity eliminated the need for extraordinary actions. The president and Congress agreed on many issues—primarily providing support for the growth of the economy. This policy consensus required little direction. The only major new issue was the character of the political system, and civil service reform was at the heart of that issue.

But as the old policies of the postwar period began to run up against new issues and problems, the tensions between the president and Congress became more obvious. They were resolved in favor of Congress only for a very brief period—the Harrison presidency. This was the period in American history when we came closest to having legislative supremacy—in fact we had virtually a parliamentary system. This resulted from two factors. First, Congress itself acted to fill the void left by too little executive leadership. The strong speakership emerged under Thomas B. Reed and allowed Congress to set and implement a legislative agenda. Second, Harrison acquiesced and actually became one of the few presidents to accept a Whig view of the presidency. It was not an altogether unproductive period. Congress began to address some of the new problems facing the nation, the Sherman Anti-Trust Act being the most important accomplishment.

This period could not and did not last for long. The strong speakership was anathema to the representative function of Congress. As long as there was substantial agreement between the Speaker and the members, the system might survive. But when disagreement arose between Speaker Joseph Cannon and moderate House Republicans, the Speaker had no popular source of authority or legitimacy to fall back on. He could not claim to be the spokesman for the nation, and without a parliamentary system and the disciplined parties it requires, the strong speakership was doomed to failure.

Even before the speakership declined, presidential power was reasserted. Harrison was a one term president, in part because the policies adopted by Congress ultimately did not appear adequate to the current problems. And if we could do some retrospective polling, I suspect we would find that Harrison was rejected in large part because of his view of the presidency. The nation believed that certain issues needed to be addressed. They wanted and expected leadership on these issues to come from the president, as it always had before. Congress was incapable of exercising that kind of national leadership. Neither Reed nor Cannon could appeal to the people over the heads of members of Congress or their party. They were creatures of Congress and of their party.

If there was a period of congressional ascendancy following the Civil War, there was never a period in which Congress took over the functions of the presidency. The elements of the modern presidency identified by Greenstein can be found in numerous nineteenth century presidencies, but never in Congress. Congress did not strike out with broad policy initiatives. The nation was not in the mood for major new government programs. Congress did not use its control over appointments to direct policy—it used it almost exclusively to promote spoils. Congress did not deprive the president of the exercise of unilateral authority. The occasion for the exercise of that kind of unilateral authority was largely missing. And finally, no one in Congress, nor the body as a whole, came to exercise the moral leadership of the presidency. No group of individuals could embody the nation and no individual in Congress had a legitimate claim to such a function.

It is not surprising that in the wake of the Civil War there was a retreat from presidential power. We should recognize, however, that it was not just a retreat from presidential power, it was a retreat from government initiative. This retreat was masked by the fact that the Republican victory had carried with it the adoption of many of the Whig policies of the pre-war period that had failed to gain ascendancy in the absence of effective presidential leadership.

In general, government policy was aimed at supporting private interests and private activity. So many had already given so much in support of the political community during the Civil War that people were asking what their country could do for them. The nation was not in the mood for moral crusades and heroic political efforts. For a while heroism would be reserved for the building of private rather than public empires. There was little scope for presidential leadership, because there was little scope for political leadership.

THE REEMERGENCE OF PRESIDENTIAL LEADERSHIP

When the opportunity for such leadership reemerged sporadically in such issues as civil service reform, and more dramatically in the host of issues facing the nation at the turn of the century, the presidency began to reemerge. While the office of the presidency became the focal point for Progressive reform during the administrations of Theodore Roosevelt and Woodrow Wilson, both Wilson and Roosevelt rejected the notion that their constitutional office was the source of their authority. The Progressives believed that they had to invent presidential leadership to deal with the current problems.

At the end of the nineteenth century, Woodrow Wilson identified what he regarded as a dangerous lack of direction in American politics. He spoke of leaderless government and the problems it posed for the future of American politics. Initially he thought these difficulties could be overcome by creating a more parliamentary system in which the Speaker would take over the role of chief executive and the president would be reduced to a mere administrator.[7] The Speaker would supply the legislature, the government, and the country with the unity and direction it was sorely lacking. But by 1908, when he wrote *Constitutional Government,*[8] Wilson had clearly changed his mind.

Wilson came to believe that "greatly as the practice and influence of Presidents has varied, there can be no mistaking the fact that we have grown more and more inclined from generation to generation to look to the President as the unifying force in our complex system, the leader both of his party and of the nation."[9] In Wilson's view, the Founders had created a "Newtonian Consti-

---

[7]Woodrow Wilson, *Congressional Government* (Boston: Houghton Mifflin, 1885).
[8]Woodrow Wilson, *Constitutional Government* (New York: Columbia University Press, 1908).
[9]Ibid., 60.

tution" that emphasized checks and balances as opposed to growth and change. In particular they had created a fairly limited presidential office. But the office has gradually been transformed by its individual occupants and the variety of circumstances they faced. From Washington and Jefferson to Jackson, Lincoln and Cleveland, Wilson saw a possibility of presidential strength not envisioned by the authors of the Constitution.[10]

Wilson was not willing to rest content with the occasional signs of presidential strength. He thought that a more radical and more fundamental change was needed. He no longer believed that a major change in the written Constitution was possible, but he also believed that such a change might be unnecessary. In writing *Constitutional Government*, Wilson sought to transform public opinion. As James Ceaser has explained, "The 'living constitution'—the actual regime as fixed not only by Constitutional provisions, but by opinion and practice—would have to be changed by means of a basic transformation of the public's views under which the people would come to regard the executive as the most legitimate source of political authority."[11] The president was to be released from the narrow legal constraints of the Constitution and find a new source of authority in popular leadership.

Theodore Roosevelt provided the most succinct explanation of the Progressive transformation of the presidency in his stewardship theory. He claimed that whereas the Constitution did place some specific limits on the president, those limits should be understood very narrowly. The president's power, however, did not depend on the Constitution. It was based on his ability to promote the public interest. As long as the president violated no specific law or constitutional provision, he was free to pursue the public interest in whatever way he saw fit.[12] The Constitution limits political power, but popular support and popular mandates would provide legitimacy for a president to undertake broad actions in the public interest.

That belief was partially justified. Because conservatives of that day often confused the idea of limited government with a kind of libertarianism, virtually no one saw the Constitution as a source of energy. It was almost universally viewed as a document of limits. When this theory was applied to the presidency, the impli-

[10]Ibid., 55-9.

[11]James W. Ceaser, *Presidential Selection* (Princeton: Princeton University Press, 1979), 172.

[12]Theodore Roosevelt, *The Works of Theodore Roosevelt* (New York: Scribner's, 1926) 20:347.

cations were clear: The purpose of the Constitution was to prevent tyranny. Thus the purpose of the constitutional provisions regarding the presidency was to prevent the president from becoming a tyrant.

In this context, the Progressives naturally looked outside the framework of the Constitution in order to address the problems they faced. They looked outside the Constitution for a source of governmental authority and executive power, leaving the Constitution in the custody of a libertarian Whig perspective. Popular legitimacy, administrative support, and extra-legal authority were the key to a strong presidency for the Progressives, and in their view these elements could not be found within the Constitution. But if the libertarians of the late nineteenth century ignored the need for government action, the Progressives ignored the desirability and need for institutional sources of strength and authority, and they failed to see the potential instability of simple direct democracy as the sole support for presidential authority. The Progressives "recovered" the democratic energy of the presidency only by wrenching it from its constitutional origins and denying it the complementary support of institutional authority. The Progressive idea led us to believe that elements of the modern presidency could only exist outside the Constitution.

Second, and more important, the Progressives attempted to transform the idea of the ends of democratic government. It was not just the constraints of the separation of powers that the Progressives thought must be escaped, it was the very notion of limited constitutional government. The Constitution placed limits on the will of democracy, and prevented the government from responding to the needs of the people. At its most fundamental level, the Progressive movement wished to transform American politics from a system aimed at the protection of individual rights to a system that promotes the growth of national community. Once the idea of rights had been replaced by the idea of community, and once the limits of constitutional government were replaced by the legitimacy of unchecked popular leadership, the "promise of American life" could be fulfilled.[13]

Although this idea of national community has met with only mixed success, it has helped to justify a major change in American government, a change that is usually described as a shift from limited government to positive government. This shift is responsible for the tremendous growth in activity on the part of the national

[13]See Herbert Croly, *The Promise of American Life* (New York: Macmillan Company, 1909).

government in general and the president in particular. The presidency was to be unleashed from the constraints of the Constitution and the law so that the government as a whole could move unfettered into the twentieth century.

THE RETREAT FROM THE PROGRESSIVE PRESIDENCY

If we look at some of the "weak" presidents of the early twentieth century, we will find that in many cases it was not a strong presidency to which they were opposed, but merely the Progressives' conception of a strong presidency and the end which that presidency was to serve.

William Howard Taft is usually seen as a leading opponent of a powerful presidency, and his presidency could hardly be characterized as a practical success. But Taft's view of the presidency is somewhat more complicated than is usually recognized. Taft did oppose Theodore Roosevelt's version of a strong presidency, but he was hardly a champion of legislative supremacy.

Why is Taft seen as the quintessential defender of the weak presidency? First of all, he explicitly rejected Roosevelt's stewardship theory. He claimed that there was no residue of power to be found outside the Constitution. The president was not free to act in the public interest without legal or constitutional sanction. During the closing days of his administration, Roosevelt had created a number of national forests by executive order. When Taft came to office he immediately sought legislation to provide legal sanction for what Roosevelt had done unilaterally.

Although Taft did propose a major piece of legislation, a tariff reduction bill, he allowed the Congress to water down the bill to such an extent that he lost the support of Progressive legislators. This rift between Taft and the Progressives led Taft actively to campaign against Republican Progressives in the 1910 congressional elections. Taft's campaign was a failure, however, and served as a prelude to his third place finish in the 1912 presidential race.

Nonetheless, a closer look at Taft's presidency and Taft's views on the presidency provides us with some interesting insights into presidential power. Although Taft did not believe in extra-constitutional presidential powers, he did believe that a strong presidency was essential to the healthy operation of the separation of powers. In later life, as a Supreme Court Justice, Taft handed down one of the most important decisions regarding presidential power in the history of the Court, the opinion in *Myers v. United*

States.[14] In that decision Taft defended the president's unilateral authority to fire executive branch officials. In so doing he settled a conflict over the separation of powers that had begun in the first Congress, flared up during Jackson's administration and led to the impeachment of Andrew Johnson. What is most important is that he settled it in favor of a strong and independent executive branch.

Even while in office, Taft made a number of proposals for increasing the president's power over the budget process, including the suggestion that Congress should be free to appropriate funds up to a level proposed in a presidential budget, but would be forbidden by law from appropriating more than the president proposed. If a contemporary president made a similar suggestion as a means of dealing with the current deficit, I sincerely doubt that he would be accused of being a weak president.

As a legislative leader, Taft met with limited success. But one should remember that although Congress diluted his tariff reduction bill, he did introduce and pass a tariff reduction bill. Theodore Roosevelt, on the other hand, had never been willing to risk his political capital even to introduce a serious proposal for tariff reform. Taft's inability to defeat his Progressive opponents in 1910 was surely a personal failure, but the attempt to do so was hardly the mark of a president unwilling to use his personal influence to promote his policies. Franklin Roosevelt met with a similar failure when he tried to campaign against his congressional foes, but he did not have a young, popular former president waiting in the wings ready to reclaim his political mantle. Taft did, and he paid the price in the 1912 election.

Taft's electoral defeat should not prevent us from taking seriously his objections to the Progressive view of the presidency. When Taft sought to codify the "midnight forests" created by Theodore Roosevelt, he was not repudiating Roosevelt's actions. To the contrary he sought a more stable foundation for Roosevelt's policies. Taft knew that policies created at the last minute by executive orders could be undone as quickly. Institutions and laws do not exist merely to prevent action, they may in fact be the best means of insuring that action will continue even after personal popularity has faded. Just as actions supported by laws may be better able to stand against the winds of change, a strong president within the Constitution may maintain his vitality far longer than

[14] 272 U.S. 52 (1926).

one who must chase short-term popular support in order constantly to renew his strength.

The other "weak" presidents of the early twentieth century—Harding, Coolidge and Hoover—also deserve another look. Harding began his administration by rejecting any active role in promoting a legislative agenda, and his death ended his presidency just before a series of scandals that would permanently tarnish his reputation became known to the public. But we will better understand Harding's presidency if we understand the context in which he was operating.

The United States had become a world power in World War I, but the experience of the war was exhausting and frightening. Woodrow Wilson had come to office holding out the promise of the Progressive presidency, but he left office having shown its potential weakness. His popular leadership had proved inadequate to the task of turning his vision of a new world order into a reality.

Harding's campaign slogan was "return to normalcy." He knew that the nation had grown tired and suspicious of heroic policies and heroic presidents. Though his agenda was less ambitious than that of his predecessor, he did have an agenda of higher tariffs and lower taxes. Although he initially refused to lobby actively for his proposals with the legislature, by July of 1921 he was addressing Congress in support of his proposals.

Harding was unsuccessful in his efforts at legislative leadership, but the significant fact is that he eventually came to see such leadership as part of his job. What is also worth noting is that Congress did not fill the leadership void. Harding's failure resulted not in congressional dominance but in inaction. It was in this period of policy lethargy or drift that the political scandals of the Harding administration took root, much as such scandal came to dominate the Grant administration in a similar period following the Civil War.

Ironically, Harding was a very popular president, even at the time of his death. The scandals did not come to light fully until after he was gone. Moreover, that popularity was not without foundation. The Bureau of the Budget that had been proposed by Theodore Roosevelt, Taft, and Wilson finally became a reality during Harding's administration. This may have been the single most important institutional development in the budgetary process in the history of the nation. The executive branch for the first time had an institutional mechanism for overseeing the budget as a whole, something that Congress itself would not develop until 1974.

Harding also took seriously the role of popular leadership that has become so associated with the Progressive or modern presidency. Harding hired the first official presidential speech writer and, more importantly, used his background as a former newspaper editor to great advantage in cultivating the press. He revived the practice of holding regular press conferences, a practice that had been neglected by Wilson during his second term. And he instituted the practice of holding daily off-the-record briefings with reporters. He even built a cottage near his house for the use of the press corps.

None of these factors make Harding a great president, or even a particularly good one, but they do explain how a president with limited legislative accomplishments and numerous corrupt associates could remain popular throughout his presidency. They also demonstrate that even a president of modest ability and limited goals might find within the concept of a limited constitutional government many of the tools of the "modern presidency."

It was Coolidge rather than Harding, however, who realized the potential of using the office of the presidency to promote the goal of limited government. Coolidge is known as a president of few words and fewer accomplishments. But to some extent that evaluation is the result of our acceptance of the Progressive standard of the presidency. The Progressives wanted to develop a strong presidency in order to energize a more active government. But what would a president who wanted to use his office to limit government look like? The answer might be, a lot like Coolidge.

Not only did Coolidge leave office as a popular president, he also managed to overcome the stench of corruption left over from the Harding administration. He did not have a broad legislative agenda, but he was successful in pushing his tax cut bill through Congress. More importantly, he was able to lower the expectations of government, and thereby increase the possibility that government would be able to meet popular expectations.

In spite of his infamous silence, Coolidge pursued his goals by carefully cultivating public support. He was the king of the photo opportunity; one can find pictures of Coolidge in an unbelievable range of settings. It was also Coolidge, and not Franklin Roosevelt, who pioneered the use of radio. Coolidge's radio addresses will never obtain the historical status of Roosevelt's fireside chats, but it was he who first showed the possibility of using the radio to establish a personal relationship between the president and the American people.

Coolidge demonstrated that legislative leadership and popular leadership were in principle and in practice consistent with the idea of limited government. Coolidge was a modern president, but he differed from the Progressives as to the proper role of modern government.

If Coolidge is at least a modest success story, Hoover's presidency is synonymous with failure. At the beginning of his administration, Hoover appeared to be following in the footsteps of Coolidge. His personal reticence was perfectly compatible with his limited view of government. When crisis struck, Hoover refused to change his approach. In the view of most commentators he continued to cling to a nineteenth century view of the presidency as the world of the twentieth century came crashing down around him.

Hoover's view of the presidency and of government did come from the nineteenth century. In particular it came from that libertarian Whig perspective which saw no room for an active government or an active president. But that view was a distortion of the Constitution and the constitutional presidency. When Congress passed the Smoot-Hawley Tariff, Hoover saw the potential problems but refused to exercise his unquestioned constitutional authority to veto the bill. Even the stock market crash and the Depression that followed failed to lead Hoover to search for sources of energy and authority within the Constitution.

Hoover's response, or lack thereof, was not inevitable. There was a tradition of presidential leadership in the nineteenth century to which Hoover could have appealed, the tradition of Lincoln, Jackson, Jefferson and others. That appeal was possible because, from the beginning, the Constitution provided the potential for an energetic modern executive. Hoover's failure to see this fact in a time of national crisis meant that, once again, those who followed would look outside the Constitution for energy and strength.

CONCLUSION

In recent years there has been much criticism of the growth of presidential power, much talk of an imperial presidency. But many of the criticisms of the growth of executive power have been misplaced. Does the president wield too much discretionary authority? Does he control too large an administrative staff? Does he actively promote too broad of a legislative agenda? One might answer yes to all these questions, but not find the source of that problem in the growth of executive power vis-à-vis the other branches of government. The problem is instead the growth of government as a whole. If we want a government whose activities are as wide ranging as ours, there is no substitute for the modern presidency as it exists. The president provides the unity and energy that allows such a system to function. This was true with the more limited government of the nineteenth century and it is true today. If the system does not function as well today, we should not look to the size of the presidency, but to the size of the government as a whole.

The presidency may, in fact, offer one of the greatest possible sources of protection for the doctrine of limited government. There has been a tendency to identify proponents of a more active presidency with proponents of a more active national government, but there have been important exceptions. In addition to Taft, Harding and Coolidge, the names of Andrew Jackson and perhaps Ronald Reagan come to mind as examples of activist presidents who supported the idea and practice of limited government. They believed in using the powers of their office to restrain what they saw as the unchecked growth of the national government, and to reestablish an appreciation for the constitutional concept of limited government.

But if expanding the national government is a sure way of expanding the power of the presidency, why would any president resist such an expansion? Perhaps because when faced with the need to exercise the powers of the presidency, it becomes obvious that less is sometimes more. The doctrine of limited government teaches that government should not do more than is necessary to maintain the peace and security of the community. This may still be quite a lot, but by limiting the tasks of government, the task of governing becomes more manageable. The solution to the problems of contemporary American politics cannot be a mere lowering of expectations for the presidency, it must be a lowering of expectations for the government as a whole. A more modest presidency in the face of a more immodest government would be a recipe for disaster, for it is primarily through the presidency that the activity of the government gains coherence and direction.

Even a limited government requires a powerful executive if it is to function effectively. Limited government is not a synonym for weak government. What the authors of the Constitution realized is that a limited government must be a powerful government, and it can be that only if there is adequate provision for the exercise of executive power.

In their reaction against the reactionaries, the Progressives lost sight of the full dimensions of the problem. The libertarian Whigs couldn't escape the belief that government should do nothing, while the Progressives were blinded by the belief that government can do everything. The American Constitution offers an alternative to both perspectives. It shows that the doctrine of limited government is truly a middle ground between tyranny and anarchy. At the center of that Constitution is the office of the presidency.

What Has Happened to the Separation of Powers?

Hugh Heclo

INTRODUCTION

THE SEPARATION OF POWERS is a subject that invites compartmentalized thinking. Protagonists proclaim the unfettered or hamstrung condition of this or the other branch of government. If one side is up, the other must be down; one side more powerful, the other less so. The clarity of a development in one part of the system easily obscures the reverberations set off in other parts of the governmental web. It is very difficult to gain a view of the whole, steadily and with perspective.

The discussion that follows begins with one of the most neglected "holistic" aspects of the separation of powers: its durability. We then turn to what has been discussed at extensive (and, some might say, banal) length: the growing overall role of the presidency in the separation of powers. The picture becomes more complex and hopefully less banal as we move on to show how congressional delegation of power to the executive and legislative strings of control have grown hand in hand. And because institutions in our system of government are inescapably interconnected, our discussion reaches out to include the role of the courts in the unfolding development of the separation of powers: often limited in terms of "constitutional review" and increasingly extensive in terms of "statutory review." The final sections offer evidence and analysis relevant to thinking about the important question of whether the system works. On the whole there is reason to feel sanguine about what appears as a moving balance of overlapping and separate powers. When it comes to the particular issue of the president's warmaking powers, however, there are trends that should give Americans more cause for worry.

THE FORGOTTEN SUCCESS

Political writers have fallen into the habit of using shorthand labels to characterize the state of our national institutions. One hears about the "imperial presidency," or the "resurgent Congress," the "fettered presidency," or the "imperial Congress." Above all, in recent years we hear about a government of "stalemate," "gridlock," and "immobilism."

Leaving aside for the moment how accurate these labels might be, they all miss the most important and least commented upon feature about our separation of powers system: its durability. With the basic constitutional design of separated powers still in place after 200 years, durability is something we simply take for granted.

It was not always so. The minds of the Founders—both those who designed the American Constitution and the larger, diverse groups who debated its ratification—were preoccupied with the problem of durability. Of course, institutional survival was "only" a means to the larger ends of government. The chief object in the separation of governing power was liberty, a safeguarding of each person's unalienable rights from arbitrary power. Also, contrary to some more recent interpretations,[1] efficiency was an important objective. Having lived through the chaos of government-by-committee in the Continental Congress, as well as having witnessed the upheavals in domestic affairs resulting from executive feebleness in state governments, many of the Founders saw the separation and balancing of different powers as essential to efficient government. A bumbling, ineffective government could threaten liberty as surely as could an unrepresentative government of concentrated powers. As Justice Robert Jackson would later put it, "While the Constitution diffuses power the better to secure liberty, it also contemplates that practice will integrate the dispersed powers into a *workable* government. It enjoins upon its branches separateness but interdependence, autonomy but reciprocity."[2]

If goals such as liberty and efficiency were in the back of the Founders' minds, the question of viability was in the front. In those days any college graduate or other learned person could be expected to have studied the history of the ancient republics and

---

[1] In a theme that has been repeated many places, Justice Brandeis observed in 1926 that our system of checks and balances was designed "not to promote efficiency but to preclude the exercise of arbitrary power." *Myers* v. *United States*, 272 U.S. 52, 293 (1926).

[2] *Youngstown Sheet and Tube Co.* v. *Sawyer*, 343 U.S.579, 635 (1952), emphasis added.

the seemingly inevitable decline of such governments. The one-way life cycle of the republican form of government—from public virtue and liberty, to licentiousness and the corruption of public-mindedness, and thence to anarchy and eventual tyranny—was part of the common currency of late eighteenth century political thought. Or, as the patriot-orator Thomas Dawes, Jr., put it, "Half our learning is their epitaph."[3]

Given these familiar historical lessons, given their experience with the Articles of Confederation and the accompanying turmoil in state governments, it seems fair to say that those debating the Constitution were fairly haunted by the fear that such a form of government as they were proposing could not endure.

Hence the first and, historically speaking, most astonishing answer to the question of what has happened to the separation of powers system is that it has survived. The design has proven robust and resilient throughout immense transformations in our national life. For us today it is difficult to grasp the enormity of that achievement. It is a government design that has accommodated the metamorphosis from a seacoast strip of a nation with under four million inhabitants to a continental world power with over one-quarter billion people. No other political framework in place in the late eighteenth century managed to survive the transformation to modernity. The enormous and easily overlooked historical fact of regime durability should be the starting point for any discussion of what troubles American constitutionalism.

EXPLAINING THE SUCCESS

How has the separation of powers design managed to be so durable? Not, perhaps, because of any unique wisdom or virtue inherent in the American people. The Founders' mixed view of human nature seems to have gotten it about right: people are bad enough not to be trusted with power but virtuous enough to govern themselves within properly designed constitutional institutions for allocating power.

Three other reasons carry more weight in explaining the durability of the separation of powers. For one thing, popular reverence for the Constitution itself—something which the nation's early leaders successfully enshrined as central to Americans' self-identity—has aided regime survival. Although few Americans

---

[3]Quoted in Forrest McDonald, *Novus Ordo Seclorum: The Intellectual Origins of the Constitution* (Lawrence, KS: The University Press of Kansas, 1985), 70.

have detailed knowledge about its contents, reverence for the very idea of the Constitution has served as a huge sheet anchor of stability amid the turmoil of events. Any politician, no matter how popular, incurs immense penalties if he is perceived as somehow playing fast and loose with the Constitution. This is what befell President Franklin Roosevelt and his Supreme Court "packing" plan after the 1936 election landslide, and the results were even more disastrous for President Richard Nixon and the Watergate cover-up after his own landslide victory in 1972.

In the second place, the framework of 1787 has proven durable because the dynamics set up in its allocations of power have usually operated more or less as intended. Ambitions of legislators, with their own electoral base and legislative powers, and ambitions of presidents, with their different electoral base and executive powers, have indeed checked each other and thereby reduced the risk of either branch usurping the functions of the other. Likewise no "faction" has been able to gain control over the whole system and independently work its will. For important things to get done, very large coalitions are needed throughout the dispersed centers of power. From the outset, the intention behind the design was not simply to produce self-cancelling vetoes on any action but, by delaying and checking the exercise of power, to facilitate the kind of action that recognizes joint concerns across many interests (*Federalist* 51). Something of that hope was operational approximately 100 years later when James Bryce observed that "there is an excessive friction in the American system, a waste of force in the strife of various bodies and persons created to check and balance one another." It is "only when a distinct majority of the people are so clearly of one mind" that concerted action becomes possible.[4] And today on matters such as Social Security reform, the environment, health insurance or educational reform, something of the same tendency can be discerned, though we often have to call those common concerns a "crisis."

The third point is that the separation of powers system has proven durable because it has been adaptable. Practical-minded people in and around Washington have kept adjusting to circumstances and acting out of the belief that, as a character in Lampedusa's novel *The Leopard* puts it, "If we're going to keep things the same there are going to have to be some changes made around here." Since this phenomenon of stability-enhancing change is central to what has happened to the separation of powers, the point deserves a fuller discussion.

[4]James Bryce, *The American Commonwealth*, 3d ed., 2 vols. (New York: Macmillan, 1899), 1:302.

IMPROVISATION AND JOINT CONSTRUCTION

Political adjustment and accommodation, events and experience rather than doctrine have been the lifeblood of the separation of powers. It has been so from the beginning. Amid our current confusions one is tempted to assume that the Founders had a clear idea of how the separation of powers would operate. It is more accurate to say that they had a clear idea of the opposite—how the concentration and abuse of power would operate. They knew this from hard experience, and it accounts for some of the provisions in the Constitution that seem obscure today but that the Founders regarded as very important. For example, they knew from British politics how executive leaders could dominate the legislature by bribing lawmakers with sinecures. Hence the Constitution prohibits members of Congress from concurrently holding any other civil office and also forbids former congressmen from being appointed to any federal position the salary of which has been increased during their term of office (Article I, sec. 6). Then too, the Founders had also seen from state experiences how legislatures could be inflamed and ride roughshod over executive and judicial officials. Thus the Constitution prohibits Congress from reducing the compensation of the president and federal judges while they are in office, and makes it difficult for Congress to remove them from office (Article II, sec. 1 & sec. 4; Article III, sec. 1).

As to how the separation of powers would actually function in a more positive way, the Founders were no different from their successors in having to experiment, adjust and, as we would say, work things out. The most famous early improvisation was the matter of the removal powers of the president versus Congress, but there were many others. Thus, as the Constitutional Convention's presiding officer, George Washington presumably learned as much as anyone about the document's intentions. But even Washington could only improvise as he pondered what form of communications to adopt in order to carry out the Constitution's "advice and consent" requirement regarding presidential nominations to office and the submission of foreign treaties to the Senate. At first Washington thought it essential to communicate orally and in advance of negotiating the terms of such treaties. Accordingly the president and his secretary of war came to the floor of the Senate on August 22, 1789, and submitted papers for discussing the terms of a new Indian treaty. It was not a happy experiment and was never repeated. Likewise, in the early Congress some members of the House sought to have cabinet secretaries appear on the floor of the House for discussion and questioning. The House's leader, James Madison, effectively squelched that idea, thereby helping preserve not only the integrity of strictly legislative debate on the floor of Congress but also the president's control over executive departments.[5]

Such political adjustments have continued down to the present day. The ongoing process of interaction by which the executive and legislative branches have tried to work out the practical meaning of the Constitution's separation of powers has sometimes been called coordinate or joint construction (as opposed to strictly judicial constitutional construction).[6] With a few important exceptions, the courts have played a fairly marginal role in sorting out what the Constitution requires with regard to the operation of the separation of executive and legislative powers. Judges have prudently regarded this as a political matter to be worked out between the other two branches. Hence, unlike with questions of individual rights or the power of the federal government vis-à-vis the states, there has grown up no extensive body of court-sanctioned doctrine to consult and apply when disputes about the relative roles of the executive and legislative branches arise. As we shall see, some recent Supreme Court decisions have sought, with dubious results, to move in a more doctrinal direction in this matter.

THE RISE OF PRESIDENTIALISM

The most obvious development in the twentieth century separation of powers is the growth of the president's role as policy leader. By this I mean that presidents, who with a few exceptions were overshadowed in the nineteenth century by Congress, have in this century become expected to be the nation's leading agenda setters, policy initiators, problem solvers, and all-round leaders with a "vision." How that occurred in the last one hundred years is a complex story that has been told in many presidency textbooks. Here I wish to sketch just a few, sometimes forgotten, highlights.

To say that developments in the separation of powers have been ad hoc, experimental and event-driven is not to suggest that things have just happened without rhyme or reason. The president's growing prominence as policy leader is directly connected to the increasingly complex demands on government that have come

[5]See David M. Matteson, "The Organization of the Government under the Constitution," in *United States Constitution Sesquicentennial Commission, History of the Formation of the Union Under the Constitution* (Washington: U.S. Government Printing Office, 1943).

[6]Louis Fisher, "Separation of Powers: Interpretation Outside the Courts," 18 *Pepperdine Law Review* 57 (1990).

in the wake of rapid economic, technological, and social changes. These demands strained Congress's ability to legislate in sufficient detail. Bureaucracy grew in Washington, as it did in the states and in other developed countries; and the president as head of the executive bureaucracy became a focal point for policy management.

It is important to recall that in the early part of this century the presidency was given new coordinating chores, not to enhance presidential power but to help Congress get on with its work. For example, Congress had traditionally produced a federal budget by summing up the separate budgets negotiated individually with each executive bureau, a process that was proving unmanageable before the First World War. Finally in 1921 the Budget Control and Accounting Act recognized the inability of a multiheaded Congress to produce a coherent budget for the government without executive leadership. The president, with the aid of a new professional budget staff housed in the Treasury Department, was charged by Congress with the responsibility to prepare a single, coordinated budget proposal for the executive branch as a whole and to submit such a proposal to Congress each year. It may be difficult to believe today, but the orienting idea in those days was that, by helping the president prepare and execute a unified executive branch budget, a professional budget staff would enhance the power of Congress, not the presidency, to effect its will. To a significant extent, the same motivation of using presidential coordination to facilitate Congress's deliberative ability underlay legislative authorization for the president to negotiate individual tariff rates, reorganize executive branch agencies, and report on the condition of the economy.

Although some of the relevant developments were underway before the 1930s, the Depression and Franklin Roosevelt's administration set the mold for the more modern, powerful presidency. Previous presidents such as Jackson or Lincoln had made vigorous use of presidential power, but these were sporadic, crisis-driven responses that produced few lasting institutional changes. By contrast, developments after 1932 institutionalized the presidency as the focal point of national government leadership, no matter who held the office and whether or not there was a national crisis.[7] By

[7] This change became evident in a variety of ways. From the first half-dozen special assistants provided by legislation to the president in 1939, the White House Office evolved into a 400- to 500-member complex of specialized staffs looking after presidents' personal political and policy interests. The Executive Office of the president was created in the same year and soon came to house presidential agencies concerned with the budget (the Budget Bureau was transferred from the Trea-

mid-century, the president's "legislative program" was expected to set the main agenda for Congress and the nation each year. Executive agency proposals for legislation, testimonies to Congress, and comments on pending legislation had to be "cleared" through the president's Office of Management and Budget staff. After 1981 their proposed regulations had to be cleared as well.

Overarching these particular developments was a growing aura, a seeming awesomeness that surrounded the presidency. The emergence of the United States as a world power, the onset of the Cold War against which stood "the leader of the free world," images of the presidential finger on the atomic button—this was the stuff for creating a White House aureole. At the same time, growth of the mass electronic media offered presidents unique advantages for focussing public attention on the presidential persona, against which the hydra-headed and usually undramatic work of Congress could not compete.

DELEGATION AND CONTROL

Although the growing prominence of the president has been a dramatic development, it is scarcely the whole or most of the story about what has happened to the separation of powers. Congress has been far more than a passive participant in or observer of this trend. Like a moving counterweight to what has been happening in the presidency, congressional adaptations have been made in the ongoing struggle to control policy. Congress has delegated legislative power not only to the president but also to executive agencies and independent commissions. Partly this has been due to the practical difficulty of legislating complex public policies in sufficient detail and in part it has been a way for Congress to avoid politically tough decisions.

Delegation has certainly not meant that Congress has given free rein to presidents or the executive agencies on the matters so delegated. The familiar theme has continued to be not a neat separation but an overlapping or, as the Founders might have said, "blending" of powers. For example, major delegations of power to

---

sury Department in 1939 and later renamed the Office of Management and Budget, or OMB, in 1970) and the economy (Council of Economic Advisers, 1946). Eventually Executive Office staffs were added to advise presidents on defense and foreign policy (National Security Council, 1948), science policy (Office of Science and Technology, 1962), trade relations (Special Representative for Trade Negotiations, 1963), the environment (Council on Environmental Quality, 1970) and domestic policy in general (Domestic Council/Office of Policy Development, 1971).

regulatory agencies have, even apart from any other congressional
"strings," prevented presidents from removing commissioners of
these organizations except for "good cause." After much political
and legal wrangling, the Supreme Court held that the Congress
could indeed restrict presidential removals to specified causes—
i.e., not simply policy disagreements with commissioners.[8] This has
been seen as a way to protect the quasi-legislative, quasi-judicial
position of "independent" regulatory commissions from White
House policy control.

Much more pervasive than any fights over the removal of personnel has been Congress's insistence on maintaining a voice and
ultimate policy control, even while it has authorized the executive
bureaucracy to do more and delegated power to that end. At this
point we come to the essence of how the separation of powers
framework has managed to change and in some ways stay the
same. Beyond the formal congressional power to pass laws authorizing and appropriating funds for federal activities—an immense
power over the life of the bureaucracy—the legislature has continued to evolve a vast, informal system of control based on political
negotiations and quid pro quos. In addition to the requirements
it writes into laws, Congress watches, nudges, and in many instances directs executive agency activities in ways that never have
made or will make the nightly news. The language in committee
reports, understandings reached with executive officials in hearings, correspondence and reviews, informal concordants reached
between staffs in the two branches—these are the workaday means
through which the separation of powers has adapted and survived.
Congress has usually found means to combine delegation and
control, but doing so is a messy political process that can never satisfy those who wish to see clear bright lines drawn between the
branches of government.

The legislative veto is a good example of the way the separation of powers design has been adapted through a combination of
delegation and control. Although there were a few early precedents, the modern legislative veto came into major use in the
1930s when executive officials sought authority to take actions
that would normally have required congressional legislation. In return for this authority, such executive action was made subject to
some form of congressional approval or disapproval before it could
take effect.

[8]*Humphrey's Executor v. United States,* 295 U.S. 602 (1935).

Thus in 1932 President Herbert Hoover obtained congressional authority to reorganize executive departments through reorganization plans that would take effect unless either house of Congress passed a resolution rejecting the president's reorganization plan. Use of the legislative veto soon spread to other policy areas. Congress experimented with provisions requiring a positive vote to sustain the presidential action in question as well as provisions that required merely the absence of a negative vote. Legislative vetoes could sometimes be registered by both houses, or one house, or even just one committee of Congress. Presidents and their advisers objected to such vetoes as unconstitutional infringements on executive functions, but usually acquiesced and signed the legislation containing veto provisions. As a rule, they wanted the new authority more than they disliked the veto strings. When executive-legislative relations deteriorated from late in the Johnson administration through the Nixon administration, Congress made increasing use of legislative vetoes to reassert its position in areas such as presidential war powers, agency regulations, and budget impoundments.

Both the Carter and the Reagan administrations expressed their determination to raise constitutional challenges to the legislative veto, and in 1983 the Supreme Court responded with the decision *INS* v. *Chadha*.[9] The Court declared that legislative veto provisions were unconstitutional, arguing that the exercise of such congressional actions was the equivalent to lawmaking and that therefore congressional vetoes should have to follow the normal constitutional requirements of passing both houses of Congress and being presented to the president for his signature or veto. Although acknowledging that the laws containing legislative veto provisions had themselves been signed by presidents and that such provisions facilitated working relations between the branches, the Court repeated the familiar refrain that "convenience and efficiency are not the primary objectives—or the hallmarks—of democratic government." According to the Court, the Constitution separated government into "three defined categories, Legislative, Executive, and Judicial," and it is the duty of the Court to resist the "hydraulic pressures inherent within each of the separate Branches to exceed the outer limits of its power."[10]

In 1986 the Court reiterated in even stronger language the doctrine of compartmentalized powers by declaring unconstitutional a provision in the Gramm-Rudman-Hollings Budget Act

[9]462 U.S. 919 (1983).
[10]Id. at 951.

that allowed the comptroller general to order executive spending cuts if a schedule of deficit reduction targets was not met. Since the comptroller general is removable only by a congressional joint resolution, these executive duties given to that officer by the act were said to interfere with the powers of the president in what was "a separate and wholly independent Executive Branch." The Court argued that, apart from impeachment, the president is "responsible not to the Congress but to the people" and that "once Congress makes its choice in enacting legislation, its participation ends. Congress can thereafter control the execution of its enactment only indirectly—by passing new legislation." The Court went on to quote the sweeping language of the 1935 *Humphrey's Executor* case to the effect that "the fundamental necessity of maintaining each of the three general departments of government entirely free from the control or coercive influence, direct or indirect, of either of the others, has often been stressed and is hardly open to serious question."[1]

Despite these declarations of the mid-1980s, the legislative veto and equivalent informal arrangements have continued in the practical political world of joint construction. Between the time of the *Chadha* decision in 1983 and the end of 1990, over 200 new legislative veto provisions were passed into law under the signatures of Presidents Reagan and Bush. A legal purist might well wonder what is going on here. The answer is, an exercise in pragmatic accommodation to political realities, realities created in large part by the constitutional design itself.

One thing Congress did after the *Chadha* decision was to rewrite certain laws to eliminate legislative vetoes, thereby making life more difficult for executive officials seeking discretionary authority to act. For example, statutes on executive branch reorganization were changed to require the president to obtain approval from both houses of Congress for a reorganization resolution that would then be presented to the president for signature or veto. This was actually a more stringent hurdle for presidents than the earlier pre-*Chadha* situation when presidents had discretion to reorganize unless there was a resolution of disapproval passed by one house.

Formal amendments to statutes were less important, however, than post-*Chadha* reassertions of informal strings that Congress continued to tie to executive branch activities. For example, congressional appropriation committees have threatened to withdraw

[1]*Bowsher v. Synar*, 478 U.S. 714, 722, 725 (1986).

authority for particular executive agencies to transfer funds or exceed specified spending caps unless prior notification has been given to the committees and their approval obtained. Executive officials have generally agreed to such informal understandings as the price of the discretion they desire. They have proceeded just as if a legislative veto had been written into the laws.

The courts have acquiesced to this bypassing of the strict separation of powers doctrine laid down in the *Chadha* and *Bowsher* cases of the mid-1980s. Indeed, in recent decisions the courts have returned to the more traditional, pragmatic approach that accepts the political reality of overlapping powers. For example, the Supreme Court in 1988 ruled that the act authorizing the creation of independent counsels to prosecute high level executive branch officials was constitutional, even though the counsels investigating executive personnel are appointed by a panel of judges rather than the president and not removable except for good cause (rather than serving at the pleasure of the chief executive). As the Court put it, "We have never held that the Constitution requires that the three Branches of Government 'operate with absolute independence.' "[12] In a case the next year the Court went on to recommend "a flexible understanding of the separation of powers." Unlike the reasoning in the 1983 *Chadha* case, the Justices now observed that "the Framers did not require—and indeed rejected—the notion that the three Branches must be entirely separate and distinct." According to the Court, the Constitution created branches with "a degree of overlapping responsibility, a duty of interdependence as well as independence."[13]

DISTRUST, MICROMANAGEMENT AND FUDGED LEGISLATION

In retrospect we can now see that congressional delegations of rule-making power in the 1930s were accompanied by a good deal of faith in the efficiency of the bureaucracy and confidence that executive officials would carry out Congress's policy intentions. As the story of the legislative veto implies, since the 1960s that faith has largely disappeared and distrust between the two branches has grown. Typically the term used to identify what has been lost is "comity," a kind of mutual, courteous respect. Why has this occurred?

[12]*Morrison v. Olson*, 487 U.S. 654, 693 (1988).
[13]*Mistretta v. United States*, 488 U.S. 361, 380, 381 (1989). See more generally Harold J. Krent, "Separating the Strands in Separation of Powers Controversies," 74 *Virginia Law Review* 1253 (1988).

Trust depends on honesty. Of course a degree of deception and manipulation is nothing new in politics. But, starting with the Johnson administration and intensifying in the Nixon administration, there was a growing perception in Congress that the president and his representatives simply could not be counted on to deal in good faith with the legislature and the American public. This "credibility gap"—a term coined midway through the Johnson presidency—applied not only to the exceptional circumstances of high stakes politics, but also to the routine facts and numbers from the executive branch which Congress heretofore had counted on in order to do its legislative work. Information on the course of the Vietnam War, budget and spending transfers, conditions in the economy, implementation of congressional statutes, the Watergate affair, and a broad variety of other government concerns were seen as subject to self-serving political influences from the White House, and thus suspect.

Mistrust has in turn fed an explosion in congressional staffing to counter the growing presidential establishment. To enhance its own independent sources of information and give greater scrutiny—or oversight as it is called—to executive branch activities, Congress has produced a virtual revolution in the supply of people to support the work of Congress.[14] These additions to the political scene have been different from the folksy, political generalists that typically staffed the pre-1960s Congresses. The newer types of people are more likely to be young professionals, often well trained in the ways of policy analysis and interested in the substantive details of government programs. These interests and abilities can, of course, put the newer breed of congressional staffers into competition with the policy expertise claimed by executive branch officials, producing ever more intricate and arcane conflicts between executive and legislative bureaucracies.

Other developments undermining the chances for comity have also been at work. Certainly it has not helped that divided government, with one party controlling the White House and the

[14]New congressional agencies have been created (Office of Technology Assessment, 1974; Congressional Budget Office, 1975), the size of the Congressional Research Service quadrupled between 1960 and 1980, and, most dramatic of all, the number of persons employed in congressmen's personal offices rose from 3,556 in 1957 to 11,625 in 1985. The number working for the standing committees of Congress rose from less than 900 to over 3,000 persons in the same period. Standard accounts of these developments can be found in *The New Congress*, ed. Thomas Mann and Norman Ornstein (Washington: American Enterprise Institute, 1981); and in Nelson W. Polsby, *Congress and the Presidency* (Englewood Cliffs: Prentice-Hall, 1986).

other the Congress or at least one house of Congress, has become the norm in recent decades. In only five of the last 25 years (the Carter and Clinton administrations) have the presidency and both houses of Congress been controlled by the same political party. Nothing like this condition has ever prevailed for so long in American history, and it means that the natural institutional jealousies established in the Constitution's separation of powers are intensified by the overlay of divided partisan control.

Then too, the general trend in the same period has been toward a more ideologically strident politics. Evidence indicates that those who are active in the two political parties have increasingly grounded their political involvement in a concern for "the issues" and that the activists' attitudes toward policy issues have become increasingly polarized and "truly antagonistic" between the two parties.[15] To appreciate what has happened to the separation of powers, we need to understand the corrosive impact on working relations between the branches produced by this combination of deceit and mistrust, competitive staffing, divided government and ideological activism in the past 25 years.

At the same time, demands on government continued to grow. In order to deal with contemporary concerns about the environment, health, energy, education and many other matters, Congress has still found it necessary to delegate rule making and other powers. Distrustful that executive officials will vigorously carry out its legislation, however, Congress has often resorted to detailed instructions telling agencies when and how to enforce its laws—what its critics call "micromanagement."

Some modern conservatives critical of Congress have argued that if Congress cannot legislate in sufficient detail on a given issue, then what it is delegating was never legislative power in the first place but rather an attempt to usurp the executive function. This may be a reassuringly tidy view of government, but it immediately runs afoul of political reality. Congress has shown that if it wishes to, it can legislate in very great detail indeed, leaving executives little of the discretionary power they so highly value.

Trying to find the essence of the legislative or executive function is beside the point, if not positively counterproductive, in the political bargaining over policy. For example, the 1976 Resource Conservation and Recovery Act had delegated broad regulatory powers and general guidelines to the Environmental Protection

---

[15]See Warren E. Miller and M. Kent Jennings, *Parties in Transition: A Longitudinal Study of Party Elites and Party Supporters* (New York: Russell Sage Foundation, 1986), 167.

Agency for protecting the environment against hazardous wastes. After a series of highly publicized disasters such as Love Canal and clear evidence of EPA foot-dragging in implementing the 1976 Act, Congress passed a much different sort of act in 1984. The 1984 Hazardous and Solid Waste Amendments recaptured the regulatory role that had been delegated and did so by enacting a highly detailed policy framework with specific standards of protection, clear deadlines, and an implementation schedule studded with penalties that would take effect if the timetable was not met. All of these so-called "land ban hammers" were meant to counter the prevailing "bury and forget it" mentality in hazardous waste disposal and would strike unless EPA produced acceptable alternatives by a certain date. In the end EPA met the congressional deadlines. Purists, but not politicians, might wonder how a manifestation of the executive power had transmogrified to legislative power and back again.

Techniques for congressional micromanagement are legion. They include not only traditional budget controls and legislative veto-type provisions discussed earlier, but also reporting and certification requirements laid on executive agencies, mandated agency reorganizations, grillings of executive officials at congressional hearings, and many other methods. As power in Congress has become more decentralized into committees and subcommittees—a post-1960s reflection of more open participation by increasingly independent political entrepreneurs—the possibilities for more specialized and detailed congressional controls have become very great indeed. And this in turn has been made possible by and helped encourage the growth of congressional staff.

Despite the conventional wisdom, the results of this trend are not necessarily counterproductive for government policy. In the early 1990s, a panel of the National Academy of Public Administration selected ten important case studies to illustrate the nature and supposedly deleterious effects of congressional micromanagement. The cases ranged from the "land ban hammer" just mentioned to hospital reimbursement rules under Medicare, foreign arms sales, and international human rights policy.[16] All ten cases showed a shift from an original, broad delegation of authority under legislation passed in the 1940s, 1950s and early 1960s to much more detailed and continuous congressional guidance of the executive in the 1970s and 1980s. Often these changes were made after policy differences erupted between the branches, chronic ad-

[16]National Academy of Public Administration, *Beyond Distrust* (Washington: National Academy of Public Administration, 1992).

ministrative difficulties or crises occurred, and/or executive officials were perceived as failing to carry out the legislation as Congress had intended. But, to the surprise of the panel of management and academic experts, these cases showed that the results of congressional micromanagement were more sustained and constructive for the administration of policy than critics assumed.[17] That does not change the fact that, as a reflection of the increased distrust between the branches, micromanagement is one of two major characteristics more frequently found in legislation of the last 25 years.

The second characteristic affecting the overlap and separation of powers is what might be called "fudged legislation." It too is a response to a changed political environment. Since the early 1960s there has been a proliferation and mobilization of interest groups and policy networks, both those favoring and those opposing various forms of government activism. At the same time, legislative power in Congress has become more decentralized in the hands of congressmen whose political careers owe little to their party and almost everything to their personal campaign organizations and fund-raising capacities. The result has been an increase in the range of contending groups and in the number of available veto points, and an every-man-for-himself mentality in the legislative process. In order for anything to pass in this situation, legislation typically has to be "fudged," embodying a host of concessions that render the statute ambiguous if not contradictory on key points in order to assemble the unpredictable votes and pass through the numerous roadblocks.[18] For example, liberal pro-activist forces are likely to be strong enough to write broad language about purposes of the legislation and "rights" to a clean environment or access of the handicapped to various facilities. But other forces are likely to have to be appeased by special exemptions or qualifying language

[17]For example, congressional intervention pushed the Federal Aviation Administration to act on a new system for avoiding mid-air collisions, reduced the number of American arms that would have otherwise been sold abroad in volatile situations, and forced the Department of Energy to shift its focus from the production of high-level nuclear waste to public protection and environmental restoration in its disposal. Congress created new reporting and certification requirements that made the State Department give more attention to human rights records in foreign aid decisions and established a new technical capacity to advise on standardized formulae to control Medicare payments.

[18]See Martin Shapiro, "The Supreme Court from Early Burger to Early Rehnquist," in *The New American Political System*, 2d ed., ed. Anthony King (Washington: American Enterprise Institute, 1990), 47–85.

that sets down ambigious requirements for administrators' actions to be "reasonable," "cost-effective," "feasible," and the like.

Fudged legislation means that, although Congress has delegated legislative rule-making power, how that power is to be used is often open to a variety of plausible interpretations. Enter the courts. Challenges to the validity of agency decisions have mushroomed in the past 25 years, especially since much of the domestic legislation passed in this time literally invites disgruntled groups to litigate agency actions. Federal district and appeals courts in particular have become intimately involved in deciding what agency rules should look like, and when and how they should apply in areas of education, health, the environment and consumer safety, to mention just a few areas. In the name of assuring a fair rule-making process, judges have required agencies to develop and maintain thorough records of all the information that has gone into making a given rule. This record is then used by judges to take a close look at challenged agency decisions in light of statutes that, being both detailed and ambiguous, almost invariably point in several different directions. By such statutory review—deciding whether an agency action accords with congressional legislation and fair procedures—judges are frequently the final word on what action is "reasonable," and therefore what public policy is to be. Generally speaking, it is this statutory review of agency decisions, rather than the constitutional review of statutes under any separation of powers doctrine, that has thrown the federal courts into the middle of political squabbles about legislative versus executive control over policy.

Whether this trend helps the president or Congress depends on the ideology and policy preferences of judges as well as the distribution of partisan power in the executive and legislative branches. For example, a traditional constraint on judicial review of agency decision making has been deference to the presumed administrative expertise in the bureaucracy. But in the contemporary political environment, deference to administrative expertise has become a means for courts to make policy by determining whether agencies have used reasonable means to achieve reasonable results.[19]

Thus if Congress has become more involved in managing administration, it can also be said that the executive and courts have become more involved in lawmaking. The various threads might

---

[19]Abortion counseling is one of many such issues. See *Rust* v. *Sullivan*, 111 S.Ct. 1759 (1991).

be drawn together in the following way: The formal, constitutional separation of powers has in recent years occasionally been affected by legal doctrine expressed by the courts (*Chadha, Bowsher*). But usually a more pragmatic, flexible approach has prevailed as the courts have accommodated the executive/legislative politicking (joint construction) through which the meaning of the separation of powers has developed. Thus despite attacks on the constitutionality of the legislative veto, congressional micromanagement has continued. The political incentives to pass "fudged" legislation, however, have brought the courts to engage in widespread statutory review. This, and not constitutional review, has given judges an important policy-making role by allowing them to decide just what a congressional delegation of rule-making power to the executive requires and allows.

Is the System Working?

Fine, one might say. The durability of our basic institutional framework is admirable. And if stability-enhancing change is achieved in the everyday politicking through which the separation of powers evolves, that surely helps explain some of the durability. But we are now stuck in political gridlock, with policy stalemated between the branches of government. An immobilized, eighteenth century system is not working to solve the nation's problems.

Certainly there is no denying the widespread perception that our political system is not working as it should. But we ought to be careful not to leap to the conclusion that this sense of the system not working is necessarily associated with what has happened to the separation of powers. In many areas where people feel there is policy gridlock, the issues are immensely complex and difficult. Matters such as improving race relations, protecting the environment, reviving long-term economic growth, and so on, are not so much "problems" to be "solved" as they are collective nouns for an enormous web of challenges that have to be addressed again and again on one front after another in both government and civil society.

It is true that divided party government, which became the norm in the last 25 years, can intensify the political jealousies already inherent in the institutional separation of powers. With distrust already thriving, it has been easy for each side to play the blame-avoidance game and condemn the irresponsibility of the other. Divided party government was undoubtedly an important force preventing effective action on one of the country's mounting problems since the early 1980s—the budget deficit. On the other hand, unified party control of government may not have helped either, since there is little evidence that voters at state or national levels reward parties for balancing budgets.

We should be careful to look at the actual evidence before accepting any blanket indictment about the separation of powers and divided government producing an immobilized "system that doesn't work." In the first place, it is important to recall that the normal pattern in our political history is one of moving in fits and starts. Going back well before this century and continuing down to the present, one finds alternating and somewhat overlapping phases of activism, innovation and reform, followed by longer periods of inactivity, stock taking. and stalemate.[20] Congressional and executive coordination and productiveness are not the norm for our system. Stalemate is not the norm. But both alternating occurrences are.[21] Thus when we find ourselves in a period of inactivity we should not automatically conclude that the system is not working. We may need to look deeper into the longer-term dynamics of policy development and the if-at-first-you-don't-succeed rhythm. For example, after President Reagan's initial burst of legislative success during his first year in office, commentators spoke of the policy stalemate that seemed to persist year after year. Then at the end of the Reagan presidency, to almost everyone's surprise, the 100th Congress passed (among other things) a comprehensive tax reform that was supposed to be impossible, the most important reform of the welfare system in three generations, and the most sweeping change in immigration policy since 1965, not to mention major laws on trade policy, medical care and drugs.

In the second place, there is little evidence that divided party control of the executive and legislative branches has had the general effect of stalemating important government initiatives. A recent study has examined whether there is any systematic relationship between the frequency of two important types of government activity and the periods when party control of the two branches has been unified or divided.[22] The first such activity is highly publicized congressional investigations of misconduct in the executive branch, the theory being that in periods of unified party

[20]Arthur M. Schlesinger, Jr., *The Cycles of American History* (Boston: Houghton Mifflin, 1986); Kevin Phillips, *The Politics of Rich and Poor* (New York: Random House, 1990); and more generally, Albert o. Hirschman, *Shifting Involvements* (Princeton: Princeton University Press, 1981).

[21]See Nelson W. Polsby, "Political Change and the Character of the Contemporary Congress," in *The New American Political System*, ed. King, 29–30.

[22]David R. Mayhew, *Divided We Govern: Party Control, Lawmaking, and Investigations, 1946–1990* (New Haven: Yale University Press, 1991).

control there may well be a greater tendency to "hush up" such misdeeds. Of the 30 such investigations between 1947 and 1990, half took place in periods of divided party control and half during periods of unified party government. The second government activity is enactment of major legislation during the same period. Using a variety of expert and historical accounts, the study selected a total of 267 important enactments during the 1947–1990 period, ranging from the Marshall Plan of 1947–48 to the Clean Air Act of 1990. The conventional "stalemate" view would expect major legislation to be more difficult to pass in periods of divided party control. The reality is more complex, however. Periods of unified party control of the presidency and both houses of Congress averaged 12.8 enactments of important laws per Congress, while periods of divided government averaged 11.7 enactments. The difference is minor and can easily be accounted for by the technical artifact that in the 1980s (a period of divided government) important acts were more frequently folded into omnibus budget measures and therefore counted as only one enactment.

A third reason to question the stalemate thesis and slogans of congressional or presidential dominance comes from looking at the detailed legislative history of executive/legislative relations in the postwar period. One recent study has conducted such an examination for domestic policies, studying the intricate fates of some three hundred major legislative proposals submitted by presidents from the first year of the Eisenhower administration in 1953 to the midpoint of the Reagan administration in 1984.[23] The results do not show presidential dominance in the postwar period. Neither do they show congressional intractability. Rather the results indicate that both, and more, have occurred.

In about one-third of the cases, there was outright conflict where either the president defeated his opponents or his congressional opponents defeated him. In about one-quarter of the cases the president's proposals were accepted with little or no organized opposition, and in another quarter the proposals were simply ignored. In the remainder of the cases (19%) the result was a compromise where the president got some but by no means all of what he wanted. Looked at in another way, presidents from Eisenhower through Reagan seem to have pretty much gotten their way a little over one-third of the time when they submitted major domestic initiatives to Congress. Thus, as with activism and stalemate, neither

[23]Mark A. Peterson, *Legislating Together* (Cambridge: Harvard University Press, 1990). The 299 cases are a random sample, stratified by year, and drawn from 5019 presidential domestic proposals to Congress over these 31 years.

cooperation nor conflict has been the norm, but both together have characterized the legislative relationships between postwar presidents and Congress. The overall picture is hardly one of a system that is not working—unless one assumes all presidential proposals have to be enacted by Congress for the system to be judged effective. The mixed relationship that emerges in the data is what the Framers probably would have called "balance," where the separate institutions are at various times contending and cooperating in the work of government.

Within this overall picture, there is also evidence of the post-Sixties changes and declining comity noted earlier in our discussion. A combination of conflict and cooperation can be found in every administration, but shifts in the balance of congressional responses to presidential proposals are also apparent after the late 1960s. In the past 25 years or so, the overall shift has been toward more outright conflict, with the proportion of presidential proposals agreed to by consensus declining to zero by the end of Reagan's first term. In this more recent period, defeat by opponents in Congress has become somewhat more frequent, and clear presidential successes (i.e., cases in which a president prevails by consensus or by defeating opponents without major compromises) have become more rare.

Obviously the indicators we have been discussing are crude, but they do help fill in the sketch of what has happened to the separation of powers. The story these measures tell is consistent with a sense of diminished comity between the branches in recent decades, of more ideological and conflictual politics. Not only that, but the separation of powers system in this recent period has also had to operate in a context where the nature of many policy choices has been changing, quite apart from happenings in the political world. Since the early 1970s, American economic performance has lagged well behind what was achieved in the earlier postwar period. At the same time, demands on government to deal with ever more complex problems of technology, environmental side-effects, and the like have continued to grow.

In recent decades this more congested policy agenda, in a context of weak and intermittent economic growth, has forced more difficult zero-sum policy choices to the fore. The myriad of policy demands from newly mobilized groups has heightened the political agony of making tradeoffs between one policy goal, such as environmental protection, and another, such as jobs. The same applies to equal opportunity and affirmative action, worker protection and economic competitiveness, low taxes to spur the economy and decent public services to meet collective needs, and the list could go on. Not everything on the public agenda has moved in this direction, but enough has that it is scarcely any wonder that in recent decades the separation of powers system has reflected a politics that is more conflictual and confused.

Some have argued that the American separation of powers has exacerbated these policy problems and is virtually certain to produce a regime that does not work under modern circumstances.[24] By blurring any clear lines of accountability for what government does and making coordination of interrelated choices in the crowded policy agenda difficult if not impossible, the separation of powers is said to be a recipe for irresponsible government. Hard choices will be ducked, blame passed around like a beanbag, and incoherent courses of action will be the norm.

For a critique that is so often heard, there is remarkably little concrete evidence adduced as to the comparative responsibility and effectiveness of democratic governments based on a separation of powers system versus parliamentary governments of unified powers. One recent study has set out to gather and weigh such evidence.[25] Although the various findings in this exercise are complex, they lend little support to any claim that the separation of powers is an arrangement that does not work, or works significantly less well than democratic governments with unified executive and legislative powers. Using information from a variety of policy areas and different developed, democratic nations, the authors find a few general but very limited differences in the capabilities of the two broad types of government. For example, the study provides evidence that unified parliamentary institutions can, though not necessarily always will, do a better job than the American system of separation of powers in targeting resources in a coordinated industrial policy. On the other hand the study of environmental policy suggests that the American system has done somewhat better than parliamentary systems in representing diffuse, less well-organized interests in society. And when it comes to imposing losses on powerful groups, *any* form of government that can be held accountable to its people finds it very difficult to make the hard choices that impose losses.

---

[24]Lloyd N. Cutler, "To Form A Government," *Foreign Affairs* 59 (Fall 1980): 126–143; James L. Sundquist, *Constitutional Reform and Effective Government* (Washington: Brookings Institution, 1986).

[25]Kent Weaver and Bertrum Rockman, eds., *Do Institutions Matter?* (Washington: Brookings Institution, 1992). See also Thomas O. Sargentich, "The Limits of the Parliamentary Critique of the Separation of Powers," 34 *William and Mary Law Review* 679 (1993).

The evidence we have surveyed regarding whether or not the separation of powers "works" can hardly be regarded as definitive. But it should be enough to make the reader skeptical of easy conclusions that are often drawn from the conventional wisdom about "imperial" branches of government or "stalemate" throughout the system. Apart from the policy-making role of the courts, the mixed picture presented so far would probably not, could they see it, surprise many of the Founders. Certainly a system where there is a good deal of delay, but also periodic action, is something they expected. Likewise, being the practical politicians that they were, the Founders probably would not have found it particularly remarkable that postwar presidential domestic initiatives have continually faced a mixture of congressional responses ranging from conflict to cooperation. And if, as they thought in creating separate "departments" of government, "ambition [is] made to counteract ambition" and if "in republican government the legislative authority, necessarily, predominates" (*Federalist* 51), how could the Framers of the Constitution be surprised at the modern skirmishing over delegation and control that we have described?

As for the diffusion of responsibility and its apparently variable effect on policy-making capabilities, that too seems to speak to a durable vision of government.[26] The Founders were not in the business of creating a government guaranteed to "solve" particular policy problems. They wanted a government that could act when necessary, but almost nowhere was there to be the conclusive, preclusive power to act unilaterally. What some today condemn as the diffusion of responsibility, they commended as a protection against the concentrated and arbitrary abuse of power.

A SYSTEM NOT WORKING

There is, however, one area where serious doubts can be raised as to whether the separation of powers is working as intended. The relative roles of president and Congress in foreign policy generally and war making in particular have been hotly contested grounds, especially after the United States emerged as a world power following World War II. There is no space here to explore the topic fully, but the basic issues are too important to omit from the discussion.

In modern times essentially two contrasting interpretations have been invoked, and they find emblematic expression in two

[26]Charles O. Jones, "The Diffusion of Responsibility," *Governance* 4, no. 2 (April 1991): 150–67.

Supreme Court cases. According to one view, the president is supreme in foreign affairs, inherently possessing independent, implied, even "extra-constitutional" powers that are constrained only by what the Constitution expressly forbids. Those who believe that the dominant authority in foreign policy lies with the president rely on the 1936 Supreme Court decision in *United States* v. *Curtiss-Wright Export Corporation.*[27] In this case the Court not only upheld Congress's delegation to the president of broad discretionary power to impose criminal sanctions on arms sales (when in the president's view such sales would promote domestic violence in two warring South American countries). In his opinion for the Court, Justice Sutherland laid down a doctrine he had long argued when a United States Senator. In this view there was no excessive delegation of congressional power over foreign affairs because external sovereignty—the sole power of transacting with the outside world—had passed directly from Great Britain to the Union and the president as its representative.

The second view contends that there are no such inherent, extraconstitutional powers in the presidency and that the conduct of foreign policy is shared between the two branches, with the president the executive agent but Congress the basic lawmaker for both domestic and foreign affairs. Champions of this vision rely heavily on the 1952 Supreme Court case *Youngstown Sheet and Tube Co.* v. *Sawyer.*[28] While American troops were fighting in the Korean "police action," President Truman ordered the seizure of American steel mills to prevent a threatened nationwide strike from halting the flow of war materials to the Korean front. The president defended his action by claiming inherent powers as president and commander-in-chief, reasoning that directly descended from the doctrine of external sovereignty.

In its *Youngstown* decision, the Court vigorously rejected the president's action as an unconstitutional usurpation of legislative authority. Justice Robert Jackson, who as Franklin Roosevelt's Attorney General had supported numerous expansive uses of presidential power, wrote the concurring opinion which has come to be regarded as the classic statement of the pragmatic view of shared foreign policy powers. While not denying that the president has some powers to act alone, these were said to exist in only very limited areas (as in the Constitution's textually enumerated power unilaterally to recognize foreign governments). Beyond that, Jackson argued, the setting of broader foreign policy is conceived un-

---

[27] 299 U.S. 304 (1936).
[28] 343 U.S. 579 (1952).

der the Constitution as a concurrent congressional-executive
activity. The president's powers to act depend centrally on the degree of congressional endorsement of those actions and thus on
the political dialectic between the two branches. According to this
view, "Presidential powers are not fixed but fluctuate, depending
upon their disjunction or conjunction with those of Congress."[29]

Each of these two views has been vigorously contested in the
postwar period, both in the legal arena and in partisan political
debates. On balance, the outcome in the legal sphere during the
four decades following the *Youngstown* decision is fairly clear. The
Supreme Court, from Warren through Rehnquist (Robert Jackson's law clerk), has consistently deferred to presidential power
in foreign and national security affairs. In doing so, judges speaking for the Court majority have routinely invoked *Curtiss-Wright*
and its view of expansive executive authority in foreign affairs.
Whether or not the legal personification of the nation's sovereignty in the presidency strikes a blow at the heart of American
constitutionalism is a subject that can and should be debated.[30]

On the political front the picture is somewhat more mixed.
Under the Constitution the Congress obviously possesses and has
employed important powers over foreign affairs. This authority includes Senate ratification of treaties, the powers to raise and support the military forces, to lay and collect foreign trade duties, and
to regulate commerce with foreign nations, and the overarching
power to grant or deny funds to any aspect of foreign policy requiring government spending (which encompasses almost everything in the field).

Politically speaking, these formal congressional powers simply
provide the backdrop against which the two branches routinely
struggle over control of foreign policy. For example, presidents
have made increasing use of executive agreements with other na-

[29]Id. at 635–37. Jackson described a three-part version of this political dialectic.
First, presidential authority is at its maximum when the president acts with the authorization of Congress, for then he acts with all the authority possessed in his own
right as well as all that Congress can delegate. The president's power is at its lowest
ebb when his actions are incompatible with the expressed or implied will of Congress, for then he can count on only his own constitutional powers minus those
powers of Congress over the matter at hand. Finally, in between these two situations, there is a "zone of twilight" where Congress has neither granted nor denied
authority. Here too the president can rely only upon his own independent powers,
but such congressional inaction can, as a practical matter "enable, if not invite,
measures of independent presidential responsibility."

[30]Two informative recent surveys are Louis Henkin, *Constitutionalism, Democracy,
and Foreign Affairs* (New York: Columbia University Press, 1991); and Michael J.
Glennon, *Constitutional Diplomacy* (Princeton: Princeton University Press, 1991).

tions to accomplish their policy purposes without having to go through the Constitution's treaty ratification process in the Senate. Likewise, even when a ratified treaty exists, presidents in recent decades have undertaken to reinterpret or terminate existing treaties in order to accomplish their policy purposes without congressional participation.[31]

At the same time we have already seen how Congress has used its panoply of powers to intervene in foreign policy matters such as arms sales, human rights conditions attached to foreign aid, and humanitarian assistance to the Nicaraguan Contras. Likewise the distrust bred by Vietnam and nurtured by other revelations has led Congress to demand increased access to national security intelligence information. New requirements were put into place in the 1970s requiring executive intelligence agencies to keep newly created congressional intelligence committees "fully and currently informed" about their activities (including planned covert actions). Although these requirements were often circumvented in the 1980s, the contemporary Congress has vastly improved its access to secret national security information as compared with the situation 20 or 30 years ago.

Rather than in foreign affairs generally, it is in the use of military force that the separation of powers has become most seriously unbalanced in favor of the president. This has happened largely within the last half century. The capacities of the president to take the nation into armed hostilities and war itself have grown as a major postwar disjuncture in American history. If there is anywhere the system is broken, it is here.

Partisan affiliations of the moment can be counted on to generate strenuous debate about the appropriateness of any particular exercise of military power by a president. Some experienced participants in recent administrations simply dismiss the whole matter as a political issue to be settled one way or another by relative partisan strength.[32] If constitutionalism is to be taken seriously, however, we should try to rise above the expedient question

---

[31]Thus President Carter unilaterally terminated the nation's defense treaty with Taiwan (and was upheld in the 1979 Supreme Court decision of *Goldwater* v. *Carter*, 444 U.S. 996). President Reagan unilaterally terminated treaties involving relations with Nicaragua, membership in UNESCO and the compulsory jurisdiction of the World Court over American actions abroad. Thus too, the Reagan administration in 1985, contrary to what the Senate thought it had approved in a treaty, reinterpreted the 1972 Anti-Ballistic Missile Treaty so as to allow the initiation of the president's Strategic Defence Initiative (SDI) program.

[32]John Lehman, *Making War* (New York: Scribners, 1992).

of whose ox is being gored at any given time and think about the matter as if we did not know which party was in the White House.

On this subject the Founders' intentions for the separation of powers are about as clear as anything can be when it comes to original intent. The power to take the country into war should rest with the legislature, not the executive.[33] This break from British precedent, where powers of war and peace were said to rest with the executive, was explicit, self-consciously discussed, and widely accepted at the time the Constitution was adopted. The Constitution not only gave Congress the power to declare war. It also gave to the Congress and not the president the power to issue letters of marque and reprisal (authorizing military action by private citizens), to raise and regulate the armies and fleets, and to call forth the state militia.

Defenders of presidential prerogatives have argued that, in the constitutional debates, the Founders considered and explicitly rejected language giving Congress the power to "make" war and settled for the formality allowing Congress to "declare" war. Yet the evidence in the record is overwhelming that this wording change was viewed simply as a refinement that would permit the president to repel sudden attacks in case of an emergency—a reasonable precaution, given that Congress was expected to meet only once for a brief part of the year. No one at the time regarded this wording change as authorizing the president to commence war or engage in offensive military operations. Once Congress had taken the country into war, it was the president's job as civilian commander-in-chief to conduct and direct that war in the unified way required for effectiveness (*Federalist* 74).

Modern defenders of presidential war powers have also pointed to the numerous occasions throughout American history when presidents have engaged in military operations without congressional declarations of war. The favorite statistic invariably cited is that presidents have sent military forces to fight abroad more than 200 times, while there have been only five official declarations of war by Congress.[34] Any serious examination of the

[33]An excellent review is David Gray Adler's "The Constitution and Presidential Warmaking," *Political Science Quarterly* 103 (1986): 1–36.

[34]A recent example is the testimony of Secretary of Defense Richard Cheney in anticipation of the Gulf War, "Crisis in the Persian Gulf Region," Hearings before the Senate Committee on Armed Services, 101st Cong., 2d Sess. (1990). It is interesting to note that this list (originally with 85 entries) began to be kept in the summer of 1941, when Democratic senators sought evidence to defend President Roosevelt's dispatch of 80,000 American troops to Greenland and Iceland, relying

much cited list shows that it consists almost entirely of minor incidents (fights with pirates, chasing cattle rustlers across the Mexican border), distant military escapades unauthorized by the president, actions approved by Congress without a formal declaration of war, and so on.[35]

The few major incidents on the list give no support to modern defenders of a presidential prerogative power in this matter. What they in fact show is that in the time of the nation's greatest insecurity in the world—during the country's first several decades and Civil War—the war power was not considered exempt from the established constitutional system of checks and balances.[36] Only Congress was regarded as having the power to take the country into war. Thus, to take the most extreme example of presidential warmaking power, Lincoln admitted that his actions in the first months of the Civil War were beyond his constitutional authority and required the sanction of Congress. At the first opportunity Lincoln sought and gained that sanction on the explicit assumption that if any of his acts were illegal, they were certainly not beyond the constitutional competency of Congress. Legislation was passed legalizing the president's actions and orders "as if they had been issued and done under the previous express authority and direction of the Congress of the United States."[37] Here as in other instances on the list, presidents have never claimed authority, independent of Congress, to initiate and wage war. That claim has had to wait until our own postwar period.

The Korean "police action" was a major turning point. On June 25, 1950, the communist regime in North Korea invaded South Korea. On June 26 President Truman ordered American military forces to the assistance of South Korea. There was no formal defense treaty requiring such action, and it was only the next day, June 27, that the UN Security Council requested military assistance from UN member states to repel the attack. The president did not seek the approval of Congress, claiming instead to rely on his constitutional powers as president and commander-in-chief

---

on an executive agreement with Britain that circumvented Congress and its powers of treaty ratification. At this time it was conservative Republicans, such as Sen. Robert Taft, who attacked such presidential actions as unconstitutional, a situation that would be reversed in the 1980s.

[35]Francis Wormuth and Edwin Firmage, *To Chain the Dog of War* (Dallas: Southern Methodist University Press, 1986); Edward S. Corwin, "The President's Power," *The New Republic*, 29 January 1951, 15–16.

[36]Harold Hongju Koh, *The National Security Constitution* (New Haven: Yale University Press, 1990), ch. 3.

[37] 12 Stat. 326 (1861).

and acting, as Secretary of State Dean Acheson said on June 29th, "under the aegis of the United Nations."[38] Although presented to the public as a defensive action, the president's commitment of military forces was in clear violation of the congressional act that authorized American participation in the United Nations and of presidential assurances given at the time of the passage of that act.[39] A central feature of this law was the requirement that the president could commit armed forces to UN military actions only after authorization by both houses of Congress. This authorization was neither sought nor granted in the Korean conflict. Although Senator Robert Taft declared that Truman "had no authority whatever to commit troops to Korea without consulting Congress," efforts to restrict funding to terminate the conflict could not be passed, largely for fear of political retribution that would follow from not supporting "American boys abroad" fighting communist aggression. Leading presidential scholars sympathetic to the Democrats, such as Henry Steele Commager and Arthur S. Schlesinger, Jr., defended the legality of presidential war powers in a nuclear age threatened by communism.

President Eisenhower's uses of military force, as in the Formosa Straits and Lebanese crises, were all taken with the support of congressional authorizing legislation. But with Vietnam in the 1960s, presidential dissembling to Congress reached new heights (or lows). First under President Kennedy and then President Johnson, the number of "military advisers" that were secretly being used in combat roles in South Vietnam was gradually increased. In August 1964, minor North Vietnamese engagements with two American spy ships operating in the Tonkin Gulf were used as a pretext by President Johnson to order the first bombing of North Vietnam. The president then sought and gained overwhelming congressional support for the Tonkin Gulf Resolution, which offered broad support for presidential actions in Vietnam. When the president subsequently used the resolution as a blanket congressional authorization to launch and continually escalate a major ground war in Southeast Asia with U. S. forces, many in and out of Congress came to regard the Tonkin Gulf Resolution as a trick. By the end of the Johnson administration, both Professors Commager and Schlesinger had publicly apologized for their ear-

[38]*Department of State Bulletin* 23, No. 575, July 10, 1950, 43. An account is contained in Glenn D. Paige, *The Korean Decision* (New York: The Free Press, 1968), and elaborated in Edward Keynes, *Undeclared War* (Philadelphia: Pennsylvania State University Press, 1982).

[39]UN Participation Act of 1945, as amended in 1949.

lier endorsements of presidential war powers.[40] In 1970, President Nixon expanded secret strikes and military aid into Cambodia, using special funds and budget transfers without prior congressional approval.

Despite the increasing unpopularity of the war, it was only in 1973 and 1974 that Congress mustered the votes to enact legislation denying the use of funds for military operations in Southeast Asia. With resentment against the drift into an undeclared war at its height and the presidency reeling under the Watergate revelations, Congress sought to reassert its war powers. The 1973 War Powers Resolution, passed over President Nixon's veto, imposed requirements that the president report to Congress within 48 hours after introducing U. S. troops into areas where hostilities have occurred or "are imminent," as well as a 60-day limit on any such presidential commitment of troops without express congressional authorization to continue the deployment.

But this was hardly the end of the story. Denying the constitutionality of the War Powers Resolution, presidents since its passage have circumvented this and other congressional restrictions on military force and have done so with increasing boldness in the 1980s and 1990s. The circumventions have taken a variety of forms: engaging in covert, paramilitary operations that are not covered by the resolution; denying that hostilities are "imminent" where troops are sent; simply ignoring congressional reporting requirements; and using the resolution's 60-day time period as de facto permission for military operations that can be begun and completed within that period.

In a long succession of cases, the courts have steadfastly refused to enter disputes between the other two branches over warmaking powers. In doing so the courts have mainly relied on two arguments. First, such issues are considered "political" questions to be settled between the branches themselves. Second, the courts have argued that Congress, through its power over spending, has adequate means to remedy the situation should the legislature conclude that its power to declare war has been encroached upon.[41]

---

[40]Louis Fisher, *Constitutional Conflicts Between Congress and the President*, 3d ed. (Lawrence: University Press of Kansas, 1991), 251.

[41]See, for example, the legal challenges and decisions involving Reagan administration activities in El Salvador, Nicaragua and the Persian Gulf, respectively: *Crockett v. Reagan*, 558 F. Supp. 893 (D.D.C. 1982), cert. denied, 467 U.S. 1251 (1984); *Sanchez-Espinoza v. Reagan*, 568 F. Supp. 596 (D.D.C. 1983); and *Lowry v. Reagan*, 676 F. Supp. 333 (D.D.C. 1987).

Precisely as an attempt to use the spending power in this way, Congress passed the Boland amendments in successive appropriation acts between 1982 and 1986. Similar to earlier spending restrictions for military operations in Southeast Asia and Angola, the Boland amendments barred any "agency or entity of the United States involved in intelligence activities" from spending funds "to support military or paramilitary operations in Nicaragua." It was to circumvent this congressional constraint on presidential military operations that Reagan officials involved in the Iran-Contra affair raised money from abroad, transferred funds from the sale of arms to Iran, and essentially created a separate sub-branch of government operations outside the bounds of the Constitution. The historical contrast with extraconstitutional presidential conduct in times of truly great threats to national security is instructive. Lincoln publicly stepped outside the Constitution in circumstances that left him with no alternative if the Union was literally to avoid destruction, and almost immediately sought congressional sanction for his actions. The Reagan White House secretly went outside the Constitution simply to avoid legitimately imposed congressional constraints on military initiatives it wanted to take abroad, and never willingly disclosed anything to Congress or the public. Whatever precedents exist for the Iran-Contra affair lie wholly within our own postwar period and its pattern of presidential aggrandizement in the warmaking power.[42]

The Korean precedent was taken a step further in the 1991 Persian Gulf War with assertions of an inherent presidential authority to take the nation into major offensive operations without congressional approval and under UN auspices. In fact Korea appears to have been used to reassure White House decision makers about the legitimacy of their contemplated military offensive.[43] Following the Iraqi invasion of Kuwait in August 1990, President Bush began sending American military forces to the Mideast with the assignment of defending Saudi Arabia. Administration officials later acknowledged that there existed no official record, written or otherwise, "establishing the commitments of the United States for the defense of any of the Gulf nations, including Kuwait and Saudi Arabia."[44] In November 1990, the president doubled the size of American forces on the Arabian peninsula to half a mil-

[42]Koh, *The National Security Constitution*, chs. 2, 4.

[43]Bob Woodward, *The Commanders* (New York: Simon and Schuster, 1991), 357.

[44]Testimony of Assistant Secretary of State for Near Eastern and South Asian Affairs, "Relations in a Multipolar World," Hearings before the Committee on Foreign Relations, Senate transcripts, November 26–30, 1990, Pt. 1, 150.

lion persons, a capability specified as sufficient to wage an offensive attack. At the same time the Bush administration, rather than seeking authority from Congress, negotiated with other nations to obtain UN Security Council approval for the use of force against Iraq. The UN resolution that followed on November 29th authorized but did not require member nations to take all necessary means to enforce Security Council resolutions. From then on and throughout the Gulf War, the president and his representatives claimed that no further authorization, particularly from Congress, was required before launching an attack on Iraq.[45]

The courts briefly entered the scene on December 13th, when a U. S. District Court ruled on a lawsuit brought by 54 congressmen challenging Bush's power to attack Iraq without a congressional declaration of war. The Court refused to decide the issue at that time, partly on grounds that it was unclear that war was imminent and in part because a decision would be premature until the attitude of Congress had become known. However, in a departure from the usual contention that such issues were political questions beyond the courts' competence, the ruling foresaw that court action would appear to be the only available means of breaking a deadlock (should one develop between a majority of Congress and the president) and went on to reject sweeping claims of independent presidential war-making power put forward by the president's lawyers. The District Court ruling pointed out that if the president alone "had the sole power to determine that any particular offensive military operation, no matter how vast, does not constitute war-making but only an offensive military attack, the congressional power to declare war will be at the mercy of a semantic decision by the Executive. Such an 'interpretation' would evade the plain language of the Constitution, and it cannot stand. . . . The Court is not prepared to read out of the Constitution the clause granting to the Congress, and to it alone, the authority 'to declare war.' "[46]

Still denying that any congressional authorization was necessary, but possibly influenced by this court decision, the Bush administration on January 8, 1991, sought legislation supporting the president and a showdown was avoided when Congress voted on January 12th to authorize offensive actions against Iraq. But the assertion of inherent presidential power to take the country into

---

[45]The debate between the president's legal defenders and critics is joined in the Spring and Summer 1991 issues of *Foreign Affairs.*
[46]*Dellums* v. *Bush,* 752, F. Supp. 1141 (D.D.D. 1990).

war remained. In signing the authorizing legislation, President Bush declared that "my request for congressional support did not, and my signing this resolution does not, constitute any change in the longstanding positions of the executive branch on either the president's constitutional authority to use the Armed Forces to defend vital U. S. interests, or the constitutionality of the War Powers Resolution."[47] In his May 1991 commencement address at Princeton, President Bush elaborated his position, not only repeating the *Curtiss-Wright* doctrine, but going beyond it by in effect claiming inherent presidential power to decide when, if at all, to seek congressional approval or even inform Congress before using UN authorizations to attack a nation with which we are not at war. In Bush's words,

It is the president who is responsible for guiding and directing the nation's foreign policy. The Executive Branch alone may conduct international negotiations, appoint ambassadors, and conduct foreign policy. . . . The president also serves as commander-in-chief of our armed forces—as it was my role to do in the Persian Gulf.

This does not mean that the executive may conduct foreign business in a vacuum. I have great respect for congress and I prefer to work cooperatively with it *wherever possible*. Though I felt after studying the question that I had the *inherent power* to commit our forces to battle after the U.N. resolution, I solicited congressional support before committing our forces to the Gulf war. So while a President bears special foreign policy obligations, those obligations do not imply any liberty to keep Congress *unnecessarily* in the dark.[48]

The implication clearly is that it is up to the president to choose when or whether to involve Congress in the decision to go to war.

As everyone knows, American troops were quickly victorious, and the vital matter of war making under the separation of powers system was something in which ordinary Americans took virtually no interest. The issue has been left for another day. The troubling fact is that this is one area where Congress is poorly positioned to counterbalance the executive and protect its institutional responsibilities. When it comes to appeals for Americans to rally around the flag, presidents' influence on public opinion can be immense. Experience has also shown that presidents have an ability to ma-

[47]Weekly Compilation of Presidential Documents, 27, no. 3, 14 January 1991, 48.

[48]George Bush, "Remarks by the President at Building Dedication of the Social Sciences Complex," Press Release, Office of the Press Secretary, The White House, 10 May 1991, 2, emphasis added.

nipulate foreign events and back Congress into a corner in a way that is not possible in domestic affairs. All of this can easily have a debilitating effect on Congress's will to stand up in defense of its war-making power and can break the link connecting, as the Founders put it, "the interest of the man . . . with the constitutional rights of the place." (*Federalist* 51). Once the rigorous guardian against forays in presidential war making under FDR and Truman, conservative political opinion has by now traded places with liberal Democrats in supporting the notion of inherent presidential power in foreign and military affairs. Few people seem worried about the expedient, and perhaps Faustian, bargain that has recently enhanced presidential war powers by making American policy dependent on UN rather than congressional approval. A decent respect for American constitutionalism would seem to deserve something better.

CONCLUSION

Clearly there is no single or simple answer to the question of what has happened to the separation of powers. Where once the defining problem had been the potential instability of our republican political institutions, the problem now is conventionally seen as an excess of stability, to the point of immobilism.

In this discussion, however, we have seen reasons to be wary of the conventional slogans about stalemate or consistent dominance of one branch by another. No one has ever doubted that it is difficult to get things done in Washington, and it has probably become more difficult in the last 25 years or so. Institutional developments under the separation of powers system are only one complex part of an even larger, more complex picture of our public life. As a sharp observer of American politics observed some 50 years ago, "Our government works as it does, not entirely because the machinery is cumbersome, but rather because the propelling power is sporadic and the load is heavy."[49] The propelling power is ultimately the will of the people, in all its variegated, contradictory and differently organized forms. The load is the accumulation of public expectations on government and its congested legacy of policies and programs. To judge if the system is working we need to inquire about something deeper than the matter of whether or not government is "solving" any particular problem that you or I

[49]Pendleton Herring, *The Politics of Democracy* (New York: W. W. Norton, 1940), 408.

might care about. It is asking us to judge the state of American constitutionalism.

Taking the large view: In the bulk of our affairs, domestic and, to a lesser extent perhaps, foreign developments in the separation of powers seem to have flowed through fairly familiar constitutional channels—so long as we understand those channels in a politically pragmatic rather than narrowly legalistic way. What we find in domestic and much of foreign affairs is neither presidential or congressional dominance but a mixed picture, depending on time and circumstance. Certainly today's executive branch is more prominent in sharing in the legislative power than anything with which the Framers were familiar. And too, Congress's and the courts' interventions in the "execution" of the law is more extensive than they ever imagined. This should not be surprising or alarming since, as we noted, the Founders were much clearer on what the separation of powers was to prevent and how it was to prevent it than on how such a novel system would positively do its work. The overall "holistic" picture is one of a moving balance—both a checking and balancing, a separation and overlap between the spheres of government. As the Founders seem to have intended, it is a kinetic design where institutions must practice a relationship.

Where this portrait breaks down, I have suggested, is in the postwar shift in war-making powers toward the president. This is a contentious view. But in a post-Cold War era, when for the first time in its history the United States lacks a major foreign military threat—indeed when for the first time in all human history the world has one dominant military power, and that power supposedly a government of, by, and for the people—this is an issue to which more citizens should pay serious attention.

PART III

On Contemporary Practice

THE PARTY GOVERNMENT
SCHOOL OF THOUGHT
IN ACTION

William F. Connelly, Jr.

FOR CONSTITUTIONAL REFORMERS, the grass always seems greener on the other side of the fence. British parliamentary reformers frequently look longingly at the American "strong executive" model of governance, while American reformers regularly turn to the British (though not the Italian) model of parliamentary government. At least since Woodrow Wilson, "party government" reformers in the United States have sought to engraft disciplined or "responsible" British-style parties onto our constitutional system. Unfortunately for these would-be reformers, the "responsible party" ideal runs contrary to the Constitution's separation of powers. Worse yet, the reformers' dreams are often predicated on a fundamental misunderstanding of the separation of powers. Nowhere is this better seen than in congressional reform over the past fifty years.

Contrary to the party government reformers' understanding, the separation of powers makes Congress *more* effective as a legislature, not less effective as so often presumed. Institutional reformers frequently ignore this in their never ending efforts to improve Congress by trying to make Congress more like the executive or more like Parliament. The argument of this essay is simple: Congress is not the president, nor is it the British Parliament. Rather, congressional reformers should let Congress be Congress. Different institutions do different things. Institutional tinkerers should allow Congress to function as it is best designed to function: as a legislature, not as the executive. A case in point is the creation and evolution of party policy committees in the House of Representatives over the past five decades.

PARTY POLICY COMMITTEES IN CONGRESS

House Democrats and House Republicans both established party "steering committees" during the Progressive Era, yet the LaFollette-Monroney Joint Committee on the Reorganization of Congress in 1945 concluded that such steering committees "seldom meet and never steer." The LaFollette-Monroney Joint Committee recommended creation of formal seven-member party policy committees "for the determination and expression of policy." The Joint Committee clearly reflected the arguments of party government academic reformers at the time. In retrospect, the party policy committees represent a major failed experiment in party government, a failure due in large part to the reformers' misunderstanding of the Founders' separation of powers.

Congress organizes itself for action along two distinct, and perhaps contradictory, lines: party and committee. Each Congress begins with the election of party leaders by Democrats and Republicans in the House and Senate. These include the Speaker of the House and the President pro tempore of the Senate, as well as the Majority and Minority Leaders of the two chambers. Each Congress also sees the election or re-election of the chairs of the standing (or permanent) legislative committees. Generally, chairmen are re-elected in deference to the principle of seniority, although on occasion more junior members revolt and replace the most senior majority party member of the committee with a "younger" chair.

Party leaders and committee leaders often conflict. Dan Rostenkowski (D-IL), the powerful Chairman of the House Ways and Means Committee, rarely kowtows to his party's leaders. Likewise, the late Silvio Conte (R-MA), as Appropriations Committee Ranking Member (or Vice-Chairman, as Republicans like to say), was known for his independence from the dictates of his more conservative fellow House Republicans. Party leaders have little control over the electoral fate of congressmen; hence committee leaders—and for that matter, rank-and-file committee members—often exhibit little allegiance to the party line. Party policy committees were originally designed to bridge this gap between party and committee organization by promoting (to call it "enforcing" or "ensuring" would be too strong) greater party discipline. In a manner of speaking, party policy committees fell between the stools of party and committee organization of Congress.

What are the party policy committees? They are *not* the bipartisan standing legislative committees known as the "workshops" of Congress. Indeed, the party policy committees (or "policy committees") stand outside the normal stream of the legislative process. There are four policy committees, one for each party in each chamber: the House Republican Policy Committee (HRPC), the House Democratic Steering and Policy Committee (HDSPC), the Senate Republican Policy Committee (SRPC) and the Senate Democratic Policy Committee (SDPC). All four have their roots in the responsible party school reforms of the 1940s.

Policy committees are part of the party leadership organizations in each chamber. The party apparatus for the majority party in the House (the Democrats for the past four decades) includes the Speaker, the Majority Leader, the Whip, the party caucus, the House Democratic Steering and Policy Committee, and the Democratic Congressional Campaign Committee. A parallel organization, minus the Speaker, exists among House Republicans: the Minority Leader, the Whip, the Republican Conference (caucus), the House Republican Policy Committee, the Research Committee, and the National Republican Campaign Committee.

The two House policy committees have roughly similar memberships. For example, the House Republican Policy Committee has thirty-four members, including eight ex officio party leaders, four designated ranking members of key standing committees, eight regional representatives, ten appointed members-at-large, and two members each from the two most recently elected classes. Curiously, the regional representatives are perceived as the core of the House Republican Policy Committee; at-large members provide balance, including additional geographic balance. The thirty-one member House Democratic Steering and Policy Committee includes twelve regional members, thus emphasizing geographic balance even more than the Republicans. The size and composition of the two Senate policy committees, however, does not matter since they never actually meet as such.

What purpose do the policy committees serve? The original reformers hoped the party policy committees would help promote greater party discipline. Historian George Galloway wrote in 1953 that the reformers' intentions were to create a leadership committee "to plan the legislative program, coordinate and guide committee activity, focus party leadership, and strengthen party responsibility and accountability."[1] In other words, the intent was to create executive committees for the parties in each chamber and for coordination between chambers. In effect, the House majority party policy committee was meant to act as a "domestic council" for the Speaker of the House.

[1] George Galloway, *The Legislative Process in Congress* (New York: Thomas Y. Crowell Company, 1953), 602.

Ideally, from the reformers' perspective, a policy committee should: (1) *analyze* the substance of issues, in order to (2) *advocate* party positions, (3) engage in proactive legislative *clearance* including *tracking* and *scheduling*, (4) determine party floor *strategy* and *tactics*, and finally, (5) *coordinate* floor and electoral strategy. Such analysis, advocacy and clearance activities would require policy committees to be actively involved in the legislative process early enough so as to guide, rather than be guided by, the standing committees. In addition, congressional party policy committees ideally should coordinate bicameral House and Senate party efforts, and, in turn, coordinate legislative party policy efforts with the executive branch.

Today party policy committees do not seem to meet the ideals of the original reformers. The first function, long range issue analysis, is done largely by the standing committee system. The powerful House Rules Committee and Senate leaders exercise the third function, legislative clearance. The party Whip operations determine floor strategy. And, to the extent function five is done at all, coordination of floor and electoral strategy is the domain of the independent congressional campaign committees. Intraparty coordination between chambers and between branches is primarily a function of the Leaders' offices and not the policy committees. Function two, advocating party positions, is the responsibility of the House party policy committees, though the timing of such advocacy limits its efficacy.

The policy committees in the House meet just before legislation reaches the floor and sometimes place their imprimatur on a bill, while issuing a (usually one page) "policy statement" articulating the rationale for supporting or opposing the bill. Coming this late in the legislative process, after a bill has incubated in committee, seriously limits the effectiveness of such policy committee advocacy. Many, and perhaps most, members have taken a position on legislation before the policy committees have had a chance to act. Two Congress scholars, Lawrence Dodd and Bruce Oppenheimer, note that the "lofty goals" for the House Democratic Steering and Policy Committee of "long-range scheduling and setting legislative priorities and goals for committees and subcommittees . . . often are neglected as the leadership finds itself under the day-to-day press of legislation."[2]

In the Senate, the policy committees do not advocate legislation; rather they act as reservoirs for leadership staff, and they

---

[2] Lawrence C. Dodd and Bruce I. Oppenheimer, eds., *Congress Reconsidered*, 3d ed. (Washington, D.C.: CQ Press, 1985), 59.

host weekly "policy committee lunches" on Tuesdays when Senators congregate in an informal, off-the-record format to discuss the week's legislative business. Each of the four policy committee staffs occasionally produces long-range studies. The House Democratic Steering and Policy Committee does exercise one very important function, namely acting as the party's "committee on committees." Each party's "committee on committees" allocates to members their standing committee assignments. Such a responsibility, exercised at the beginning of each Congress, thus makes service on the HDSPC desirable. Nevertheless, the HDSPC is not the Rules Committee, and it does not play the gatekeeper function envisioned by reformers.

Ultimately, the party policy committees are of marginal consequence. They are certainly not the central locus of party activity as intended by the reformers. Indeed, the reformers failed to produce policy committees that make policy. The evidence to support this conclusion is overwhelming.

EMPIRICAL EVIDENCE OF FAILED PARTY GOVERNMENT REFORM

Contrary to the postwar party government reformers' intentions, Congress today remains more a committee-centered, than a party-centered, decision making process. The permanent standing committees, especially in the House, play a much more significant role in policy making than do the party policy committees. Two earlier academic studies, one by Charles O. Jones in the 1960s and the other by Evelyn Schipske in the 1970s, both concluded that the policy committees are weak, ineffective and reactive.[3] My research interviews during the 1980s with policy committee members and staff elicited the common observation that the reformers' intentions were "naive," or a "waste of time," and that the reformers basically "misunderstood the character of Congress." Indeed, some members laughed when told of the original aspirations for the policy committees.

One former policy committee chairman went so far as to suggest that his policy committee position served little useful purpose other than providing another "leadership slot." For this reason, all four policy committees tend to be, in the words of another chairman, "creatures of the chairman." The policy committees take on

---

[3]Charles O. Jones, *Party and Policymaking: the House Republican Policy Committee* (New Brunswick: Rutgers University Press, 1964), and Evelyn G. Schipske, "Policy Statements and Policy Making," U.S. Congress, House Republican Policy Committee files, 1974.

the personality of the chairman, and policy committee staff clearly work for the chairman, not for the party or its membership.

The policy committees have evolved away from the reformers' original plan. Far from being the seven-member executive committees envisioned, the policy committees quickly grew in size. When first created, the House Republican Policy Committee consisted of twenty-one members, and today stands at over thirty. As noted above, HRPC membership currently includes eight party leaders, four standing committee ranking members, four recent class representatives, eight regional representatives, and finally, ten "at-large" members added *not* for party discipline, but for "balance." Balance includes considerations of ideology, geography, standing committee representation, and generational equity. Again, the perceived core of the policy committees is the regional representation, reflecting the local or parochial nature of congressional elections. The ex officio and at-large standing committee representation reflects the reality of a committee-dominated decision making process in Congress.

Representing diversity. The local or parochial orientation of Congress differentiates our national legislature from the British Parliament. For Congress, local concerns typically supersede ideational concerns; that is, parochial interests commonly take precedence over ideology or party principle. Congress's strength as a legislature is rooted in its particularity, which may be appropriate given the conditions and circumstances of the American political culture. Alexis de Tocqueville, the author of the classic *Democracy in America,* notes that different forms of government may be appropriate or inappropriate for a nation depending on its history, circumstances and political context. Our separation of powers system may be a more fitting form of representative democracy for the United States than a pure parliamentary form of government, especially given the enormous diversity of the country.

Richard Fenno, possibly the foremost contemporary scholar of Congress, recognizes the virtue of the institution's diversity. Fenno's research for his book *Homestyle* included extensive travel with members in their districts. He concluded that "any claim by anybody to have a feel for the whole country would be preposterous. For ill or good, no one can comprehend the United States. . . . Only institutionally, not individually, can it be done."[4] The particularity of Congress and the tendency of its members to reflect parochial interests may be virtues rather than weaknesses of our

[4]Richard F. Fenno, Jr., *Homestyle* (Boston: Little, Brown & Company, 1978), 293.

legislative process. Party government reformers, with their desire to create a legislative process more inclined to reflect broad national concerns or broad ideological differences, may be ignoring the insights of Tocqueville and Fenno. The evolution of party policy committees in Congress suggests that despite reformers' good intentions, the nature of Congress remains a function of the founding fathers' understanding of the separation of powers and federalism.

Short term focus. Further evidence that party policy committee reforms failed to create disciplined party government can be seen in the short term, reactive character of the current policy committees. Policy committee success at influencing legislation, including the issuing of "policy statements," is marginal at best, in part because of the timing of such efforts late in the legislative process. Also, the flow of information, from standing committees *to* the policy committees, is telling. Senate policy committee staff organize weekly sets of meetings, first with standing committee staff directors, and then with the legislative directors from Senators' personal staffs. Up-to-date information crucial to the press of legislative business then flows from the standing committees to the policy committees and on to members' staffs. Policy committee staff are in no position to direct the standing committee staff in molding legislation; at best, the policy committee staff act as facilitators and disseminators of standing committee information. Little in the way of long-range policy analysis occurs at the above meetings.

The absence of any serious role for the policy committees in legislative clearance is further evidence of the failure of responsible party reformers. A thirty-year old observation by Hugh Bone about the Senate policy committees holds true for all four policy committees today:

Some have compared the policy committees with the House Rules Committee. In terms of legislative scheduling, this in not an apt comparison. The latter enjoys the status of a standing committee with authority to issue specific rules, impose limitations, and bottle up measures; the policy bodies possess none of these powers. Scheduling in the real sense of the word involves discussion of strategy, decision as to sequence, and consideration of timing. Neither policy committee, as a committee, appears to have gone into these matters with any degree of regularity.[5]

[5]Hugh Bone, *Party Committees and National Politics* (Seattle: University of Washington Press, 1958), 181.

The Rules Committee in the House, and the Majority and Minority Leaders in the Senate through the unanimous consent process, hold primary responsibility for legislative clearance and scheduling. In this regard, the party policy committees play a secondary role at best.

Even what the policy committees do *not* do tells us much about the limitations of party government reform. First, the policy committees do *not* take positions on most legislation that passes through Congress, because most legislation does not involve questions of party principle. Second, the policy committees are limited in that they react to bills rather than issues. This is reflected in the fact that the "policy statements" policy committees issue just before some bills reach the floor are seen as more important than the policy research papers their staffs occasionally produce. By implication, short range efforts to discover existing party consensus take precedence over long-range efforts to build such consensus. As Charles O. Jones noted in his 1964 study of the House Republican Policy Committee, "Long range policy studies—designed to develop consensus among party members on policy alternatives—are not only difficult to produce, given the present structure and resources of congressional political parties, but also difficult to have accepted and understood by party members. Further, and potentially more important, this procedure represents a significant departure from, and a direct challenge to, the existing standing committee seniority system."[6]

Bicameralism. Additional evidence on the limitations of party government reform can be seen in the lack of cooperation, and even sympathy or understanding, between the House and Senate policy committees of the same party. The staffs of the two Democratic policy committees seemed fairly ignorant of the workings of each other, despite the fact that two decades earlier the SDPC had assisted in rejuvenating the HDSPC. A similar lack of understanding was reflected in a SRPC staffer's praise for the "discipline" of the House Republican Policy Committee—praise that most House Republicans would not recognize as applying to them. In turn, HRPC members and staff actually expressed delight during interviews at the loss of majority status by their fellow Senate partisans in 1986. Republicans in each chamber saw the minority or majority burdens they bore as relatively greater than that of their counterparts in the other chamber. In general, the interviews

---

[6]Jones, *Party and Policymaking*, 155.

revealed a remarkable lack of bicameral sympathy between fellow Republicans.

Seventy-five years ago, Robert Luce complained that the lack of "harmonious cooperation for the public welfare" between the House and Senate "is the most serious defect in the machinery of Congress."[7] This "defect," however, was intentional on the part of the Framers of the Constitution. In *Federalist* 51, Madison observed that in a republican government "the legislative authority necessarily predominates." He went on to suggest, however, that "the remedy for this inconveniency is to divide the legislature into different branches; and to render them, by different modes of election and different principles of action, as little connected with each other as the nature of their common functions and their common dependence on the society will admit."[8] Reformers since the Progressive era have sought to overcome this "defect" in our national legislature. In 1946, for example, the LaFollette-Monroney Committee recommended joint House and Senate policy committee meetings, a prescription which has been largely ignored in practice. Why this disagreement between reformers' intentions and Congress's practice?

The original policy committee reformers may have misunderstood Madison's intent in creating a bicameral legislature. Madison sought not simply to "weaken," but also to strengthen Congress as an institution. Clearly, as seen in the above quotation, Madison saw bicameralism as a means of limiting legislative power relative to the executive branch. But he also saw bicameralism as a way to strengthen the legislative function. In principle, a legislature should represent and deliberate. Two chambers chosen "by different modes of election" can better represent, albeit somewhat redundantly, the needs of their constituents. Furthermore, two chambers motivated by "different principles of action" will inevitably clash. House and Senate conflict and competition will just as inevitably augment the twin virtues or functions of any democratic legislature, namely public deliberation and consensus building. Walter Kravitz argues, for example, that "reasonable consensus, not efficiency, is the measure of congressional effectiveness in policymaking."[9]

[7]See Walter Kravitz, "Relations Between the Senate and the House of Representatives: The Party Leaderships," U.S. Congress, Commission on the Operation of the Senate, *Policymaking Role of Leadership in the Senate*, 94th Congress, 2d sess. 1976, Committee Print, 121.

[8]Alexander Hamilton, James Madison, and John Jay, *The Federalist Papers*, introduction by Clinton Rossiter (New York: New American Library, 1961), 322.

[9]Kravitz, "Relations Between the Senate and House of Representatives: The Party Leaderships," 132.

Bicameralism accounts in part for the differences in the evolution of the four party policy committees. The obstacle bicameralism raises to cooperation and coordination within and between parties occurs not simply because this "defect" limits congressional efficiency, as is so often assumed by successive generations of reformers. Rather the policy committees have failed to bridge the gap between the two chambers because bicameralism succeeds in making Congress more effectively representative of our enormous diversity as a nation and more deliberative in adjudicating among our differing interests and opinions. Perhaps party policy committees have not been successful because Congress does not need them in order to be effective at representing and deliberating. Indeed, strong party policy committees might conceivably weaken congressional representation, deliberation, and consensus building.

Separation of powers paradox. The final evidence of the failure of policy committee reform takes the form of an observation that, on first blush, appears counterintuitive. Party policy committees in Congress are strongest when in opposition to a president of the other party; their role fades when confronted with a president of their own party. For example, during the Reagan presidency, the House and Senate Republican Policy Committees were less assertive than during the Carter years. One Republican congressman observed that the House Republican Policy Committee "is very inhibited when there is a Republican president in the White House" and "much more aggressive and free-wheeling when there is a Democrat in the White House." Former Senate Republican Policy Committee chairman John Tower acknowledged that following the 1976 election, "I felt that with the Republicans out of the White House, I wanted to do more to arrive at Republican positions here in Congress. During the Republican Administration, of course, we were generally taking the initiative from the White House."[10] The implication here may be that partisan or programmatic policy initiative may best reside with the president.

FAILURE OF PARTY GOVERNMENT REFORM

In neither chamber do party policy committees play an aggressive proactive role in legislative analysis or clearance as intended by the original reformers. House policy committees may be mar-

---

[10]Christopher J. Bailey, *The Republican Party in the U.S. Senate* (New York: St. Martin's Press, 1988), 88.

ginally more involved than their Senate counterparts in explicit advocacy by adopting policy statements. Conversely, Senate policy committees may be more significantly engaged, through party leader consultations during Policy Lunches, in legislative clearance. Nevertheless, neither House nor Senate policy committees match the reformers' ideal. The analysis and advocacy role of standing committees dwarfs that of all the policy committees. Similarly, the scheduling and clearance role of the Rules Committee in the House, and party leader consultation in the Senate, largely preempt any significant role in this area for the policy committees. The flow of legislative business remains largely determined by standing committee activity. Limited policy committee involvement in legislative clearance or scheduling and in analysis or advocacy serves the purpose of accommodating standing committees, more than it does the original reformers' hope of directing policy.

The policy committees have not fulfilled the original reformers' dreams; they remain the creatures of a decision-making process dominated by the standing committees. The legislative process is not policy committee centered. Instead, it is diffused and dispersed throughout a larger institution that is, in turn, influenced by its environment. Committees within, and congressional elections without, limit the effectiveness of the four party policy committees. The legislative process invites the demand for party government at the same time that it thwarts the same.

CONCLUSION: THE SEPARATION OF POWERS

The original policy committee reforms failed because the party government reformers fundamentally misunderstood the nature of the separation of powers. The "checks and balances" are not all there is to the separation of powers. The separation of powers does not merely limit the abuse of power; it also provides for the effective use of power. Congress is a powerful national legislature because of the institutional independence afforded by the separation of powers. The institutional independence or separation of Congress from the executive means that as a legislature it has more affirmative responsibility for policymaking than its counterpart in a parliamentary system. Michael Mezey's definitive work, *Comparative Legislatures*, concludes that the United States Congress is the only major national legislature that clearly exercises an active, policymaking role.[11]

---

[11]Michael Mezey, *Comparative Legislatures* (North Carolina: Duke University Press, 1979), chs. 1 and 12.

Different Institutions Do Different Things. Herbert Storing understood that the separation of powers is "not aimed primarily at mutual checking but at the efficient performance of certain kinds of tasks," based on the assumption that "all governments perform certain kinds of functions, which are best performed in distinctive ways and by distinctive kinds of bodies."[12] For example, making general laws requires a detailed knowledge of the diverse interests, opinions, and passions of the people; many representatives, frequently elected, can do this better than one individual, especially if they deliberate in open session. On the other hand, "executive action" is more naturally the preserve of one person, especially if it requires "energy, secrecy and dispatch." Similarly, the judiciary is more judicious for being independent and appointed, not elected, for what amounts to life tenure. The structure of institutions and their "different modes of election" determine what kind of power or function each can best exercise.

Congress is more democratically responsive because of its independence from the executive. Members are better able to represent the particular needs of their constituents, and the frequency of elections requires that they do so. But if the separation of powers makes Congress more responsive, it also makes it more responsible for national policy. Unlike a parliamentary system, Congress cannot force a consensus. If, for example, a general consensus on how to solve the budget deficit is lacking, Congress cannot create such a consensus. In this sense, Congress is more responsive to the whole as well as the parts. But at the same time Congress is designed to be more responsive, it also has more independent responsibility for policy making. Only in our separation of powers system could the legislature, for example, declare the executive's annual budget proposal "dead on arrival."

The functional separation of powers means that the two "political branches" can compete while they complement one another. The competition between the president and Congress introduces more energy into the policy process.[13] The competition also invites

---

[12]Herbert J. Storing, *What the Anti-Federalists Were For* (Chicago: University of Chicago Press, 1981), 60.

[13]Nelson Polsby argues that the separation of powers adds, rather than subtracts, energy from the political process. He concludes that there are "incentives to search for innovations" which are "incorporated into the constitutional routines of the American political process as they affect the ambitions of politicians—routines associated with the electoral cycle and routines associated with the separation of powers." *Political Innovation in America: The Politics of Policy Initiation* (New Haven: Yale University Press, 1985), 165.

a more open and public deliberation between the branches, which in turn invites greater policy responsiveness. But the separation of powers also accounts for a greater need for Congress to be responsible, as well as responsive. Congress is a more powerful legislature with national responsibility because of its independence from the executive. Unlike parliamentary legislatures, Congress never surrenders its responsibility to the executive. Because the separation of powers removes the executive from exercising decisive control over the legislative process, Congress needed to develop its own internal devices for fulfilling its responsibility.

Standing Committees in Congress. The congressional committee system stands as the most enduring, and perhaps most successful, effort to fill the "vacuum" caused by the severing of executive and legislature in a separation of powers system.[14] The committee system also remains the single most significant internal factor limiting the party policy committees. The reforms establishing the policy committees have not enabled party leaders to assume a more assertive posture in dealing with the standing committees. Smith and Deering concluded that party leaders "are not in a position, except in isolated cases, to direct either committees or their caucuses in a concerted action to develop coherent party policy."[15] Even when party leaders are able to assert themselves, such as with Howard Baker's Senate Republicans following the 1980 election, committee politics eventually reasserts itself.

Why does Congress remain, much to the frustration of generation after generation of reformers, a committee-centered decision-making process? Perhaps it is because the committee system offers a fitting "solution" to the "defect" of the separation of powers. The committee-based legislative process enables Congress to shoulder effectively its affirmative national institutional responsibility as a co-equal branch *and* it allows Congress to be highly responsive to diverse interests. An effective committee system allows Congress to compete effectively with the executive. The committee system also invites a specialization and division of labor that arguably augments the deliberative character of the legislative process. The same committee system that allows narrow interests to influence legislation also concentrates the expertise of members and staff.

[14]David E. Price, "Congressional Committees in the Policy Process," in *Congress Reconsidered*, 3d ed., ed. Lawrence C. Dodd and Bruce I. Oppenheimer (Washington, D.C.: CQ Press, 1985), 165, 168 and 175.

[15]Christopher J. Deering and Steven Smith, *Committees in Congress* (Washington, D.C.: CQ Press, 1984), 259.

Moreover, committees must be responsible to the parent chamber. The overall process can "refine and enlarge the public views."[16]

The original reformers correctly identified the essential defect of our legislative process: congressional party discipline is difficult, not to say impossible, in a separation of powers system. For this reason, hope for reform springs eternal among so-called party government reformers: they are forever attempting to patch over this "defect" with one artifice or another. But such reforms, including the policy committees, are doomed, not because they fail to identify the weakness of the separation of powers, but again because they fail to appreciate the strengths of the separation of powers. The separation of powers makes Congress more responsive to its electoral environment *and* it makes Congress more institutionally responsible for national policy. The separation of powers makes Congress more dependent on electoral pressures *and* more in need of cooperating with the executive. As a result, the party policy committees are epiphenomenal; they cannot overcome the limitations placed on them by the constitutional design of Congress. The parochial, pragmatic, and incremental character of Congress may always frustrate the burning desire of policy intellectuals for sweeping political change.

The function, the virtue, and "the genius of Congress is democracy, diversity, debate. . . . Congress nurtures creativity."[17] Congress needs the president, the public, and the pressure groups to make policy. That need is the strength of Congress, not its weakness. Congress is a pluralistic institution responding to a pluralistic environment. Congressional reforms should be based on an understanding of the institution's strengths and weaknesses. At best, structural reforms may augment Congress's ability to represent, deliberate, and build consensus. Reforms can no more artificially impose consensus than can Congress.

Divided Government. Today we hear that Americans are deeply frustrated with the partisan gridlock that prevents solutions to enduring problems such as the burgeoning budget deficit. Some blame the separation of powers and call for constitutional reform. Divided government, however, is not fundamentally a constitutional problem. We have not always had policy gridlock, though we have always had the separation of powers. Why then the gridlock?

The president and Congress have not solved the budget deficit for two basic reasons. First, there is no consensus in the country as

---

[16]*Federalist* No. 10, 82.

[17]I.M. Destler, "Executive-Congressional Conflict in Foreign Policy: Explaining It, Coping With It," in *Congress Reconsidered*, ed. Dodd and Oppenheimer, 345.

to how to eliminate the deficit—whether, for example, to raise taxes or cut entitlement programs. Second, divided government is an artificial condition caused, in part, by the last round of misguided reforms in Congress. In the name of a "more open and more democratic" Congress, reformers in the early 1970s attacked the committee system. Reformers weakened "committee government" by, in effect, creating "subcommittee government," and thus made Congress even less manageable than usual. At the same time, reformers weakened political parties by means of campaign finance reform and they liberated individual members of Congress from the parties by, among other things, increasing members' staff budgets and the perquisites of office. The incumbency advantages that reformers voted themselves in effect froze into place the Democrats' dominance of Congress following the Watergate scandal. Today's congressional scandals may be directly attributable to the "reforms" of the early 1970s. Perhaps it is time to reform the reforms.

Congress and the Separation of Powers Today: Practice in Search of a Theory

L. Peter Schultz

Introduction

"Congress bashing" is, undoubtedly, one of the more interesting and abiding features of the dialogue that surrounds the American political order. Although some might think that this practice is recent or that it has reached new heights in recent times, as with President Bush wanting to make Congress the centerpiece of his 1992 reelection campaign, clearly this is wrong. "Congress bashing" has been a favorite pastime of Americans for a very long time. Mark Twain once quipped: "It could probably be shown by facts and figures that there is no distinctly American criminal class except Congress." Will Rogers said, "Congress is the best money can buy," a statement that Mark Green and Ralph Nader would agree with.[1] And Woodrow Wilson, the only political scientist elected to the presidency, began his career with a critique of what he called "Congressional Government."[2] So, despite the impression that criticism of Congress is something new, such criticism is a venerable part of American political discourse. Even President Bush's complaints about Congress and his assertion that Congress should just "go home" and let him "govern" is nothing new. We need only

---

[1] The Mark Twain and Will Rogers quotations are found in Mark Green, *Who Runs Congress?* 4th ed. (New York: Dell Publishing Co., 1984), 21, 221. See also Nelson W. Polsby, "Congress Bashing for Beginners," *The Public Interest* (Winter 1987): 15–23.

[2] Woodrow Wilson, *Congressional Government* (Baltimore: Johns Hopkins University Press, 1981).

remember such presidents as Theodore Roosevelt and Harry Truman to realize that "Congress bashing" is not unique to the 1990s.[3]

Given that this phenomenon is so deeply ingrained in the American psyche and political rhetoric, it is reasonable to admit that Congress deserves to be bashed. Numerous examples of congressional incompetence are available for those who want to use them.[4]

However, there are some reasons to think that Congress bashing, while fun, understandable, and even reasonable, is often less than illuminating about Congress as an institution. After all, alongside the numerous examples of Congress doing more to hinder than advance the cause of good government, there are other examples of Congress acting as a competent and capable legislature, one that can do things well and that can respond, even with some dispatch, to the exigencies of the moment.[5] In fact, often a recognition of Congress's competencies and capabilities is embedded in critiques of that institution.

Consider, for example, Woodrow Wilson's *Congressional Government*, the classic critique of Congress as a governing institution. Despite the book's reputation as a blistering attack on Congress, Wilson alluded to the fact that Congress is competent, although he did so in an oblique way:

To speak very plainly, it is wonderful that under such a system of government legislation is not oftener at sixes and sevens than it actually is. The infinitely varied and various interests of fifty millions of active people would be hard enough to harmonize and serve, one would think, were parties efficiently organized in the pursuit of definite, steady, consistent policies; and it is therefore amazing to find how few outrageously and fatally foolish, how few bad or disastrous, things have been done by means of our disintegrated methods of legislation.[6]

---

[3]"Congressmen are very often demagogues; they are very often blind partisans; they are often exceedingly short-sighted, narrow-minded, and bigoted; but they are usually not corrupt; and to accuse a narrow-minded demagogue of corruption when he is perfectly honest is merely to set him firmly in his evil course and to help him with his constituents, who recognize that the charge is entirely unjust, and in repelling it lose sight of the man's real shortcomings." Theodore Roosevelt made this statement in a public address when he was chairman of the Civil Service Commission in 1893. *The Writings of Theodore Roosevelt*, ed. William H. Harbaugh (New York: Bobbs-Merrill, 1967), 12.

[4]One of the best sources in which to find such examples is *The Public Interest*, no. 100 (Summer 1990). See also Green, *Who Runs Congress*.

[5]See William F. Connelly, Jr., "In Defense of Congress," in *Readings in American Government*, 3d ed., ed. Mary Nichols and David Nichols (Dubuque: Kendall-Hunt Publishing Co., 1990), 209–219. Also see Michael J. Malbin, "Factions and Incentives in Congress," *The Public Interest*, no. 86 (Winter 1987): 91–108.

[6]Wilson, *Congressional Government*, 88–89.

In fact, Wilson explains why Congress has a certain competence, namely, its organization into committees. Describing the development of Congress, Wilson wrote, "Congress was very quick and apt in learning what it could do and in getting into thoroughly good trim to do it. It very early divided itself into standing committees which it equipped with very comprehensive and thorough-going privileges of legislative initiative and control, and set itself through these to administer the government."[7] This led Wilson to conclude, again offhandedly complimenting Congress, "I am inclined to think, therefore, that the enlarged powers of Congress are the fruits of an *immensely increased efficiency of organization,* and of the redoubled activity consequent upon *the facility of action* secured by such organization, than of any definite and persistent scheme of conscious usurpation."[8]

In sum, Woodrow Wilson thought that Congress was competent, that it could do certain things, and even that it was "immensely" efficient and possessed a "facility of action." Whatever was wrong with Congress in his time, Wilson *did not* argue that Congress was simply incompetent or incapacitated. Perhaps the problem for Wilson, and for others like him, is not so much what Congress cannot do as what it can do.[9]

The purpose of the above is to underscore the importance, when we criticize Congress, of understanding it as an institution embedded in a particular kind of society. It bears repeating that Woodrow Wilson did not fault Congress as being unable to legislate. According to Wilson, Congress could legislate and it could do so competently or after a certain manner. As Wilson wrote in *Congressional Government:* "Our legislation is conglomerate, not homogeneous. The doings of one and the same Congress are foolish in pieces and wise in spots. They can never, except by accident, have any common features."[10] In other words, Congress could legislate but it could not legislate in the manner Wilson deemed most desirable.

Underlying Wilson's critique of Congress and congressional government is the assumption, quite common even today, that

---

[7]Ibid., 49.
[8]Ibid., 50, emphasis added.
[9]"Congress always makes what haste it can to legislate. It is the prime object of its rules to expedite law-making. . . . Its temper is strenuously legislative. . . . If legislation, therefore, were the only or the chief object for which it should live, it would not be possible to withhold admiration from those clever hurrying rules and those inexorable customs which seek to facilitate it. Nothing but a doubt as to whether or not Congress should confine itself to law-making can challenge with a question the ability of its organization as a facile statute-devising machine." Ibid., 193.
[10]Ibid., 89.

legislation ought to be "homogeneous" or "homogenizing." How many times has it been written that when Congress legislates, it does so in a piecemeal fashion? How many times has it been written that Congress makes policy "incrementally" and, therefore, badly? Quite often, to say the least. But it is fair to ask: Is this assumption in favor of homogeneity justified?

Consider, in contrast to Wilson's preference for homogeneity, James Madison's characterization of the act of legislating in *Federalist* 10. After cataloguing the interests that "grow up of necessity in civilized nations, and [that] divide them into classes actuated by different sentiments and views," Madison asserts that "the regulation of these various and interfering interests forms the principal task of modern legislation and involves the spirit of party and faction in the necessary and ordinary operations of government."[11] Madison here argues that legislation in a "modern" republic would be, to use Wilson's language, more "conglomerate" than "homogeneous." For Madison, however, such legislation is defensible because of the difficulties of trying to regulate these different interests from the point of view of "the public good." As Madison went on to write, "shall domestic manufactures be encouraged, and in what degree, by restrictions of foreign manufactures? are questions which would be differently decided by the landed and the manufacturing classes, and probably by neither with a sole regard to justice and the public good."[12] Madison here recognized that "justice and the public good" are unlikely to guide the behavior of the many different interests composing "civilized nations." Thus it is more reasonable and practical not to try to "render them all subservient to the public good," a task Madison suggested could occur only under the most propitious circumstances with the guidance of statesmen not always available.[13] Without denying that there is a "public good," Madison preferred the kind of legislation, "conglomerate," that Wilson rejected.

Emerging from Madison's argument in *Federalist* 10 is, at least in part, a "definition" of Congress as an institution that has a particular responsibility and would "behave" in a certain manner in fulfilling that responsibility. Congress, in fulfilling its responsibility to legislate, would regulate in the sense of accommodating or adjusting those "clashing interests" that compose a "civilized nation." Put differently, Madison's Congress would not seek by means

[11]Alexander Hamilton, James Madison, and John Jay, *The Federalist Papers*, introduction by Clinton Rossiter (New York: New American Library, 1961), 79.
[12]Ibid., 80.
[13]Ibid.

of legislation to order, "homogenize," or harmonize these clashing
interests to "render them all subservient to the public good." However troubling this may seem today, when Wilson's point of view
predominates, Madison understood Congress to be an institution
that aims at accommodation and adjustment, not at order, homogeneity, or harmony. We might even say that for Madison "modern
legislation" is unique in that it does not seek to order those interests that compose civil society.[14] As Madison wrote immediately
after denying the efficacy of trying to render the interests "subservient to the public good," "The inference to which we are
brought is that the *causes* of faction cannot be removed and that
relief is only to be sought in the means of controlling its *effects*."[15]

CONGRESS AS A LEGISLATURE: WHAT IT DOES NOT DO

The preceding is meant to prepare the way for a more nuanced assessment of Congress as an institution of government
than is usually found in descriptions and assessments of the American political order. In the argument made here, it is essential to
think of Congress as a particular kind of institution, namely a legislature, because this encourages us to make explicit just what we
expect or should expect from Congress. The relevant questions
are: what does it mean to say that Congress is a legislature, and
what should we expect—and not expect—from Congress as a
legislature?

[14]Of course, this view of Madison is controversial. Theodore Lowi, for example,
has argued that Madison sought to "regulate," not "accommodate," interest groups.
For Lowi, the whole difference between Madison's pluralism and "contemporary
pluralism" is that for the latter, "Groups become virtuous; they must be *accommodated*, not *regulated*." And, again: "Note, for example, the contrast between the traditional and the modern view of the group: Madison in *Federalist* no. 10 defined the
group ("faction") as 'a number of citizens, whether amounting to a majority or a
minority of the whole who are united and actuated by some common impulse of
passion, or of interest, *adverse to the rights of other citizens, or to the permanent and ag-
gregate interests of the community.'* Modern political science usage took that definition
and cut the quotation just before the emphasized part. In such a manner pluralist
theory became the handmaiden of interest-group liberalism, and interest-group
liberalism became the handmaiden of modern American positive national state-
hood, and the First Republic became the Second Republic." Theodore Lowi, *The
End of Liberalism: The Second Republic of the United States*, 2d ed. (New York: Norton
Publishing Co., 1979), 36, 55. Suffice it to say that, in my view, Lowi does not
appreciate Madison's use of the word "regulation," and its connection to the
uniqueness of "modern legislation." Such legislation focuses on accommodating
or controlling the effects of faction, not removing their causes or changing their
character.

[15]*Federalist* No. 10, 80.

Although it seems trite to say so, Congress is first and foremost a legislature. Since its primary function is to legislate, we should assess it in light of its capacity to make law. To emphasize that Congress's primary function is to legislate is not as meaningless as it might appear. For example, when one reads Woodrow Wilson's *Congressional Government* with this in mind, it is clear that Wilson does not argue that Congress cannot legislate. As noted above, Wilson admitted Congress could legislate, even that Congress could legislate with facility and in a reasonably prudent way. For Wilson, the committee system was created to promote and did promote Congress's ability to legislate. He was critical of Congress because even though Congress could legislate, it was not organized to promote "leadership."[16]

Wilson was correct to fault Congress for a lack of leadership, but he was too quick to depreciate legislation while doing so. Wilson wanted to "gear" Congress for leadership because he was convinced that the central function of good government was leadership, not legislation.[17] This is a legitimate argument but it leads to an assessment of Congress that highlights its defects, not its strengths. In fact, some of Congress's strengths as a legislature become defects when viewed through Wilsonian lenses. Thus, we need to emphasize that Congress is a legislature in order to arrive at a more nuanced treatment of that institution than is found in Wilson's *Congressional Government*.

Most importantly, emphasizing that Congress is a legislature allows us to appreciate anew what are often billed as "failures of Congress." For example, Congress is often criticized for inadequately "overseeing" the executive department with regard to executing the laws.[18] But it is not at all clear that "legislative over-

---

[16]"It is this multiplicity of leaders, the many-headed leadership, which makes the organization of the House [of Representatives] too complex to afford uninformed people and unskilled observers any easy clue to its methods of rule. . . . They do not consult and concur in the adoption of homogenous and mutually helpful measures; there is no thought of acting in concert. Each Committee goes its own way at its own pace. It is impossible to discover any unity or method in the disconnected and therefore unsystematic, confused, and desultory action of the House, or any common purpose in the measures which its Committees from time to time recommend." Wilson, *Congressional Government*, 59.

[17]"Eight words contain the sum of the present degradation of our political parties: *No leaders, no principles; no principles, no parties.*" "Cabinet Government in the United States," *International Review* III (August 1879), in *The Political Thought of Woodrow Wilson*, ed. E. David Cronon (New York: Bobbs-Merrill, 1965), 48.

[18]"In addition to the political disincentives for vigorous pursuit of oversight by Congress, there is also the fact that the very broad delegations of power Congress has given the bureaucracy over the years . . . makes [sic] oversight difficult." Randall B. Ripley, *Congress*, 4th ed. (New York: Norton Publishing Co., 1988), 360.

sight" is an essential function of a legislature. In fact, legislating and overseeing can be understood as two distinct functions insofar as legislating provides the authority for executive officials to exercise discretion, while oversight attempts to control that discretion. To assume, as many do, that Congress was intended to control the exercise of executive discretion obscures the difference between executing the laws and legislating. By keeping in mind that Congress's primary function is legislating, a more nuanced view of "oversight" emerges, one that helps define the kind of oversight we can expect from Congress.[19] And by doing so, we can better appreciate why Congress often displays a surprising degree of deference toward administrators, even toward administrators who have shown a certain degree of independence from, if not downright surliness toward, Congress.[20]

Again, by focusing on Congress as a legislature, we can clarify the kind of deliberations we should expect from Congress. Often, Congress is faulted for not debating the grand issues of politics, for example, the meaning of liberty, equality, or property.[21] But, first and foremost, legislating means writing laws, which more clearly involves deciding how a particular law should be written than it does debating and deciding the grand issues of politics. To be sure, such grand concepts will influence Congress when it legislates, but to say that great congressional debates should be typical ignores what legislating requires. Thus the fact that congressional debates most often are mundane and legalistic is merely a reflection of congressional responsibilities and not simply a defect.

[19]Rarely is the question asked: What kind of oversight should Congress engage in? Most often, we assume Congress should oversee the actual execution of the laws and so we expect Congress to ask: "How are executive officials executing the laws?" The argument herein implies that a more appropriate question would be: "Are the laws working?" In practice, it is the latter question Congress most often raises, which helps explain why "there is a great amount of cooperation between Congress and the bureaucracy and it is in good measure based on mutual self-interest." Ibid., 359. In sum, Congress and the bureaucracy cooperate because both have an interest in having the laws "work."

[20]One recent illustration of this deference to administrators is the Senate's decision to confirm the nomination of Robert Gates as Director of the Central Intelligence Agency despite some evidence that he misinformed Congress while serving as Deputy Director of that agency.

[21]"We are thus again brought into the presence of the cardinal fact of this discussion—that *debate* is the essential function of a popular representative body. In the severe, distinct, and sharp enunciation of underlying principles . . . we see the best, the only effective, means of educating public opinion." Wilson, "Cabinet Government," 35–36. See also Joseph M. Bessette, "Is Congress a Deliberative Body?" in *The United States Congress*, Proceedings of the Thomas P. O'Neill, Jr. Symposium on the United States Congress (Leominster: Eusey Press, 1982), 3–11.

Furthermore, by remembering that Congress is primarily a legislature, we can appreciate the often-commented upon reluctance of Congress to debate and decide certain other kinds of questions, most importantly, the question of war.[22] Whether the nation goes to war does not involve legislating in the typical sense. The question of war is not like questions concerning gun control or a new commercial code. Legislating on matters such as these is not like the decision to go to war because after deciding to legislate, Congress must still draft the legislation and can revise it as necessary. However, a decision to go to war is irrevocable and, once taken, not subject to revision or amendment. So, it is precisely because Congress is a legislature that it most often follows the lead of the commander in chief with regard to war and warmaking. Again, this "congressional failure" can be understood as a reflection of Congress's institutional responsibilities. To expect Congress to reject the recommendations of the commander in chief ignores the differences between legislators and the commander in chief.

In addition, remembering that Congress is primarily a legislature helps us appreciate why Congress is not more representative than it is. Of course, as is frequently noticed, Congress is far from reflecting the characteristics of the American people.[23] Men are greatly overrepresented, as are white Americans and, among the professions, lawyers. But because Congress is primarily engaged in legislating, underrepresentation of certain groups is less troubling than if Congress were primarily a representative body meant to speak and act for the people. Moreover, a lawmaking body is properly composed of lawyers insofar as lawyers should be more knowledgeable as legislators than others might be. Indeed, in a legislature, those who are adept at lawmaking have a certain claim to govern, even when they behave in ways their constituen-

---

[22]"The Constitution has conferred the power to go to war on Congress. . . . Two centuries after independence the congressional role had evaporated. . . . The constitutional goal—that no one man should hold the power of committing the nation to war or keeping it at war—was still valid and must prevail. But the Constitution had manifestly failed to provide the machinery by which that goal could be surely attained." Arthur M. Schlesinger, Jr., The Imperial Presidency (New York: Atlantic Monthly Co., 1974), 270, 274–75. See also J. W. Peltason, Understanding the Constitution (New York: Harcourt Brace Jovanovich, 1991), 115: "Throughout our history, Congress has resisted, but with little success, the president's predominant role in controlling our military forces."

[23]"The winners of seats in the House and the Senate are by no means a cross section of the American population. By almost any measure, they come from a social and economic elite." Ripley, Congress, 86–87.

cies find morally questionable or suspect.[24] From this perspective, the fact often bemoaned by critics that Congress does not more accurately reflect the composition of the American people is less troubling than it seems at first glance. In a lawmaking institution, that the representatives truly reflect the people is less important than that they know how to legislate.[25]

Finally, to understand Congress as a legislature is to better appreciate why certain congressional activities seem ineffective or suspect. For example, it is quite common for Congress to be understood as a "checking" institution, one that checks the other two departments of the government.[26] But more often than not, this function is inconsistent with Congress's legislative function because legislation empowers the other departments. By passing laws, Congress gives the executive the opportunity to implement them and thereby allows the executive to exercise its discretion and influence public policy.[27] Similarly, by passing laws, Congress creates the opportunity for the courts to adjudicate disputes that arise under those laws. In resolving such disputes courts use their discretion and thereby influence public policy. Thus, Congress's often-remarked upon "inability" to check the other departments of the government is due in large part to the fact that it is a legislature.

And, when Congress seeks to "expose" individuals or practices, its activity is suspect insofar as it lacks a connection to lawmaking.[28] As a legislature, Congress should not be in the business of enforcing public morality through exposure rather than through legislation. "Exposing" loan sharks, disreputable business persons, organized crime figures, communists, or even patriots like Ollie North is not the business of a legislature, except insofar as it contributes to legislating. Again, Madison's argument in *Federalist* 10 is illuminating because it reminds us that Congress's

[24]The scandal involving Representative Barney Frank (D-Mass.) comes to mind as illustrative of this phenomenon.

[25]See *Federalist* Nos. 55–58.

[26]Ripley, *Congress*, 87.

[27]William Howard Taft, in analyzing the president's authority to take care that the laws were being executed, wrote: "Someone has said, 'Let me make the ballads of the country, and I care not who makes the laws.' One might also say, paraphrasing this, 'Let anyone make the laws of the country, if I can construe them.'" And, further, Taft argued that "statutory construction is practically one of the greatest executive powers." William Howard Taft, *The President and His Powers* (New York: Columbia University Press, 1967), 78.

[28]*Kilbourn v. Thompson*, 103 U.S. 168 (1881); *McGrain v. Daugherty*, 273 U.S. 135 (1927); *Eastland v. United States Serviceman's Fund*, 421 U.S. 491 (1975).

"principal task" is to legislate. In sum, Congress is first and foremost a legislature and this fact has implications for how Congress
does and should behave.

CONGRESS AS LEGISLATURE: WHAT IT DOES, WHAT IT SHOULD DO

Up to this point, I have considered the negative implications
of arguing that Congress is a legislature. Mainly, I have focused on
what Congress does not do. Now, the issue is: What is it that Congress does or should do?

Of course, as is already obvious, Congress's primary responsibility is legislating. But what does this mean? Does it mean that
Congress should legislate frequently and easily? And, secondly,
what kind of legislation should we expect from Congress?

Very often it is assumed that Congress should legislate frequently and easily. For example, one way of assessing any particular Congress is in terms of the number of bills passed.
Commentators most often compare the number of laws enacted
with the number of bills introduced.[29] As might be expected, far
fewer laws are passed than bills introduced, which reinforces the
image of Congress as an inefficient and ineffective legislature.

This approach is not devoid of merit. It recognizes that Congress is, first and foremost, a legislature. Particular Congresses,
then, are not assessed by the quality of their floor debates or of the
material found in the *Congressional Record*. Similarly, they are not
assessed in terms of their representativeness, by the number of
legislative vetoes exercised, by the number of nominations rejected, or by the number of committee hearings that exposed some
shameful or illicit activity. Rather, Congresses are assessed by the
work they were intended to do—legislating.

But this approach is also simplistic. Comparing the ratio between bills introduced to laws passed implies that legislative activity should be measured quantitatively rather than qualitatively.
The *more* a Congress legislates, the "better" it is. And this suggests
that Congress should legislate frequently and easily. In sum,
counting the number of laws passed implies that Congress should
be continually legislating.

However, as noted in *The Federalist*, frequent and voluminous
legislation is not necessarily—or even usually—a virtue. As Madison asked in *Federalist* 62, "What indeed are all the repealing,

---

[29]For an excellent assessment of such measures, both their strengths and weaknesses, see Mark A. Peterson, *Legislating Together: The White House and Capitol Hill
from Eisenhower to Reagan* (Cambridge: Harvard University Press, 1990), Appendi-
ces B and C, 302–315.

explaining, and amending laws, which fill and disgrace our volu-minous codes, but so many monuments of deficient wisdom; so many impeachments exhibited by each succeeding against each preceding session; so many admonitions to the people of the value of those aids which may be expected from a well-constituted senate?"[30] From this perspective, government is best when its laws are not continually changing and when the laws become more rather than less permanent. Put differently, Congress should resist the temptation to legislate, unless such legislation is necessary or beneficial. As Madison noted, long-established laws are stronger than new laws because they are more likely to have the respect of the people.[31]

Madison's perspective reminds us that it is appropriate for Congress to choose not to legislate. Today, such a perspective seems odd because we prefer action to inaction, a preference re-flected by the commonplace quantitative measures used to assess particular Congresses. But criticisms of Congress resting on that institution's "failure" to enact "enough" legislation rest upon a conception about government at odds with the Constitution, and we need to recover the constitutional perspective on government and legislation.

By the constitutional perspective on government, I do not mean the familiar one which deems inactivity or inefficiency gov-ernmental virtues. Quite the contrary. Almost everywhere in the Constitution, grants of power are more prominent than limita-tions on those powers. Article I, which vests Congress with a long list of powers, contains only three explicit limitations on those powers.[32] Most limits on Congress's powers are implicit, as they are, for example, in the commerce clause. And even where limita-tions are explicit, for example, in Article I, section 9, they do not significantly compromise Congress's powers of legislation.[33] More-over, this is true of Articles II and III as well.

The Constitution then broadly grants Congress extensive leg-islative powers but it does not follow that the Constitution in-tended to make it easy for Congress to legislate. To understand this apparent contradiction, we need only recognize that govern-ment under the Constitution was to take place, by and large,

[30] *Federalist* No. 62, 379–380.
[31] Ibid., No. 49, 314–315.
[32] The explicit limitations are found in paragraphs 1, 12, and 16 of Article I, sec-tion 8.
[33] In very few instances have these limitations affected Congress's power to leg-islate. See Peltason, *Constitution*, 92–98.

within a framework of laws enacted by Congress with the president's approval.[34] By this view, Congress is responsible for establishing the legal framework within which government would take place. For this purpose, Congress has extensive powers broadly granted. But the Constitution has a bias against legislative activity, as evidenced by bicameralism and the president's qualified veto, because the established legal framework ought not be changed for light or transient reasons.[35] This is not to say, however, that the Constitution is simply opposed to change in the established legal framework. Indeed, change is anticipated, most clearly in Article II which obligates the president to recommend to Congress "such Measures as he shall judge necessary and expedient."[36] But Article II also obligates the president to "take Care that the laws be faithfully executed," which suggests that legislation and law enforcement are not less important than leadership.[37]

In practice, this means that Congress's first responsibility is not to discern and respond to those needs or situations deemed most pressing, but to create the legal framework within which the executive "governs."[38] Thus, Congress should be judged not by its

---

[34]See *Federalist* Nos. 62–66.

[35]"There are some who would be inclined to regard the servile pliancy of the executive to a prevailing current, either in the community or in the legislature, as its best recommendation. But such men entertain very crude notions, as well of the purposes for which government was instituted, as of the true means by which the public happiness may be promoted. The republican principle demands that the deliberate sense of the community should govern the conduct of those to whom they intrust the management of their affairs; but it does not require an unqualified complaisance to every sudden breeze or passion, or to every transient impulse which the people may receive from the arts of men, who flatter their prejudices to betray their interests." *Federalist* No. 71, 432.

[36]U.S. Constitution, Art. II, sec. 3.

[37]Ibid. See also *Federalist* 62 where Madison delineated "the mischievous effects of a mutable government." He wrote that "a mutable policy . . . poisons the blessings of liberty itself" because such mutability leads to "laws . . . so voluminous . . . they cannot be read, or so incoherent that they cannot be understood." *Federalist* No. 62, 381.

[38]See *Youngstown Sheet & Tube Co. v. Sawyer*, 343 U.S. 579 (1952), especially Chief Justice Vinson's dissent: "A review of executive action demonstrates that our Presidents have on many occasions exhibited the leadership contemplated by the Framers when they made the President Commander in Chief, and imposed upon him the trust to 'take Care that the laws be faithfully executed.' " Vinson's argument is more persuasive than that made by Justice Black for the Court, who argued that the President is limited to seeing "that . . . congressional policy be executed in a manner prescribed by Congress. . . ." As the Chief Justice noted, Black's view implied that "the President cannot even act to preserve legislative programs from destruction so that Congress will have something left to act upon" and reduced the President to a "messenger-boy."

capacity to meet the exigencies of the moment but by its capacity to pass the kind of legislation that establishes the "ground rules" for government. When judged in these terms, Congress is not as incompetent as many critics maintain. Throughout our history, Congress has demonstrated a capacity to establish the legal framework of government. In fact, Congress has shown a capacity to reform the established legal order, even to create what might be called "new regimes." For example, Theodore Lowi in his *End of Liberalism* distinguishes between the "first" (Madisonian) and the "second" ("interest group liberalism") republics of the United States. Lowi prefers the first republic, but insofar as a second republic exists, it does so because Congress has the capacity to change the character of government in the United States in important ways.[39] Similar arguments, although more nuanced than Lowi's, can be found elsewhere as well.[40]

It is fair to argue then that Congress has demonstrated its ability to legislate broadly or comprehensively. Moreover, Congress's capacity to legislate comprehensively is evident in recent times as well. The Civil Rights Act of 1964 is one example of Congress's capacity to change the basic "ground rules" of American politics. More recently, Congress has demonstrated its capacity to legislate, even under those presidents who seemed most inept as leaders. As one commentator, Mark Peterson, has described Congress's response to President Carter's National Energy Plan, "In response, the gears of this governmental machine whirled and sometimes sputtered, meshed and often clashed. In the end, however, energy policy was produced; perhaps not *an* energy policy, and certainly not *the* energy policy Carter desired, but policy nonetheless. The statutory provisions of the act that passed a year and a half later would alter the behavior of both suppliers and consumers of coal, natural gas, petroleum, and other forms of energy."[41] And even during extended periods of "divided government" under the Reagan and Bush administrations, Congress passed significant legisla-

---

[39]Lowi, *End of Liberalism*, 271–314.

[40]"Although the Constitution written in 1787 continues powerfully to shape our political life, many significant changes have occurred in the basic elements of our political system. . . . Some of these changes have come through Constitutional amendments. . . . Some have come through new interpretations of the Constitution. . . . *Some have come from federal laws of extraordinary important character* (such as the Civil Rights Act of 1964). . . ." James Ceaser, *American Government: Origins, Institutions, and Public Policy,* 2d ed. (Dubuque: Kendall-Hunt Publishing Co., 1992), 70, emphasis added.

[41]Peterson, *Legislating*, 100. See also Malbin, "Factions."

tion.[42] Moreover, to say Congress can legislate is not to say that its legislation is always prudent or wise. Significant or important legislation is not less significant or important because it is imprudent.

But if Congress is competent, why are we so dissatisfied with it as an institution? For two reasons, I think.

First, as Woodrow Wilson pointed out, Congress's "legislation is conglomerate, not homogeneous." Many critics are bothered not by Congress's failure to legislate but by how it legislates. These critics want "homogeneous" legislation, legislation that reflects a rational plan or order, rather than the kind of legislation that most often emerges from Congress. To use Mark Peterson's language cited above: These critics want *an* energy policy or *the* energy policy. Anything less is unsatisfactory and unacceptable.

Although such criticisms are factually accurate, it is not clear they support the charge that Congress is simply incompetent or ineffective. After all, we should remember that Congress is legislating for a large, commercial, and now ethnically diverse society. Such a "setting" is not conducive to homogeneous legislation, as Wilson recognized. In fact, given the complexity of American society, Congress's ability to legislate comprehensively as often as it has is more surprising than its tendency toward "conglomerate" legislation. At the very least, however, given the complex character of American society, Congress's ability to legislate comprehensively at all is as remarkable as its tendency to legislate incrementally.

Second, dissatisfaction with Congress runs high because we have redefined the "legislative virtues" and subordinated them to leadership. For Madison, however, "modern legislation . . . involves the spirit of party and faction" as a matter of course and is "regulatory" in the sense of accommodating the different interest groups or factions. When Madison wrote that "the cause of faction cannot be removed," he was arguing that these factions cannot be made "subservient to the public good." Madison did not think it possible, or perhaps desirable, to order or harmonize the various interest groups composing his large, commercial republic. Accommodation is distinct from harmonization and Madison sought accommodation, not harmony.

---

[42]"To portray Congress solely in terms of programs that do *not* pass misses some important lessons of the 1980s. Some major programs do become law. The House and Senate of the 1980s, despite the fact that so many of the incentives of internal cohesion have been weakened, have both shown a remarkable ability to work cohesively—sometimes across party lines and sometimes within them—on complicated and highly divisive policy issues." Malbin, "Factions," 104.

Today, however, we prefer order, harmony, and unity to accommodation. We do so because, like Woodrow Wilson, we value national unity; we think of it as *the* goal of politics. Thus, we value leadership more than legislation because leadership both reflects and promotes unity. When we agree on a leader, we are more unified and better able to reach the unity we seek.

But should we prefer leadership to legislation? For Wilson, constructing a political order based on leadership required remodeling the Constitution because an order that revolves around leadership is fundamentally different than one that revolves around legislation.[43] As understood by Wilson, leaders are distinct from and superior to legislators. They engage in the "real stuff" of politics, making legislators and legislatures look dull and incompetent by comparison. They possess the "vision thing," as President Bush would say. Not surprisingly, however, leaders eventually view legislatures either as their tools or as obstacles to be avoided when they obstruct leadership. The "vision thing" obscures the value of legislatures and of law.

It is then far from clear that we should prefer leadership to legislation. Even Aristotle chose to confound the two by calling founders "legislators."[44] More to the point, however, the scheme of the Constitution provides important roles for both legislators and leaders. In fact, under the Constitution, leadership seems to be directed toward legislating, as reflected by the president's obligation to recommend measures to the legislature he deems necessary and expedient. Thus, the Constitution directs leadership toward legislation; we might even say that the Constitution seeks to move leadership from the popular arena, where it is often indistinguishable from demagoguery, to the legislative arena, where it is less dangerous. Undoing this arrangement and subordinating legislation to leadership might well lead to a resurgence of popular demagoguery.[45]

---

[43]"We are the first Americans to hear our own countrymen ask whether the Constitution is still adapted to serve the purposes for which it was intended; the first to entertain any serious doubts about the superiority of our own institutions as compared with the systems of Europe; the first to think of remodeling the administrative machinery of the federal government, and of forcing new forms of responsibility on Congress." Wilson, *Congressional Government*, 27.

[44]Aristotle, *The Politics*, trans. Carnes Lord (Chicago: University of Chicago Press, 1988), Bk. I, ch.2; Bk II, ch. 2; and Bk III, chs.15–17.

[45]James Ceaser, *Presidential Selection: Theory and Development* (Princeton: Princeton University Press, 1979); James W. Ceaser, Glen E. Thurow, Jeffrey K. Tulis, Joseph Bessette, "The Rise of the Rhetorical Presidency," *Presidential Studies Quarterly* (Spring, 1981): 158–171.

The appropriate relationship between leadership and legislation is surely a matter of prudence, to be arranged differently at different times depending on the prevailing circumstances. But precisely because it is a prudential question, we need to fortify Congress even if the cost is less unity than we would like. And especially insofar as our current dissatisfaction with Congress is influenced by a Wilsonian preference for leadership, we should resist it in order to preserve the balance established by the Constitution between leadership and legislation. By fortifying Congress, we help prevent the impulse for leadership from becoming the handmaiden of a populistic despotism the Constitution was designed to correct.

Conclusion

No doubt some will argue that my defense of Congress reads too much into our current dissatisfaction with that institution. By this view, the current dissatisfaction reflects little more than congressional incompetence and arrogance. Moreover, little more is needed from our congressmen than simple decency and honesty, as well as the will to confront current problems. In brief, the problem is one of practice, not theory.

To a certain extent, this rejoinder makes sense. Most Americans are responding to what they see as the great failings of our contemporary Congress. They are being "realistic." "Realism," however, almost always occurs within a certain framework and rests on presumptions often not made explicit. And when we look at Congress and notice its capacity, even today, to legislate comprehensively, we may wonder why this capacity so often goes unappreciated.

Congress's capacity as a legislature is unappreciated because we do not appreciate the importance of law and lawmakers to a healthy political order. By trying to understand Congress as a legislature, we prepare ourselves to wonder why a government of laws is better than one of men. In doing so, we prepare ourselves to appreciate anew the genius of our Constitution.

Title VII from Lyndon Johnson to George Bush: Some Thoughts on Presidential Leadership

Terry Eastland

Our most popular understanding of presidential leadership sees the president using his rhetorical powers to get Congress to pass a bill of great importance to the nation. This understanding is largely a product of twentieth century liberal presidencies, which won from Congress laws that created ever larger, more intrusive and more costly federal government. What happens, however, when there is a conservative president—as we had for the twelve years preceding 1993? How do we understand leadership on the part of a conservative president not inclined to seek from Congress more of the big-government-liberalism of ages past? How do we understand leadership from such a president especially given that the government he inherits and is charged with administering is mainly a liberal one (thanks to many of the laws previously passed and the ways previous executives have enforced those laws), while the people who elected him and to whom he is accountable reasonably can expect him to pursue conservative goals? Does it make sense to continue defining presidential leadership in the old way—in terms of legislative success in behalf of big-government-liberalism? Or, at least when conservatives hold the presidency, should we regard it differently?

A good way to approach this subject is through consideration of the life of a particular law, Title VII of the Civil Rights Act of 1964, from its enactment through 1991. The Civil Rights Act was enacted during the heyday, if not the last hurrah, of American liberalism. Helping to secure its passage was President Lyndon B. Johnson, rhetorically urging Congress on, and thus meeting the popular expectation of the president as legislative leader. As enacted, Title VII, a key part of the landmark legislation, meant certain things. But in the hands of the Johnson and Nixon presidencies, with key assists from the federal courts, it soon came to acquire diametrically different meanings. When Ronald Reagan took office in 1981, his outspoken opposition to racial quotas implied, chief among other things, a return to the original meaning of Title VII. But going back to the future did not take Reagan to Congress in pursuit of a new Title VII but into his own executive branch, where his agents altered Title VII enforcement, and into the federal courts, where his agents asked for Title VII decisions consistent with his view of the statute. When, in 1989, the Supreme Court handed down a Title VII decision to his liking, but manifestly not to that of the Democratic Congress, the latter responded in 1990 by passing new law amending Title VII. President Bush successfully vetoed that law before accepting a slightly altered version of it in 1991. Thus, in the end, a conservative president was a legislator after all, although a reluctant one. Telling this history in some detail provides an opportunity to think anew about presidential leadership, especially when the president is a conservative Republican and the government is "divided."

THE ORIGINAL MEANING OF TITLE VII

In 1963, President John F. Kennedy said that it should be possible "for every American to enjoy the privileges of being American without regard to his race or his color." Seeking equality of treatment for all Americans, President Kennedy began and President Johnson completed the task of winning comprehensive civil rights legislation. The Civil Rights Act of 1964 dealt with the right to vote, access to places of public accommodation, desegregation of public facilities, public education—and equal employment opportunity. This last was treated in Title VII, which, affecting all employers, public and private, having 25 or more employees, covered roughly 75 percent of the American work force.

Title VII declares:

It shall be an unlawful employment practice for an employer— (1) to fail or refuse to hire or to discharge any individual, or otherwise to discriminate against any individual with respect to his compensation, terms, conditions, or privileges of employment, because of such individual's race, color, religion, sex, or national origin; or

(2) to limit, segregate, or classify his employees or applicants for employment in any way which would deprive or tend to deprive any in-

dividual or employment opportunities or otherwise adversely affect his status as an employee, because of such individual's race, color, religion, sex, or national origin.[1]

Nothing could be clearer: Title VII guarantees that race or sex will *not* be the basis of employment determinations. The statutory language of Title VII, as Herman Belz has succinctly stated it, "was intended to confer an individual right to equal opportunity in employment without distinguishing by color"[2] (or national origin or sex or religion).

Title VII was a supremely colorblind law. Originally understood in terms of its text and legislative history, the law embodied several propositions that worked together to create and protect the right of the individual to equal employment opportunity without regard to race or sex. The first: racial (or gender) preferences could *not* be used by an employer, nor could they be imposed by a federal court as a remedy for proven discrimination.[3] The second: discrimination did not mean "imbalance" or "underrepresentation" or "underutilization" of minorities in a given work force. The third: discrimination instead meant the unequal or different treatment motivated by racial bias; it meant "disparate treatment" of individuals on the basis of race.[4] The fourth: employers could

---

[1] 42 U.S.C. § 2000e-2(a).

[2] Herman Belz, *Equality Transformed: A Quarter Century of Affirmative Action* (New Brunswick: Transaction Publishers, 1991), 1.

[3] Thus, the floor captains of the legislation, Senators Joseph Clark and Clifford Case, said: "There is no requirement in Title VII that an employer maintain a racial balance in his work force. On the contrary, any deliberate attempt to maintain a racial balance, whatever such a balance may be, would involve a violation of Title VII because maintaining such a balance would require an employer to hire or refuse to hire on the basis of race. It must be emphasized that discrimination is prohibited as to any individual." Senator Hubert Humphrey also said: "[Title] VII does not provide that any quota systems may be established to maintain racial balance in employment. In fact, the title would prohibit preferential treatment for any particular group, and any person, whether or not a member of any minority group, would be permitted to file a complaint of discriminatory employment practices."

[4] A section of the law concerning judicial remedies thus states: "If the court finds that the respondent has intentionally engaged in or is intentionally engaging in an unlawful employment practice charged in the complaint, the court may enjoin the respondent from engaging in such unlawful employment practice, and order such affirmative action as may be appropriate. . . . " Explaining this, Senator Hubert Humphrey said the law thus would require "a showing of intentional violation . . . in order to obtain relief." He added: "The express requirement of intent is designed to make it wholly clear that inadvertent or accidental discriminations will not violate the title or result in entry of court orders."

employ professionally developed tests so long as they were not designed, intended, or used to discriminate on the basis of race; a
plaintiff in a Title VII case thus could not challenge such a test
simply by alleging its "disparate impact" upon certain minority
groups by pointing to their "underrepresentation" or "underutilization." And the fifth: the burden of proving discrimination in a
Title VII case, as in all other civil actions, fell upon the plaintiff,
not the defendant.

Title VII put severe roadblocks in any enforcement or litigation effort that, by citing "imbalance," would take employers into
court where they would be forced to justify whatever was causing
the alleged disparity. Title VII thus sought to prevent the dynamic
whereby employers would resort to preferences in the first place in
order to avoid a "disparate impact" claim.[5]

"Employees may hire and fire, promote and refuse to promote
for any reason, good or bad," said Sen. Hubert Humphrey, one of
the statute's strongest supporters, "provided only that individuals
may not be discriminated against because of race, religion, sex,
or national origin." This was a fine summary of Title VII as originally enacted. Very quickly, however, this statement of the law became obsolete.

THE REVISED VERSION OF TITLE VII

Title VII might be said to have contained the seeds of its own
revision because the new enforcement agency it created—the
Equal Employment Opportunity Commission—bears much of the

---

[5]The Illinois case of *Myart* v. *Motorola* was itself a subject of considerable congressional discussion. Under that state's fair employment practices act, a test that was
neutral and free of any intentional discrimination had been invalidated on grounds
that it had a disproportionate impact upon blacks. The employer was told he could
not use the test until he showed that it did not cause a racial imbalance within his
work force. Sen. Clifford Case, who along with Sen. Joseph Clark was the bipartisan floor captain of the legislation in the Senate, told his colleagues that such a case
could not arise under Title VII. Case said that neither the Equal Employment Opportunity Commission, which the new law would create and authorize to enforce its
terms against private employers, nor the federal courts could "order an employer to
lower or change job qualifications simply because proportionately fewer Negroes
than white[s] are able to meet them. Title VII says only that covered employers cannot refuse to hire someone simply because of his color." An authoritative Senate
memorandum maintained that bona fide qualifications tests would not have to be
abandoned where, "because of differences in background and education, members
of some groups are able to perform better on these tests than members of other
groups." An "employer may set his qualifications as high as he likes, he may test to
determine which applicants have these qualifications, and he may hire, assign, and
promote on the basis of test performance."

responsibility for transforming the statute into one that, contrary
to its original terms, makes race and sex central to employment determinations. Opening its doors in the summer of 1965, the EEOC
seemed almost from its inception to have made its main business
the rewriting of Title VII. According to its own *Administrative History,* the agency knew that the courts, if faithful to the original
terms of Title VII, would disagree with its revision of the statute.
"Eventually this will call for reconsideration of the [statute] by
Congress," said the EEOC's *Administrative History,* "or the reconsideration of its interpretation by the Commission." As will be seen,
neither had to happen, for the Supreme Court sanctioned the
EEOC's revised version of Title VII.

In his 1991 book, *Equality Transformed: A Quarter Century of Affirmative Action,* Herman Belz has described the kind of law that
as early as August 1965 the EEOC believed Title VII should be.
"Discrimination should be defined as patterns of social and economic disadvantage caused by employment practices and social
institutions in general." Employers should be required "to conduct racial surveys, generate and publicize profiles of underrepresentation problems, and hire minorities." Toward this end, an
EEOC commissioner could complain to an employer about the underrepresentation in his work force. Or, because the EEOC did
not (then) have the power to take offenders to court, a group could
initiate a class-action suit based on "disparity" in the work force.
"A *prima facie* charge thus having been made, the burden of proof
would shift to the employer, in all likelihood disposing of the
case and leading to affirmative action hiring as a remedy for
discrimination."[6] And what did affirmative action mean? Allow
the first EEOC chairman, Clifford Alexander, to answer that.
"We ... here at EEOC believe in numbers. ... Our most valid
standard is in numbers ... in a variety of categories, not just total
numbers. ... The only accomplishment is when we look at all
those numbers and see a vast improvement in the picture."[7]

Title VII quickly became what the EEOC wanted it to be: a
statute taking aim at not just intentional discrimination but also
minority imbalance in the work force; a statute favoring plaintiffs
by shifting to employers the burden of justifying that practices allegedly causing the disparity; a statute pressuring employers to
hire and promote protected groups by the numbers in order to
avoid Title VII liability. Despite relatively meager powers in its first
years, the EEOC pushed its view of the law through its statutory

[6]Belz, *Equality Transformed,* 28.
[7]Ibid., 28-29.

authority to make reasonable cause findings, issue procedural regulations, and file friend-of-court briefs.[8] To force employers toward proportional representation, the EEOC targeted such practices as job testing and seniority as devices causing statistical imbalances. Regulations issued in 1966 held that any employment test rejecting blacks at a higher rate than whites must be statistically validated with full documentation by employers, and done so separately for blacks and whites. As later revised, those regulations came to require *identical* rejection rates for minority and non-minority job applicants.[9] By 1968, writes Belz, the disparate impact theory of discrimination, focusing on statistical proofs, putting the employer on the defensive, and encouraging, not to say forcing, resort to racial preferences, had been accepted in civil rights circles, and was being advanced in the plaintiffs' bar.[10]

The EEOC hoped the courts would not do as it feared they might—read Title VII in its original terms—but according to its revised version of the statute. As history would have it, the EEOC filed an *amicus* brief in the landmark case in which the Supreme Court basically ratified the agency's transformation of the law. This was the 1971 case, *Griggs* v. *Duke Power Co.*,[11] in which the Court unanimously sided with Willie Griggs and a dozen other black employees at a Duke Power plant in North Carolina.

In a class action, the group had charged the company with discriminating against blacks in violation of Title VII by requiring a high school diploma or passage of intelligence tests as a condition of initial employment or transfer to other plant jobs. Whatever the motivation for these employment requirements, contended Griggs, they had an adverse impact upon blacks and they did not measure the ability to perform a particular job. Duke Power replied that under Title VII—correctly, if the original terms of the law were in fact the law—ability tests were permitted so long as they were not used to discriminate on the basis of race. But the Court said that the objective of Title VII is to remove "barriers that have operated in the past to favor an identifiable group of white employees over other [i.e., non-white] employees." An employment selection practice or procedure or test can be neutral on its face, "and even neutral in terms of intent," but if it operates to

[8]Ibid., 29.

[9]Hugh Davis Graham, *The Civil Rights Era: Origins and Development of National Policy* (New York: Oxford University Press, 1990), 386.

[10]Belz, *Equality Transformed*, 45.

[11] 401 U.S. 424 (1971).

"freeze" the status quo of "past discriminatory employment practices," it violates Title VII.

Basic intelligence, said the Court, cannot manifest itself fairly
in a testing process unless it has "the means of articulation." And
blacks as a group, said the Court in a passage startling for its treatment of blacks *as a group*, do not have this means because they have
"long received inferior education in segregated schools." The
Court noted U.S. census figures for 1960 showing that 34 percent
of white males but only 12 percent of black males in North Carolina had completed high school, as well as statistics from (who else)
the EEOC showing that 58 percent of whites had passed a battery
of tests including those used by Duke Power, while just six percent
of blacks had done so. The Court assumed that the failure of
blacks to do better—and presumably on a par with whites—was
"directly traceable to race." Blacks, in short, had been the victims
of societal discrimination in regard to education, and Duke Power's employment practices only continued the victimization.

Rewriting Title VII, the Court said that the statute "proscribes
not only overt [i.e., traditional] discrimination but also practices
that are fair in form, but discriminatory in operation." The touch-
stone was "business necessity." Thus, under the Court's version of
Title VII, if an employment practice that operates to exclude
blacks "cannot be shown to be related to job performance, the
practice is prohibited." Duke Power had failed to meet this standard; by its own testimony it had adopted its educational and testing requirements to improve the overall quality of its workforce,
not with any specific job assignments in mind. While Duke Power
had declared its own lack of discriminatory intent, pointing to its
efforts to help its undereducated employees by underwriting two-
thirds of the tuition for high school training, the Court was not
impressed. "Good intent does not redeem employment procedures
or testing mechanisms that operate as 'built-in headwinds' for
minority groups and are unrelated to measuring job capability."
The Court said that when Congress wrote Title VII, it was concerned about not only the motivation of employment requirements but also their consequences, and that, in fact, Congress had
placed "on the *employer* the burden of showing that any given requirement must have a manifest relationship to the employment in
question."[12] "What Congress has commanded," said the Court, "is
that any tests used must measure the person for the job and not
the person in the abstract." By way of practical guidance, the

[12]The emphasis is mine.

Court pointed to EEOC guidelines interpreting Title VII's authorization of the use of "any professionally developed ability test" that is not "designed, intended or used to discriminate because of race." The guidelines said that Title VII permitted only the use of *job-related* tests and that employers using such a test must have available data "demonstrating that the test is predictive of or significantly correlated with important elements of work behavior which comprise or are relevant to the job or jobs for which candidates are being evaluated." It was perhaps par for the revisionary course that the Court said the EEOC guidelines "comport[ed] with congressional intent."

The *Griggs* decision was the Court's first important interpretation of Title VII. It cited no rulings by lower courts, which had yet to venture so far down the disparate impact road. But as *Griggs* was now the law, those courts were obliged to follow it. And the executive branch, under both Democratic and Republican presidents, enforced it. Indeed, during the 1970s, the enforcement of Title VII was extended (as Congress authorized the Justice Department to apply the law to public employers, previously not covered) and strengthened (as Congress gave the EEOC power to bring Title VII lawsuits). Given the eager adoption of the revised version of Title VII by civil rights groups and the plaintiffs' bar, few public and private employers could escape disparate impact scrutiny by either private groups or federal agencies, or the pressure such scrutiny created to dispense with allegedly discriminatory employment practices and simply hire and promote by the numbers. The logic of *Griggs* was used in lawsuits against a variety of recruitment, hiring, assignment, testing, seniority, promotion, discharge and supervisory selection practices.[13] While *Griggs* itself did not involve the question of remedies, some lower courts, as early as 1969, had ordered quotas, despite the original meaning of Title VII. And in 1979, in *United Steelworkers of America* v. *Weber*,[14] the Supreme Court upheld a promotions quota adopted by the Kaiser Aluminum and Chemical Corporation under threat of federal enforcement policies premised on disparate impact theory; to do this, the Court quite unrealistically defined the quota as a totally private, voluntary action uninfluenced by government enforcement policies, and the Court tortured the text of Title VII to make it allow (a quota) what on its original terms it proscribed.

Thus, by the end of the 1970s, a statute designed to enforce race- and sex-neutrality in employment had been transformed by

[13]Belz, *Equality Transformed*, 54.
[14] 443 U.S. 193 (1979).

the executive bureaucracy and the courts into a law permitting if not demanding counting and hiring and promoting by race and sex. But quotas, goals, and other such devices did not win the affection of the American people, and in 1980 they elected a president who had campaigned strongly against them.[15] That was the easy part; governing against quotas proved much harder.

REAGAN'S RESPONSE

The quota culture in existence by 1981 was a product of not just the transformed law of Title VII; other laws (some also revised by executive agencies in order to effect equal results) are part of the story. But Title VII and its enforcement were the key part of the story.

In May 1981, the Department of Justice (DOJ) announced that it would no longer seek quotas as a remedy for violations of Title VII. This was an event of no small significance, as it marked the first time a federal agency had bowed out of the numbers game. The DOJ's Title VII enforcement authority extended to public employers only. For a similar change to occur with regard to the enforcement of Title VII with respect to private employers, the EEOC had to follow suit. That basically happened in 1985.

With these enforcement changes the Reagan administration recovered the original meaning of the statute with respect to the kind of remedies sought by the government in Title VII cases. But the changes did not affect the elements of disparate impact theory written into Title VII by the EEOC and the federal courts. And in fact, under Reagan, the DOJ and the EEOC pursued discrimination in both disparate treatment and disparate impact cases. While neither agency sought to expand the law of disparate impact, its vitality in the legal culture meant that there were still strong incentives for employers to avoid a lawsuit—even one that, if successful, might not lead to numerical remedies—simply by hiring and promoting by the numbers. This fact was well understood by the president's lawyers at the Justice Department. And toward the end of the administration, the DOJ finally had opportunities in litigation to seek reform of disparate impact theory.

First, however, the DOJ's litigating efforts in earlier cases deserves mention. For not only did the DOJ eliminate quotas from

---

[15]The 1980 GOP platform stated that "equal opportunity should not be jeopardized by bureaucratic regulations and decisions which rely on quotas, ratios, and numerical requirements to exclude some individuals in favor of others, thereby rendering such regulations and decisions inherently discriminatory." Reagan himself made similar statements on the campaign trail.

its Title VII enforcement; also, starting in 1982, it argued in a series of cases that Title VII did not allow courts to impose remedial quotas. The DOJ thus sought judicial affirmation of the original meaning of Title VII with respect to the question of court-ordered quotas, which had been addressed by lower courts in the 1970s and was bound to come to the Supreme Court in the 1980s. The DOJ did so not aimlessly but quite determinedly, both as an original party to a case and as a friend-of-the-court. This litigating effort, seeking to capitalize on the effects of Supreme Court rulings, envisioned decisions that in forbidding court-ordered remedial quotas would ratify the executive's anti-quota enforcement policy while establishing rules of law of more general influence.

In 1982 the DOJ asked the Supreme Court to review a layoff quota adopted by the Boston Fire Department—a case the Court accepted but later vacated. Later that year the DOJ intervened in *Williams* v. *New Orleans,* a case in the U.S. Court of Appeals for the Fifth Circuit that involved a promotions quota for the New Orleans Police Department. Although the court ruled against the quota, it did not do so on the basis of the argument advanced by the Justice Department, here offered in a federal court for the first time, namely that under Title VII judges may not order quota remedies. Failing to get the Supreme Court to take another Title VII quota case from Detroit in late 1983, the Justice Department did succeed the next year in persuading the Court to review a layoff quota ordered by a federal court in a Title VII case. In *Firefighters Local Union No. 1784* v. *Stotts,*[16] the Supreme Court held that Title VII barred the court-ordered quota under which white firefighters with greater seniority were required to be laid off before black firefighters with lesser seniority. Title VII contained a specific provision addressing layoff situations, but Justice Byron White, writing for the Court, seemed to accept the general argument, advanced by the DOJ, namely that under Title VII a court could provide make-whole relief "only to those who have been actual victims of illegal discrimination"—regardless of the context (hiring, promotions, or lay-offs).

In Title VII cases decided in 1986 and 1987, however, it was apparent that the Supreme Court did not accept that view of the statute. Again, these were cases in which the DOJ participated, either as an original party or an *amicus.* In *Local 28, Sheet Metal Workers* v. *EEOC,*[17] the Court upheld a rigid remedial quota imposed by

---

[16] 476 U.S. 561 (1984).
[17] 478 U.S. 421 (1986).

a court upon a union that had "egregiously" discriminated against nonwhites in recruiting, selection, training, and admission. And in *Local No. 93, International Ass'n of Firefighters* v. *City of Cleveland,*[18] the Court suggested that a public employer's race-conscious promotions program approved as part of a consent decree in Title VII litigation might survive legal challenge even though the same program might fail if entered as part of a court order. Thus did the Court regard a consent decree in public employment like a "voluntary" quota such as that which a private company had adopted in *Weber.* In 1987, in *Johnson* v. *Transportation Agency, Santa Clara County,*[19] the Court upheld against Title VII challenge a preference program adopted by a county government never accused of discrimination of any kind; the plan was designed to attain a work force whose composition in every job category reflected the proportion of minorities and women in the area labor market.

The Justice Department thus was not able to get the Court to recover the original meaning of Title VII as a statute absolutely forbidding the use of preferences, whether by courts in formulating remedies for proven discrimination or by public employers in ostensibly voluntary (i.e., uninfluenced by the federal government) undertakings. On the other hand, the Court did limit the situations in which courts could impose preferences in Title VII cases. In the context of proven discrimination under Title VII, court-ordered remedies in the form of layoff preferences were now unlawful, while remedies in the form of hiring or promotion quotas would have to be confined to instances where the discrimination has been long-standing, has persisted despite efforts to end it, and has remained largely indifferent to other remedial efforts.

From the administration's perspective, the biggest disappointment had to be *Johnson.* For it was here that the Court, with Justice William Brennan writing for the majority, allowed a public employer to order his work force along lines of race and gender when minorities and women are "underrepresented," not because of conscious, exclusionary discrimination against them, but because of societal patterns. If a public employer uses preferences for this reason, and a white male with superior qualifications to those of the individual benefited does not win the job or the promotion, so be it. He does not have a Title VII complaint. Concurring, Justice John Paul Stevens said that the Court's interpretation of Title VII in *Johnson* was consistent with its interpretation eight years before in *Weber,* but that "the only problem for me" is whether to adhere

[18] 478 U.S. 501 (1986).
[19] 480 U.S. 616 (1987).

to the *Weber-Johnson* view of the statute, which he candidly admitted was "at odds with my understanding of the actual intent of the authors of the legislation." That wasn't such a problem, though: "I conclude without hesitation that I must answer that question in the affirmative." What *Weber* had done for private employment, so *Johnson* did for public employment. After *Johnson*, both private and public employers could engage in preferential treatment to correct (politically incorrect) societal attitudes, in effect, without fear of a Title VII challenge from an individual who, it must be said, could only incorrectly believe that the rights that statute protected included his.

Writing in dissent, Justice Antonin Scalia, joined by Chief Justice William Rehnquist and Justice Byron White, argued not only that the majority was wrong but also that *Weber* should be overruled. "It is well to keep in mind," wrote Scalia, "just how thoroughly *Weber* rewrote the statute it purported to construe." The lawyers at the DOJ had kept that in mind—for a long time. As early as 1981 William Bradford Reynolds, the head of the Civil Rights Division, had stated publicly his disagreement with *Weber* and his belief that it should be overruled. Not only did that not happen, but *Johnson* reaffirmed and extended *Weber*.

Despite *Johnson*, the DOJ's litigating effort in regard to Title VII continued. In the 1988-89 term, the last on its watch, the Justice Department participated in *Wards Cove Packing Co.* v. *Atonio*,[20] a disparate impact case. *Wards Cove* involved Alaskan salmon canneries that employed a mainly white work force in skilled jobs and a mainly nonwhite work force in unskilled jobs. The U.S. Court of Appeals for the Ninth Circuit had ruled that this imbalance created a *prima facie* case of disparate impact against the company, thus obligating it to show that its hiring and employment practices were justified by business necessity. The Supreme Court disagreed, relying on a 1977 ruling in which it had held that the proper comparison in a disparate impact case is between "the racial composition of the qualified persons in the labor market and the persons holding at-issue jobs." Had the Court not insisted on this kind of comparison, employers would have been even more pressured to resort to quotas in order to avoid a lawsuit. The Court also addressed key aspects of disparate impact law. It held that a *prima facie* case of disparate impact cannot be made without attributing the disparity to *one or more* employment practices. Thus, a plaintiff cannot simply point to the statistical disparity and claim

---

[20] 490 U.S. 642 (1989).

discrimination; he must isolate and identify the specific employment practices allegedly causing the disparity. In this part of *Wards Cove*, the Court was correcting lower federal courts which had held that plaintiffs in disparate impact cases do *not* have to name the particular practice(s) allegedly causing the disparity. Writing for the Court, Justice Byron White observed that every one of the Supreme Court's disparate impact cases focused on the impact of a *particular* employment practice. *Wards Cove* also addressed matters involving burden of proof. The Court held that once a *prima facie* case of disparate impact is established with respect to a particular employment practice, the burden of producing evidence of a legitimate business justification for that practice shifts to the employer. The burden of *persuasion*, however, remains with the plaintiff, who must disprove an employer's evidence that his practice has a legitimate business justification; *Wards Cove*, in placing the burden of proof *at all times* upon the plaintiff, thus overruled *Griggs*, which had placed the burden upon the defendant. In this the Court unified disparate treatment and disparate impact law in a key respect, for under the former the burden of proof had since the enactment of Title VII fallen to the plaintiff. Finally, the Court relaxed the definition of "business necessity," saying that the issue in a disparate impact case is whether a challenged practice "serves, in a significant way, the legitimate employment goals of the employer."

The Reagan Justice Department had argued most of these points in its *Wards Cove* filing. Those in the Reagan presidency now employed elsewhere who had worked to reform the law of Title VII could read the Court's opinion, handed down in the summer of 1989, with great satisfaction. The reform of disparate impact theory meant that Title VII was a less effective instrument of quotas than it had been in 1981.

PRESIDENTIAL LEADERSHIP, RECONSIDERED

How did Reagan oppose the tendency of Title VII to foster quotas? The answer is: through the appointment of key executive officers, through altered law enforcement policies, through litigation in the federal courts, and through judicial appointments. Each of these means is constitutionally rooted; all of them taken together indicate the administrative nature of Reagan's leadership.

Executive appointments. No president can personally attend to what James Madison once called "the executive business." He must have help. Madison provided a good way of classifying those engaged in the executive business when he called them "the eyes and ears of the principal Magistrate, the instruments of execution." Recognizing the president's need for assistance, the Constitution gives the president the power to nominate and, with Senate approval, appoint principal executive officers. At the Justice Department, the key positions were those of Attorney General, Solicitor General, and Assistant Attorney General for the Civil Rights Division. At the EEOC, the key positions were those of the five commissioners that run the agency.

Altered law enforcement. Under the Constitution the president has the duty (and impliedly the power) to take care that the laws are faithfully executed. Title VII not only did not require but also prohibited quotas as a remedy for proven discrimination. This was the administration's conscientious view of the law (and one that scholarship has endorsed). The administration could not have maintained the pro-quota policies it inherited in 1981—and still been true to conscience or the Constitution.[21] It was therefore appropriate, indeed necessary, for the administration to alter those policies as soon as possible. Working through the presidential appointees at the DOJ and the EEOC, it did so.[22]

Litigation. Through his lawyers the president appears in federal court: to defend his law enforcement actions, to sue to enforce the laws, and to articulate his view of relevant law as a friend of the court. Justification for the presence of the president's lawyers in court can be found in the president's duty to faithfully execute the laws, including the supreme law of the land, the Constitution. And it is in the courts that the president's lawyers can pursue his view of the law. In regard to Title VII, the president's lawyers pursued the original meaning of that statute, at least in regard to its intolerance of any racial preferences, and sought reform of disparate impact theory.

Judicial appointments. Under the Constitution, the president has the power to nominate and, with Senate approval, appoint judges, including Supreme Court Justices. Consider, then, that

[21]It could not have been true to the Take Care Clause if it was enforcing an interpretation of the law it regarded as *not* faithful to its meaning. The administration also could not have enforced a pro-quota Title VII for a different constitutional reason—it read the Fourteenth Amendment as an absolute prohibition on preferences.

[22]The fact that the DOJ effected his change so quickly reflected the speed with which the president was able to appoint the key positions. That it took until 1985 at the EEOC was in part a consequence of the fact that the president was not able to appoint key people as rapidly; by statute, the commissioners—three Republicans, two Democrats—serve for five-year terms.

even as the president litigates through his lawyers, he can place on the federal benches judges who share his judicial philosophy—and who therefore might be more inclined to accept his legal arguments than those who do not share his philosophy. The 5-4 majority in *Wards Cove* was made possible by the fact that, by early 1988, Reagan had been able to fill three Supreme Court vacancies.

The appointment of executive officers or judges, the enforcement of statutes, and litigation are all elements of the president's administration of government. Thus one may call Reagan's effort against Title VII quotas an administrative one. That kind of presidential labor, especially when it pursues major policy change, can be hard and even disappointing work. Appointments (both executive and judicial) should be made after careful consideration of the candidates' qualifications, abilities, and substantive views—a difficult task. And even the best made appointments may turn out to be disasters from the president's point of view. The work involved in altering a law enforcement policy may be time consuming, especially if new rules are to be written and issued (as was not the case with the change in Title VII enforcement). And litigation is often an iffy proposition; the president cannot manufacture cases, they arise through the system as they do, and sometimes his lawyers may find themselves arguing in cases without, from their point of view, the best facts (as occurred in the 1986 Title VII cases).

Of course, none of this counsels against the administrative employment of the formal powers in behalf of a policy end. What it counsels for is the intelligent, which is to say strategic, use, of those powers. And what it shows is that excellent administration should be something we admire, indeed something we recognize for what it is: a form of presidential leadership.

Was Reagan's administration in respect to Title VII excellent, or not? Putting to one side whether or not one agrees with the policy ends, Reagan could have done more than he did in pursuit of his policies. Had he made better appointments to the EEOC during his first term, for example, the agency might have quit seeking remedial quotas *before* 1985. Also, Reagan did not reform Labor Department policies premised on disparate impact theory that encouraged both private and public employers to resort to preferences (which the Justice Department argued in litigation violated Title VII). Still, there is no question that had Reagan not been president, if his contenders (Jimmy Carter in 1980, Walter Mondale in 1984) had been elected instead, the pro-quota ratcheting of Title VII commenced in 1965 by the EEOC would have continued apace. Given different executive and judicial appointments, different law enforcement policies, and litigation strategies, the law of Title VII would have developed in predictable directions.

Whether or not one agrees with Reagan's administrative leadership regarding Title VII, it reflected the desire in the electorate for a presidency committed to limited, as opposed to expansionist, government. The trademarks of expansionist government had been government by bureaucracy often assisted by an activist judiciary. The revision of Title VII accomplished by the EEOC and the federal courts in the period from 1965 through the Seventies was clearly an example of expansionist government. Such government had not troubled liberalism. But it did bother conservatism, or at least some elements within conservatism, which argued that the rule of law requires the executive to enforce statutes, and the judiciary to interpret and apply them, according to their original terms. The Reagan labor against quotas thus also paid tribute to this understanding of the rule of law, at least in its attempt to recover the original meaning of Title VII as an absolutely antipreferential treatment statute.

That the administration did not also seek to recover the original definition of discrimination embodied in Title VII reflected a prudential judgment, of the kind it is permitted a presidency to make, and on balance the enforcers appeared to have decided that the impact of disparate impact theory, however objectionable it might be as a matter of policy and a violation of the rule of law, could be contained by opposing remedial quotas. This judgment seemed validated when the administration sought and won reform of disparate impact theory in *Wards Cove*—thus enabling it to have another department of government in agreement with its views. *Wards Cove*, however, was not the final word in the battle over Title VII, nor, as we shall see, has that word been written.

POSTSCRIPT TO ADMINISTRATION: LEGISLATION

A Democratic Congress upset with *Wards Cove* (and several other 1989 Supreme Court rulings on civil rights issues) sought to change what the Court had done. When legislation responding to *Wards Cove* (and a host of other civil rights decisions and issues) was first introduced, in early 1990, the Bush Justice Department said there was no need to revise *Wards Cove*. By the summer of 1990, however, President Bush had indicated his willingness to accept corrective legislation of some kind, although he insisted that he would not accept a "quota bill." The president did agree on shifting the burden of proof *back* to the employer—and thus recovering this aspect of *Griggs* (which was at odds with the original terms of the law). But he could not reach agreement with Congress over the degree to which employees should be forced to identify specific employment practices, nor on the definition of "business necessity." Viewing the provisions on these matters as strengthening the tendency of disparate impact theory to force employers to resort to quotas, Bush vetoed the legislation.

That proved the first half of a legislative battle between the Democratic Congress and the Republican executive. In 1991, Congress passed a similar bill. This time Bush signed it. The new statute overruled only one of the three key parts of *Wards Cove*. Under the Civil Rights Act of 1991, the burden of proof is with the employer. But a plaintiff may not bring a disparate impact case simply by complaining about an employer's practices in general; consistent with *Wards Cove*, he must specify which of the employer's practices is causing the disparate impact. And the new law does not define the hotly contested issue of "business necessity," punting it, in effect, back to the courts, still dominated by Reagan and Bush appointees. (We could see a "unified" government—i.e., a Democratic Congress and a Democratic executive—responding to the Reagan-Bush judiciary). The bill Bush signed was better, from his perspective, than the one he vetoed the year before. But consider what his approval of the bill meant: disparate impact theory had finally been codified, which is to say the revision of Title VII commenced by the EEOC in 1965 and affirmed by the Supreme Court in *Griggs* in 1971 finally gained statutory expression in 1991.

These legislative events prompt some final thoughts. A successful litigating effort by a conservative president may force an issue previously treated by the bureaucracy and the courts into the department of government closest to the people—the Congress—provided that there are enough in Congress who disagree with the Court's rulings. While such a litigating effort may do service to the idea of rule of law by forcing Congress to consider policies developed in places less visible and accessible to the people, it is no guarantee of final success on the president's part. The president may use his veto power successfully, and in this instance Bush's veto protected the litigating success of the Reagan presidency even as it fostered welcome legislative debate, as this was the first time (since 1964) Congress had legislated on matters affecting employment quotas. But the ability of the Democratic Congress to force the president to compromise and accept some correction of *Wards Cove* suggests that divided government means not only limited government in the sense of a conservative presidency opposed to the expansionist government of liberalism, but also limited government in the sense of a liberal Congress willing to limit a conservative presidency's reform of the inherited expansionist government.

The history of Title VII from 1981 to 1991 might have been different had the Reagan and Bush presidencies pursued not only an administrative but also a legislative strategy. Responding to the 1979 *Weber* decision in 1981, for example, Reagan could have asked Congress to re-enact the absolute prohibition against preferences embodied in the original Title VII. Likewise, in 1987, he could have asked Congress to overrule *Johnson*. And in 1989-91, Bush could have raised for public discussion the salient issue—that of whether we really want to codify disparate impact theory, and if so, how we want to do that—in a way that fosters quotas or reduces their possibility. Throughout the period Reagan and Bush could have made the Democratic Congress and its embrace of quotas a more pointed election issue; after all, having majorities on *your* side does matter.

Had there been such a legislative strategy, perhaps today the law of Title VII, not to mention much else besides, would be much closer to its original meaning. If the Reagan-Bush effort against Title VII quotas teaches us the oft-forgotten administrative nature of presidential leadership, it also reminds us of the enduring relevance of its legislative aspect. The truly energetic executive will attend to both.

WAS DIVIDED GOVERNMENT REALLY SUCH A BIG PROBLEM?

Michael J. Malbin

THE START of a new presidential administration is a time when most people who care about government, Republicans and Democrats, look toward the future. This time the feeling seems to have a special edge. After twelve years, the presidency, House, and Senate are all controlled by members of the same political party. For Republicans, that means some soul searching. For Democrats it is a cause for rejoicing. In addition to the political actors, however, there are some who have been rejoicing for the sake of the process. These are the people who think divided party control was behind whatever has gone wrong in recent years in the relationships between the legislative and executive branches of the government.

Studies of divided government understandably have become prominent these past dozen years.[1] For example, the newest edition of one of the leading textbooks of American constitutional history called "divided government under the separation of powers the central constitutional problem of the 1980s."[2] Note that di-

---

[1] For starters, see Gary W. Cox and Samuel Kernell, eds., *The Politics of Divided Government* (Boulder: Westview, 1991); Morris Fiorina, *Divided Government* (New York: Macmillan, 1992); Benjamin Ginsberg and Martin Shefter, *Politics By Other Means* (New York: Basic Books, 1990); David R. Mayhew, *Divided We Govern: Party Control, Lawmaking, and Investigations, 1946–1990* (New Haven: Yale, 1991); James Sundquist, "Needed: A Political Theory for the New Era of Coalition Government in the United States," *Political Science Quarterly* 103 (1988): 613–35; James A. Thurber, ed., *Divided Democracy: Cooperation and Conflict Between the President and Congress* (Washington, DC: CQ Press, 1991).

[2] Alfred H. Kelly, Winfred A. Harbison and Herman Belz, *The American Constitution: Its Origins and Development*, 7th ed. (New York: Norton, 1991), 705. I should note, for the record, that it would *not* be accurate to say that Kelly, Harbison and

vided government is described as a "problem"—not as a neutral fact of life, or as an inconvenience, or even as a symptom, but as a major *cause* of harm to the political community. And because divided government presupposes a separation of powers system, the alleged problems of divided government have been held out by some of its critics (not the above textbook) as evidence of a problem with the separation of powers per se, and with a need to move the country toward a Westminister-style parliamentary democracy.

At this junction point between two administrations, therefore, it would be worthwhile to look back at the record to see whether divided government was in fact such a big problem. Before we can do that, however, the issue needs further definition. Divided government was said to be a problem because it was said to contribute (1) to the government's alleged inability to act, (2) to intense interbranch warfare between Congress and the executive branch, and (3) to an ongoing effort by Congress to control the executive branch through "micromanagement" of the administration. This essay will consider each of these alleged failings, and then conclude with a brief explication of a different set of "problems"— political and electoral ones, rather than the structural issues that form the heart of the usual critique of divided government under the separation of powers.

POLICY PARALYSIS?

One of the country's most thoughtful critics of the separation of powers, James Sundquist, has argued that the Constitution, particularly under divided party control, has produced a paralyzed government unable to reduce the massive federal budget deficit or address the other key policy issues of the day.[3] As Congress becomes more partisan, it is said to become more determined to prevent the president from achieving his policy goals. The opposition party in Congress even is said to prefer stalemate to endorsing an action with which it fundamentally disagrees. As a result, the two parties stake out their positions and nothing gets done.

Belz believe that divided government was the root of everything that went wrong in the 1980s. However, the quotation does accurately portray their view of the concept's importance.

[3]James L. Sundquist, *Constitutional Reform and Effective Government* (Washington, D.C.: The Brookings Institution, 1986); Sundquist, "Needed: A Political Theory," 613–35. For a related and similar argument, see Lloyd Cutler, "To Form a Government," *Foreign Affairs* 59 (Fall 1980): 126–43.

If Sundquist's charges were accurate, they would be very serious. After all, if inaction had been the goal, the Framers would have been satisfied with amending the Articles of Confederation. The Constitution was meant, in part, to create a government that would be better able to act to preserve liberty than was possible under the Articles. This was to be done not only by empowering Congress, and not only by strengthening the national government's formal authority vis-à-vis the states. It was also to be done through the separation of powers. Today, the separation of powers is often portrayed (by Sundquist and others) solely in terms of checks and balances. But the idea of separation was also intended to help strengthen the government by creating a presidential office whose occupant would have the political capacity to lead, and not merely to be the passive clerk favored when the Articles of Confederation were written.[4] Therefore, if having separate legislative, executive, and judicial branches of government, under contemporary conditions, seriously weakens the government's ability to govern a free people, that would be a good reason to rethink the Constitution's adequacy to serve its own deepest purposes.

Sundquist's case is intuitively appealing, but cannot be sustained. For one thing, divided governments have not systematically been associated with stalemate in this country. In a recent book, David Mayhew showed that since World War II, divided governments have produced just about the same number of significant new laws, and have had just about the same number of highly publicized congressional investigations of the executive, as occurred under conditions of unified party control.[5] Even during the heightened partisanship of the Reagan and Bush administrations, Mayhew noted that Congress enacted and the president signed:

- the Tax Reduction Act of 1981, followed by a series of tax increases in later years;
- major shifts in budget priorities;
- a major increase, leveling, and then decrease in the defense budget;
- a 25-year renewal and major expansion of the Voting Rights Act;
- a reorganization of the Defense Department;

---

[4]Charles C. Thach, Jr., *The Creation of the Presidency, 1775–1789* (Baltimore: Johns Hopkins, 1969); Gordon S. Wood, *The Creation of the American Republic, 1776–1787* (Chapel Hill: University of North Carolina Press, 1969); Sidney Milkis and Michael Nelson, *The American Presidency: Origins and Development, 1776–1990* (Washington, D.C.: CQ Press, 1990), 1-67.

[5]Mayhew, *Divided We Govern.*

- the Tax Reform Act of 1986, which was the most thorough overhaul of the tax code in decades;
- a major revision of the federal criminal code;
- immigration reform;
- an omnibus trade measure;
- the Intermediate Nuclear Forces Treaty of 1988;
- a Savings and Loan bailout; and
- a renewal and major expansion of the Clean Air Act.

Whether one agrees or disagrees with the policies in these statutes, it seems hard by any reasonable standards to call this a record of stalemate.

DEFICIT REDUCTION

Against all these new laws, critics have pointed to the deficit. Surely, they say, the policy failures on this issue during the Reagan and Bush years were of such crucial importance as to overwhelm everything else. In reply, I would argue that the critics are confusing the government's failure to adopt the policies the critics prefer with a failure to act.

The difference can be seen most clearly by examining the "deficit reduction package" of 1990. That highly contentious budget agreement—coming after President Bush had abandoned his "no new taxes" campaign promise of 1988—was negotiated by key White House and Office of Management and Budget appointees with Republican and Democratic party leaders in the House and Senate. It then was rejected by an alliance of rank and file liberal Democrats and conservative Republicans in the House. What followed was a confusing, bitter series of negotiations that ended only after the government literally had to shut down for a brief time. The final agreement adopted by Congress largely followed the initial one that was rejected. It was supposed to reduce the deficit by a cumulative amount of $490 billion over the course of five years, but the deficit in fact ballooned during the recession of 1991–92.

Critics point to the swelling of the deficit during 1991–92 as "Exhibit A" in their argument to show that divided government leads to paralysis. The 1990 budget agreement, however, represented almost anything but inaction. It was a deliberate set of decisions that knowingly allowed the deficit to grow during an economic recession. The 1990 budget agreement replaced the firm deficit targets that had been in law since 1985 with a new set of priorities. The Gramm-Rudman-Hollings deficit reduction act of 1985 had required the government to meet a fixed budget deficit or face automatic, across the board spending cuts. That is, the deficit was the number one priority of Gramm-Rudman-Hollings, and that was precisely why the members were unhappy with it.

The difference between the two approaches comes through most clearly during a recession. Suppose the economy went into a slump after Congress met all of the required targets under Gramm-Rudman-Hollings, but before the start of a new fiscal year. Naturally, a weak economy would drive entitlement spending up and tax revenues down. Under these circumstances, the 1985 law required further rounds of spending cuts or tax increases to meet the deficit target.

In contrast, the 1990 law replaced the fixed deficit targets of 1985 with fixed ceilings for categorical spending programs and flexible deficit goals. It included separate two-year ceilings for defense spending, discretionary domestic spending, and entitlements. However, the law specifically *permitted* entitlement spending to increase if economic conditions should worsen or demographic conditions should change, as long as no new laws were passed to create new programs or to make new classes of people eligible for old programs. (New entitlements would have to be funded by cutting old ones or by raising taxes.)

Thus, the 1990 law could be read as a firm decision to rank deficit reduction lower than other budget priorities. The decision made perfect sense, given the priorities held by various party factions in Congress as well as the divisions in opinion in the public at large. The relatively low priority of the deficit is obvious for the members who opposed the 1990 agreement. Republican opponents were upset with tax increases; Democratic opponents were upset with the failure to shift more military spending to domestic programs.

More interesting conceptually were the members in both parties who supported the package. All of the package's supporters said they were doing so because of the importance of the deficit. But for everyone involved in the process, at least one priority had a higher importance. Democrats were willing to cut defense spending and raise taxes to reduce the deficit, but not to cut domestic entitlement programs. For most Republicans, the priorities were reversed. Based on the members' behavior—and placing the highest possible priority on deficit reduction consistent with that behavior—one could describe their priorities with a ranking like this:[6]

---

[6] The argument and table in this section, despite specific points of disagreement, owe a great deal to Matthew D. McCubbins, "Government on Lay-Away: Federal Spending and Deficits Under Divided Party Control," in *The Politics of Divided Government*, ed. Cox and Kernell, esp. 138–40.

Table 1
Rank Order of Budget Priorities

Rank Order	Democrats	Republicans
First	Preserve domestic programs	Preserve defense spending; low taxes
Second	Deficit reduction	Deficit reduction
Third	Reduce defense; Raise taxes	Cut domestic spending

A true stalemate could have occurred if the two parties had a direct conflict in their first priorities—for example, if the Democrats thought nothing was more important than preserving domestic spending and the Republicans had thought nothing was more important than cutting it. That was not the situation in 1990. Instead, even though the two House parties' majorities wanted different things, the importance they placed on each goal gave them room to work out a compromise. Each side was willing to put off cutting the spending programs the other cared most about, in order to get its own first spending priority. In the course of reaching this agreement, each was willing to give ground on the deficit—something they both considered to be important, but secondary.[7] It follows that if party control of the House, Senate, and presidency had been united, and if deficit reduction had in fact ranked as high as its second priority, that party probably would have made a more sustained effort to cut the deficit during the 1980s and 1990s than came out of the process under divided government.

Fair enough, but so what? How do we move from this observation to the conclusion that divided government was a stalemated failure? The situation clearly was *not* one of stalemate but a collective decision about priorities that happened not to match the priorities of any one individual or party. Was the collective decision a failure? Many economists might think so, but the point of a democratic political process is not to translate the will of the policy analyst into policy. The process managed to let each side preserve what was most important while preserving its ability to fight for a mandate to do more.

[7]Note that it would have made no difference to the actual result if deficit reduction were the second, third, or a lower priority. I am only assuming it was the second priority for most members to give the Sundquist argument its strongest possible reading.

Is that necessarily a bad result in a democracy? Not automatically. Neither party deserves to implement its first *and* second priorities, at the expense of running roughshod over the other party's first priority. To earn such a mandate, it has to make a convincing case to the American people and then get elected on that platform.

President Reagan took just such a case to the American people in 1980, won the election, and then carried a mandate into office that enabled him to achieve a great deal. By the time of the 1982 midterm election, however, recession had set in and the public clearly did not want wholesale cuts in domestic spending programs. In 1984 and 1988, the winning Republican candidate made no effort to build a 1980-style mandate for domestic cuts to control the deficit. At the same time, however, the public strongly rejected tax increases. That is, the public rejected the Democrats' third priority (tax increase), without accepting or even clearly voting on the Republicans' third priority (spending cuts). Instead, the public seemed to be endorsing both parties' top priorities (keep taxes low, preserve domestic spending). In light of that, the political system seemed to do a reasonable job of following the public's priorities.[8] If the public's priorities are problematic, the remedy would seem to lie in the realm of public persuasion. We shall return to this point later.

INSTITUTIONAL FIREWORKS

If divided government cannot be blamed for stalemate, can it be blamed for an excessively intense level of conflict that allegedly developed across the branches from 1981–93? One recent book argues, for example, that as Democrats became entrenched in the House and Republicans won the presidency, the two parties used policies cynically to make the other party look bad and to increase the power of "their own" institution.[9] Each branch sought to control federal policy from its own power base, bypassing the other branch whenever it could do so.

The classic example of this kind of behavior was the Iran-Contra affair. In the major legislative prelude to Iran-Contra,

---

[8]For a different way of reaching the same conclusion, see David A. Stockman, *The Triumph of Politics: How the Reagan Revolution Failed* (New York: Harper & Row, 1986). Stockman was the director of the Office and Management and Budget for President Reagan's first term.

[9]Benjamin Ginsberg and Martin Shefter, *Politics By Other Means* (New York: Basic Books, 1990).

Congress adopted a limitation amendment in an appropriations bill (the Boland Amendment) to prohibit all spending by U.S. intelligence agencies to help the Nicaraguan rebels, or Contras. In subsequent interpretations, many in Congress also claimed that a spending prohibition could also be used to restrict the president's ability to persuade other governments, through ordinary diplomatic conversations, to help the Contras. Meanwhile, at the same time that Congress was using its undoubted power over the purse to reach into the sphere of diplomatic communication, the president's staff was stretching the concepts of "diplomatic activity" and "inherent executive powers" to say that they included White House staff activities to help set up and then manage private "cutout" corporations that were partly funded from proceeds obtained by the covert sale of U.S. property. That is, the White House staff was taking it upon itself to spend public funds without an appropriation—a fact that cannot be disputed, however broadly or narrowly one might interpret the poorly phrased Boland Amendment. Thus, both branches were trying to gain control over a policy by straining its own constitutional powers to reach into and negate the core constitutional powers of the other. The question is whether Iran-Contra was symptomatic of contemporary divided government or an aberration.

Iran-Contra involved a two-sided constitutional-political miscalculation by President Reagan. The first side involved an error of omission. The president failed to veto a bill, or even to give Congress a clear statement of his reservations, even though the bill contained a provision that he apparently thought stepped over the bounds of Congress's constitutional authority. Instead he signed the bill, and then proceeded silently to place his own interpretation on it. The president's second miscalculation was to assume he could get away with this. He and his White House aides behaved as if Congress could be kept off guard through secrecy and would not step in jealously to protect its own constitutional position once it understood what was happening.

There is nothing in divided government that inevitably produces these kinds of misjudgments. If anything, these are the kinds of mistakes the separation of powers is best able to deter. The theory underlying *Federalist* 51 is that the occupants of any office will have a stake in defending that office's powers. The assumption is that the legislative branch will bring a natural strength to any contest between the branches because of its popular support. By implication, for the president or Supreme Court to withstand legislative attack, it too must have a base of popular support. In particular contests, that requires the president (or the

Court) to state its position openly and persuasively. To ignore the constitutional challenge and act secretly, as if nothing had happened, is to invite long term damage to the office.

In addition to openness, the theory of *Federalist* 51 would seem to require a seriousness of purpose. In a struggle for power, contestants are taken more seriously when they are seen to have core principles which they will not compromise. President Reagan was understood to be unwilling to compromise a few such substantive issues (although even on these his flexibility was much greater than its public reputation). However, he also repeatedly showed himself willing to make institutional concessions to Congress in order to win points of substantive policy. The Boland Amendment would have been easier to veto, for example, if it had not been part of a massive continuing resolution that joined many appropriations bills together in one package. Over the years, however, Congress came to see that President Reagan could be made to swallow such continuing resolutions in return for substantive compromises on specific programs.

President Bush's reputation in Washington was in some ways the opposite of President Reagan's. He was seen as being more willing than his predecessor to compromise on substance—his conservative opponents would say excessively so. However, he was also less willing (not unwilling, but less willing) to compromise on questions of institutional power.

President Bush regularly used the statements he issued at the time he signed bills into law to assert his institutional interests. Rather than feeling forced to choose between vetoing a bill and accepting it, President Bush used signing statements to announce that he intended to ignore, or interpret narrowly, provisions that he believed would violate his obligation to defend the constitutional powers of his office against the terms of an unconstitutional statute. Other presidents have issued similar signing statements, but none as systematically as Bush.[10] Eight of the president's 24 veto messages during the years 1989–91 included objections based on the bill's perceived intrusion (or intrusions) on the president's constitutional powers. In each of these cases, the disputed provision was central to the bill's purpose. In addition, President Bush issued 62 signing statements in 1989–91 with similar constitutional objections. In the case of the signing statements, the

---

[10]For a valuable discussion of vetoes and signing statements, see Terry Eastland, *Energy in the Executive: The Case for a Strong Presidency* (New York: Free Press, 1992), ch. 4.

section or sections to which the president objected generally could be ignored, or construed narrowly, without negating the bill's central purpose.[11]

At first glance, President Bush's approach might seem confrontational. Because the president was open and fairly consistent, however, the paradoxical effect was to reduce the level of interbranch procedural warfare. Or, to put the same point conversely, a firm and open willingness to defend institutional powers, on the part of both branches, tended to increase rather than decrease the level of comity between the legislature and executive. Congress still passed laws that included what would appear to be overassertions of its authority—such as when it tried to force diplomatic negotiations upon the president legislatively. At the same time, many members of Congress had equally strong objections to some of the president's constitutional interpretations. But the key point is that the disputes were reasonably self-contained. The two sides stated their constitutional positions, agreed to disagree, and then moved on to the substantive policy issues.[12]

CONGRESSIONAL MANAGEMENT OF THE EXECUTIVE BRANCH

It is no small matter to say that disputes during the Bush years, bothersome though they may have been, did not rise to the level of a constitutional confrontation.[13] That does not mean, however, that everything functioned smoothly. In this section, I shall look briefly at whether divided government contributed to excessively detailed management of the executive branch by Congress during the Reagan and Bush administrations.

In a 1992 report called *Beyond Distrust: Building Bridges Between Congress and the Executive*, a panel of the National Academy of Public Administration (NAPA) concluded, among other things, that charges of excessive congressional "micromanagement" of the executive branch were largely unfounded. What makes the study interesting is that most members of the panel had experience in both branches of government. Moreover, most went into the pro-

---

[11] A list of the relevant 1989–91 signing statements and vetoes, grouped according to the kind of objection, is presented in the Appendix.

[12] For a more general explanation of why this occurs, using some rudimentary game theory, see Michael J. Malbin, "Legislative-Executive Lessons From the Iran-Contra Affair," in *Congress Reconsidered*, 4th ed., ed. L. Dodd and B. Oppenheimer (CQ Press, 1989), 375–92.

[13] We can conjecture a set of possibilities around the beginning of the Persian Gulf War that might have produced such a confrontation, but, happily, they did not occur.

cess feeling more negative about detailed congressional intervention into executive branch operations than they felt at the end.

The heart of NAPA's work was a series of ten case studies of detailed congressional involvement in administration. These included two of transportation policy, one each involving energy, the environment, and health care costs, three of defense, and two of foreign policy. In every single case, the panel found over the course of time "a common progression from a broad delegation of authority [at the beginning of each case study starting as early as the 1940s or as late as the 1970s] to much more detailed, frequently sustained, congressional involvement" from the mid-1970s through the time of the panel's work.[14] The consistent progression toward more detailed involvement, however, was neither helpful nor harmful automatically, the panel said. In some cases, programs were languishing in indifferent bureaucracies. In others, specific units within an agency had a stake in resisting policy change, and it took congressional involvement to awaken the interest of higher level political appointees in the executive branch. As a result, the panel concluded that "difficult situations were often improved as a result of congressional intervention."[15]

I have no doubt that detailed intervention helped the substance of policy in a number of instances. Improving particular situations, however, is not the end of the story. In the course of achieving those specific results, Congress may well be overwhelming the system—making deliberation over the broad purposes of policy impossible to sustain and public accountability more difficult to pin down.

The difference between collective and individual results is sometimes hard to bear in mind, particularly for elected officials who have to make their policy decisions one at a time. To help clarify the point, consider some of the techniques Congress has used to increase the level of their involvement. As listed by NAPA, they have included:

• detailed administrative and organizational requirements written in statute;
• requiring agencies to issue formal reports to Congress;
• deadlines for regulations ("hammers");

---

[14]National Academy of Public Administration, Panel on Congress and the Executive, James R. Jones, chair, *Beyond Distrust: Building Bridges Between Congress and the Executive* (Washington, D.C.: National Academy of Public Administration, 1992), 48.
[15]Ibid., 8.

• report-and-wait or other specific requirements for agency rule-making;
• personnel floors or ceilings;
• special staffing requirements;
• special benefits, conditions or exceptions for specific interests or constituents;
• very detailed program guidance in committee reports; and
• personal interventions by members or their staffs into program particulars.[16]

Every one of these techniques can be justified in specific situations, one at a time. But consider how just one of these techniques, required reports, can accumulate in one, admittedly large, agency of government. Table 2 lists the number of reports Congress has required of the Defense Department in selected years over the past two decades.

Even a cursory look at the number of congressional reports, as well as the timing of the statutes in NAPA's ten policy case studies, show a marked increase in the level of intervention over the past twelve years of divided government. Divided government does not really explain what has been happening, however. Republican Senate committees asked for almost as many reports from the Defense Department as their Democratic House counterparts during 1981–86, when the two chambers were controlled by different political parties. In other words, there is no reason President Clinton should think the issue will go away. Partisanship is not the only issue, and, as the NAPA report should make clear, reports are only one of a long list of available control techniques.

The use of these techniques clearly serves the interests of many members, as individuals. As a result, the habit will be a hard one to break. There is no obvious solution that one can assume members of Congress will adopt voluntarily. As with the use of signing statements, the situation may call for some executive branch assertiveness. Perhaps each executive branch agency should keep complete records of all nonstatutory congressional interventions, publish the results annually, and then challenge the Congress to explain itself. If such steps are taken fairly early in the new administration, while Democratic members of Congress still feel a stake in the new president's administrative performance, then maybe the new process can have a salutary effect.

---

[16]Ibid., 32.

[17]For data through 1990, see U.S. Department of Defense, *White Paper on The Department of Defense and the Congress*, Report to the President by the Secretary of Defense (January 1990).

Table 2
Reports Required From the Defense
Department by Congress

Fiscal Year	Number of Reports
1970	36
1976	114
1977	129
1978	153
1979	177
1980	231
1981	223
1982	221
1983	325
1984	422
1985	458
1986	676
1987	680
1988	719
1989	661
1990	861
1991	676
1992	734

NOTE: The table counts required reports specified in the House and Senate versions of the Defense and Military Construction authorization and appropriations bills.
SOURCE: U.S. Department of Defense.[17]

Whatever the impetus or solution, the cumulative effects of these interventions are almost antipolitical, in two distinct ways. First, the energy in both branches is drawn toward the narrow and particular concerns of individual members or staffers, making it harder for political leaders—members of Congress as well as presidential appointees—to focus on the major policy issues they ought to be addressing. Second, and more importantly, even when the subject is a matter of general interest and importance, the effect of a nonstatutory control is to remove members of Congress from taking politically accountable actions for the power they are attempting to exercise.[18] This exercise of power without accountability or debate helps foster the public's cynicism and its doubts about the extent to which it can control what the government is doing. Perhaps that is why the scholars quoted at the start of this

paper have some basis for feeling that divided government—
although not for their reasons—may nevertheless be symptomatic
of one of "the central constitutional problem[s]" of our era.

CONCLUSION: THE PROBLEMS OF ACCOUNTABILITY AND LEGITIMACY

So far this essay has argued that (1) divided government does
not cause policy stalemate, although it does produce policies that
fail to meet the full range of priorities for any one person or faction in Congress; (2) divided government does not *inevitably* produce excessive levels of interbranch conflict; but (3) detailed management of the executive branch does lead to an excessive focus on
minor issues of interest to a few, at the expense of serious public
deliberation over major issues of national policy.

If all of these arguments prove to be correct, then what was
the problem with divided government over the past twelve years?
I would argue that the problem lay not so much with the government's ability to act as with the perceived legitimacy of its actions.
Specifically, it came from the perceived lack of connection between
election campaigning and governing. But this lack of a connection
is not caused either by the separation of powers or by divided government. Maintaining the connection between citizens and the
government can be difficult under any system of democratic representation. It is true that divided government and the separation
of powers add distinctly American features to the issue. But I shall
argue that the solution, such as it may be, will come more
readily from electoral reforms than from a wholesale change in
the Constitution.

Members of Congress, and to a lesser extent presidents, seem
to have been elected over the past fifteen years or so for reasons
that had little to do with the job they would have to perform in
government. As so many have noted, campaigning skills were becoming distinct from governing skills. More importantly, under divided government, almost everyone was able with some credibility
to blame somebody else for the government's policies. No policy
quite matched what anyone proposed. Of course, one of the virtues of an extended republic was supposed to be that no one faction could make policy by itself. Policy was supposed to be the
result of a compromise, and it is. But few people seem to have been
willing to stand up and be judged by the result. With blame avoidance a fine art, no wonder the public sometimes has felt cynical
about its ability to influence what is happening.

James Sundquist made what I think are wrong assertions about the policy consequences of divided government, but he put his finger on one of the key problems of contemporary politics. In a representative democracy, public opinion never was supposed to dictate the details of governmental policy—public opinion is too unformed to take on that kind of a job. But the public was expected to render some kind of a subsequent judgment on the performance of its representatives, and that judgment should have some reasonable connection to the main policy tasks that engage the whole representative body.

Political parties once helped simplify this task for the public, but they have not performed that role since the late 1960s. To return to the theme of a paper I wrote for a previous Ashbrook Center volume,[19] the political parties were becoming more united *inside* Congress, with the out-party more strongly opposed to the president, at precisely the same time as the parties were also becoming less important for congressional elections. There is a basic disconnection between the party's lack of a role in the government's relationships with the public and its increasingly important role in the government's relationships with itself.

The weak connection between campaigning and governing all but preoccupies parliamentary-style reformers. The way to strengthen that connection, they argue, is to implement procedures that would turn elections into mandates for governmental action. In this way of thinking, the need for a clear mandate outweighs all other potential functions free elections might perform. It leads directly to an argument for reforms that would sharply downgrade the separation of powers and aim toward a parliamentary system with disciplined political parties.

Unfortunately, the world rarely works as simply as one might wish. The idea that elections can be designed to assure mandates is based on the assumption that party platforms will force people to choose, and that people will do so. That is a big assumption. The public will be forced to make a clear cut choice only in a disciplined, two-party system, and such two-party systems will sustain themselves only in countries where the people are prepared for two and only two choices.

The problem—if it is a problem—is that disciplined two-party systems are rare and cannot be imposed from above. The key word

---

[19]Michael J. Malbin, "Political Parties Across the Separation of Powers," in *American Political Parties and Constitutional Politics*, ed. Peter W. Schramm and Bradford P. Wilson (Lanham: Rowman & Littlefield, 1993), 75–90.

here is "disciplined." Single member district systems with winner-take-all elections tend to promote two parties per district, but they cannot explain why the same two parties dominate nationwide. Having the same two parties nationally in a large, diverse country works when the local parties or candidates are free to define their positions in ways each district will accept. Two-party systems with coherent policy platforms and disciplined voting in the legislature require another set of conditions. They presuppose either a country that is much less diverse than the United States or one that is polarized around a single, deeply divisive set of issues. Thus, designing institutions to give absolute priority to producing mandates would come at a very high price. Disciplined two-party systems would work at cross-purposes with the most fundamental decision of 1787: the decision to encourage diversity as part of an effort to preserve liberty and make politics less of a life-and-death matter than it is in so many other countries.

Much more likely than two disciplined parties in a country as diverse as the United States, however, would be a splintering of electoral options to reflect the variety of opinions that exist in the country at large. Parliamentary government in the United States, therefore, would become multi-party coalition government. In such a situation, there is no reason to expect that elections would produce a clearer mandate for governmental action than do elections under a separation of powers system. One need only think about Italy, Israel, and Belgium to realize how many otherwise healthy, multi-party democracies have been unable—even immediately after an election—to come to agreement and act upon some crucial issue or another.

That being the case, one would be hard pressed to claim that multi-party parliaments automatically would do a better job than a separation of powers system at creating mandates. Priorities would still have to be compromised and the political responsibility for governmental results would still have to be muddled. The difference is that the negotiations leading to compromise policies would take place inside a cabinet or during the process of coalition formation, instead of inside the legislature.[20]

So it would seem that the problem of reconnecting campaigning to governing across the branches is not amenable to an easy institutional fix. This may be one of those arenas in which a great deal may depend upon the character of politicians and the vigilance of citizens. The main reason politicians separate campaign-

[20]For this point, see Fiorina, *Divided Government*, 117–21.

ing from governing—campaigning as isolated individuals who should not be blamed for their institution's collective decisions—is that they can get away with it. If we do not want them to get away with it, the organizations that need to be strengthened are the ones most appropriate for making the desired reconnection.

For example, campaign finance laws could make candidates more dependent on party organizations. The parties, in turn, could be given regulatory and financial incentives (e.g., free media time) for developing themes that cut across offices and individual candidates. Once this is accomplished, the parties automatically would have an incentive to hold victorious members of the opposition party accountable for the promises they made in the previous campaign. Similarly, a presidential election system could make it desirable, instead of politically dangerous, for candidates to seek national policy mandates through party-based campaigns that would involve members of Congress.[21] It may seem farfetched to think that such changes would be adequate to overcome the fragmenting effects of political careerism and modern technological politics. But if it is farfetched, it surely is less so than trying to achieve the same results by doing away with the separation of powers.

APPENDIX

Presidential Vetoes and Signing Statements, 1989–1991
　　Prepared by Christopher Grill[22]

What follows is a list of vetoes and signing statements, taken from the *Weekly Compilation of Presidential Documents,* in which President Bush made a constitutional objection to a provision in a bill that he thought overstepped or endangered his constitutional authority. These are arranged by the topic of the president's objection. Some vetoes and signing statements contained more than one objection and these are listed under each objection. Under each heading, in parentheses, is a synopsis of the objection made by the president.

I. CONDUCT OF DIPLOMACY, NEGOTIATIONS, AND FOREIGN POLICY

(The executive power of the president includes the exclusive authority to conduct negotiations on behalf of the United States,

---

[21]The Democrats took a first step in this direction during the 1980s by telling members they could be unpledged "superdelegates" to the national convention, but much more would need to be done to make much of a difference.
[22]Graduate Student in Political Science at the State University of New York at Albany.

the "fundamental responsibility" to protect the national interest, and the authority to articulate foreign policy without congressional interference.)

Vetoes

FS-X Airplane Codevelopment, SJ Res 113, July 31, 1989
Foreign Aid Appropriations Bill, HR 2939, Nov. 19, 1989
State Department Authorization, HR 1487, Nov. 21, 1989
Textile, Apparel, and Footwear Trade Act, HR 4328, Oct. 5, 1990
Omnibus Export Amendments Act, HR 4653, Nov. 16, 1990
Intelligence Authorization Act, S 2834, Nov. 30, 1990

Signing Statements

Foreign Operations, Export Financing, PL 101-167, Nov. 21, 1989
U.S.-Palau Compact, PL 101-219, Dec. 12, 1989
Steel Trade Liberalization Act, PL 101-221, Dec. 12, 1989
Anti-Terrorism and Arms Export Act, PL 101-222, Dec. 12, 1989
Assistance for Panama, PL 101-243, Feb. 14, 1990
Foreign Relations Authorization Act, PL 101-246, Feb. 16, 1990
Supplemental Appropriations Bill, PL 101-302, May 25, 1990
Oil Pollution Act, PL 101-380, Aug. 18, 1990
National Defense Act, PL 101-510, Nov. 5, 1990
Department of Defense Appropriations, PL 101-511, Nov. 5, 1990
Foreign Operations, Export Financing, HR 5114, Nov. 5, 1990
Antarctic Protection Act, PL 101-594, Nov. 16, 1990
Aviation Security Act, PL 101-604, Nov. 16, 1990
Fishery Conservation Amendments, 101-627, Nov. 28, 1990
Operation Desert Storm Supplemental Appropriations, PL 102-28, April 10, 1991
Foreign Relations Authorization Act, PL 102-138, Oct 28, 1991
Departments of Commerce, Justice, State, and Judiciary Appropriations Act, PL 102-140, Oct. 28, 1991
Trade and Unemployment Benefits, HR 1724, Dec. 4, 1991
National Defense Authorization Act, HR 2100, Dec. 5, 1991
Coast Guard Act, PL 102-241, Dec. 19, 1991
FDIC Improvement Act, PL 102-242, Dec. 19, 1991

II. Powers as Commander-in-Chief

(Congress cannot constrain the president's authority to deploy military forces to protect the nation's security.)

Signing Statements
Department of Defense Appropriations, PL 101-165, Nov. 21, 1989
Military Personnel Act, PL 101-189, Nov. 29, 1989
National Defense Authorization Act, PL 101-510, Nov. 5, 1990
Military Construction Appropriations, PL 101-519, Nov. 5, 1990
Resolution Authorizing the Use of Force Against Iraq, HJ Res. 77, Jan. 14, 1991
Operation Desert Storm Supplemental Appropriations Act, PL 102-28, April 10, 1991
National Defense Act, HR 2100, Dec. 5, 1991

III. LEGISLATIVE VETO

(Congress cannot require the president to obtain its prior approval before spending appropriated funds.)

Vetoes
Intelligence Authorization Act, S 2384, Nov. 30, 1990

Signing Statements
Treasury and Postal Service Appropriations, PL 101-136, Nov. 3, 1989
Defense Department Appropriations, PL 101-165, Nov. 21, 1989
Omnibus Budget Act, PL 101-508, Nov. 5, 1990
Interior Department Appropriations, PL 101-512, Nov. 5, 1990
National and Community Service Act, PL 101-610, Nov. 16, 1990
Earthquake Hazards Reduction Act, PL 101-614, Nov. 16, 1990
Intelligence Authorization Act, PL 102-88, August 14, 1991
Treasury and Postal Service Appropriations, HR 2622, Oct. 28, 1991
Intelligence Authorization Act, PL 102-183, Dec. 4, 1991

IV. LEGISLATIVE PREROGATIVES OF THE EXECUTIVE

(Because the Constitution gives the president the power to submit legislation he deems "necessary and expedient," Congress cannot direct the executive to make legislative recommendations or determine what the president can or should propose.)

Vetoes
Textile, Apparel, and Footwear Trade Act, HR 4328, Oct. 5, 1990

Signing Statements
    Ethics Reform Act, PL 101-194, Nov. 30, 1989
Renewable Energy and Efficiency Technology Competitiveness
Act, S 488, Dec. 11, 1989
Customs and Trade Act, HR 1594, Aug 20, 1990
Native American Higher Education Assistance, 101-477, Oct. 30,
1990
Omnibus Budget Act, PL 101-508, Nov. 5, 1990
National Defense Authorization Act, PL 101-510, Nov. 5, 1990
Energy and Water Development Act, PL 101-514, Nov. 5, 1990
Fishery Conservation Amendments, PL 101-627, Nov. 28, 1990
Rumsey Indian Rancheria Bill, PL 101-630, Nov. 28, 1990
Energy and Water Development Act, PL 102-104, Aug 17, 1991
Foreign Relations Authorization Act, HR 1415, Oct 28, 1991
Tribal Self-Governance Project Act, PL 102-184, Dec. 4, 1991
Feasibility Study, Native American Cultural Center, 102-196,
Dec. 9, 1991

V. SUPERVISION OF THE EXECUTIVE BRANCH

(Congress improperly interfered with the president's ability to
supervise his subordinates and to oversee or manage the internal
processes of the executive branch.)

Vetoes
    FS-X Airplane Codevelopment, SJRes 113, July 31, 1989
State Department Authorization, HR 1487, Nov. 21, 1989
Eastern Airlines Strike Resolution, HR 1231, Nov. 21, 1989

Signing Statements
    Foreign Relations Authorization Act, PL 101-246, Feb. 16,
1990
Vocational and Applied Technology Education Act Amendments,
PL 101-392, Sept. 25, 1990
Immigration Act, PL 101-649, Nov. 29, 1990
Energy and Water Development Appropriations, PL 101-514,
Nov. 5, 1990
Amendments to Clean Air Act, PL 101-549, Nov. 15, 1990
Earthquake Hazards Reduction, PL 101-614, Nov. 16, 1990
National Environment Education Act, S.3176, Nov 16, 1990
Treasury, Postal Service, and General Government Appropria-
tions Act, PL 102-141, Oct 28, 1991
Civil Rights Act of 1991, PL 102-166, Nov. 21, 1991
Trade and Unemployment Benefits, HR 1724, December 4, 1991

National Defense Authorization Act, HR 2100, Dec. 5, 1991
FDIC Improvement Act, PL 102-242, Dec. 19, 1991

VI. PRIOR REVIEW OF INFORMATION

(The president has the authority to protect the confidentiality of communications within the executive branch and to review executive branch reports before they are submitted to Congress.)

Signing Statements
Whistleblower Protection Act, PL 101-12, Apr. 10, 1989
Amending 1984 Arctic Research Act, PL 101-609, Nov. 16, 1990
Conventional Forces in Europe Treaty Act, PL 102-228, Dec. 12, 1991

VII. DISCLOSURES THREATENING NATIONAL SECURITY

(The president has the constitutional duty to ensure the secrecy of information whose disclosure might threaten national security.)

Signing Statements
Treasury and Postal Service Appropriations, PL 101-136, Nov. 3, 1989
Intelligence Authorization Act, HR 2748, Nov. 30, 1989
Arms Control and Disarmament Act, PL 101-216, Dec. 11, 1989
National Affordable Housing Act, S 566, Nov. 28, 1990
Intelligence Authorization Act, PL 102-88, Aug. 14, 1991
Foreign Relations Act, PL 102-138, Oct 28, 1991
National Defense Authorization Act, HR 2100, Dec. 5, 1991

VI. THE APPOINTMENT POWER

(Congress may not reserve to itself the power to appoint those who execute the laws. The president has absolute discretion over appointments subject only to the advice and consent of the Senate; Congress cannot limit the president's authority to choose, instruct, or remove members of the executive branch.)

Vetoes
Morris Udall Scholarship and Excellence in National Environmental Policy Act, S 1176, Dec. 20, 1991

Signing Statements

Departments of Commerce . . . and the Judiciary Appropria-
tions Act, PL 101-162, Nov. 21, 1989
Intelligence Authorization Act, HR 2748, Nov. 30, 1989
Interior Department Appropriations, PL 101-512, Nov. 5, 1990
Departments of Commerce . . . and the Judiciary Appropriations
Act, HR 5021, Nov. 5, 1990
Amendments to the Clean Air Act, PL 101-549, Nov 15, 1990
Great Lakes Critical Programs Act, PL 101-596, Nov. 16, 1990
National and Community Service Act, PL 101-610, Nov. 16, 1990
Earthquake Hazards Reduction Act, PL 101-614, Nov. 16, 1990
Alaska Maritime Wildlife Refuge Bill, PL 101-622, Nov. 21, 1990
International Narcotics Control Act, HR 5567, Nov. 21, 1990
National Affordable Housing Act, S 566, Nov. 28, 1990
Water Resources Development Act, PL 101-630, Nov. 28, 1990
Joint Resolution Settling the Railroad Strike, HJ Res. 222, Apr. 18,
1991
National Literacy Act, PL 102-73, July 25, 1991
Foreign Relations Act, PL 102-138, Oct. 28, 1991
D.C. Mental Health Assistance Act, HR 1720, Oct. 31, 1991
Intelligence Authorization Act, PL 102-183, Dec. 4, 1991
Intermodal Surface Transportation Act, HR 2950, Dec. 18, 1991

INDEX

CONTRIBUTORS

Joseph M. Bessette is Alice Tweed Tuohy Associate Professor of Government and Ethics at Claremont McKenna College.

James W. Ceaser is Professor of Government at the University of Virginia.

William F. Connelly, Jr., is Associate Professor of Politics at Washington & Lee University.

Terry Eastland is Editor of *Forbes MediaCritic* and a Fellow at the Ethics and Public Policy Center in Washington, D.C.

Hugh Heclo is Robinson Professor of Public Affairs at George Mason University.

Michael J. Malbin is Professor of Political Science at the State University of New York at Albany and Director of the Center for Legislative Studies at SUNY's Rockefeller Institute of Government.

Harvey C. Mansfield is the William R. Kenan, Jr. Professor of Government at Harvard University.

Terence Marshall is Maître de Conférences, U.F.R. de Sciences Juridiques et Politiques, Université de Paris-X.

David K. Nichols is Assistant Professor of Political Science at Montclair State College.

Gary J. Schmitt is a national security consultant in Washington, D.C.

Peter W. Schramm is Professor of Political Science and Associate Director of the John M. Ashbrook Center for Public Affairs at Ashland University.

L. Peter Schultz is Associate Professor of Politics at Assumption College.

Bradford P. Wilson is Professor of Political Science and Deputy Director of the John M. Ashbrook Center for Public Affairs at Ashland University.